The Pathos of Distance

The Pathos of Distance

Affects of the Moderns

Jean-Michel Rabaté

Bloomsbury Academic
An imprint of Bloomsbury Publishing Inc

B L O O M S B U R Y
NEW YORK · LONDON · OXFORD · NEW DELHI · SYDNEY

Bloomsbury Academic
An imprint of Bloomsbury Publishing Inc

1385 Broadway	50 Bedford Square
New York	London
NY 10018	WC1B 3DP
USA	UK

www.bloomsbury.com

BLOOMSBURY and the Diana logo are trademarks of Bloomsbury Publishing Plc

First published 2016

© Jean-Michel Rabaté, 2016

All rights reserved. No part of this publication may be reproduced or transmitted in any form or by any means, electronic or mechanical, including photocopying, recording, or any information storage or retrieval system, without prior permission in writing from the publishers.

No responsibility for loss caused to any individual or organization acting on or refraining from action as a result of the material in this publication can be accepted by Bloomsbury or the author.

Library of Congress Cataloging-in-Publication Data
A catalog record for this book is available from the Library of Congress.

ISBN: HB: 978-1-5013-0800-0
PB: 978-1-5013-0799-7
ePub: 978-1-5013-0798-0
ePDF: 978-1-5013-0797-3

Typeset by RefineCatch Limited, Bungay, Suffolk

Contents

Acknowledgments — vi
List of Abbreviations — vii

Introduction: Formations of Pathos: Nietzsche, Benjamin, Warburg — 1

1 "Pathos of Distance": Huneker and Barthes Reading Nietzsche — 15
2 "Hard" Modernism: Alfred Jarry — 37
3 The Birth of Irish Modernism from the Spirit of Nietzscheism (Yeats, Joyce, and Beckett) — 51
4 *Ethos* vs. *Pathos* of the New in 1910 — 69
5 Affect Effects Affects: Deleuzian Affect vs. Lacanian Pathos — 87
6 "Playing Possum": War, Death, and Distance in Eliot's Poetry — 105
7 Let the Lips of the Wound Speak: Cocteau's *Pathosformel* — 129
8 The Pathos of History: Trauma in Siri Hustvedt's *The Sorrows of an American* — 149
9 Pathos of the Future: Nihilism and Hospitality in *The Childhood of Jesus* — 163

Conclusion: When is a Door Not a Door? — 183

Notes — 191
Index — 211

Acknowledgments

I want to express my gratitude to Haaris Naqvi whose discriminating eye has helped me progress at various stages in this project, which began as an expansion of some of the theses developed in *Crimes of the Future* (Bloomsbury, 2014). All my thanks go to Camille Henrot who graciously allowed her work to be reproduced on the cover.

Parts of some chapters have been published in collections, albeit modified and rewritten for this book.

A section of chapter 1 was published in *Die Tonkunst* (April 2013) as "1913, or the Pathos of Distance," pp. 170–6.

A part of chapter 3 was published in *The Cambridge Companion to Irish Modernism*, edited by Joe Carey (Cambridge University Press, 2014) as "Intellectual and Aesthetic Influences," pp. 21–34.

A part of chapter 5 was published in *The Cambridge Companion to the Body in Literature*, edited by David Hillmann and Ulrika Maude (Cambridge University Press, 2015) as "Literature and Affect," pp. 230–44.

A section of chapter 6 was published in *T.S. Eliot, France, and the Mind of Europe*, edited by Jayme Stayer (Cambridge Scholars Publishing, 2015) as "Playing Possum: Symbolic Death and Symbolist Impotence in Eliot's French Heritage, pp. 1–23. Another part of chapter 6 was published in *The Cambridge Companion to the Waste Land*, edited by Gabrielle McIntire (Cambridge University Press, 2015) as "The World Has Seen Strange Revolutions Since I Died: *The Waste Land* and the Great War," pp. 9–23.

I am grateful to the editors for granting permission to use these texts.

List of Abbreviations

AP	*The Arcades Project*, Walter Benjamin. Trans. H. Eiland and K. McLaughlin. Cambridge: Harvard University Press, 1999.
BA	*Blue Arabesque: A Search for the Sublime*, Patricia Hampl. New York: Harcourt, 2006.
C	*Correspondance complète, suivi de lettres sur la poésie*, Stéphane Mallarmé. Ed. Bertrand Marchal. Paris: Gallimard, 1995.
CJ	*The Childhood of Jesus*, J. M. Coetzee. London: Harvill Secker, 2013.
CL	*Camera Lucida: Reflections on Photography*, Roland Barthes. Trans. Richard Howard. New York: Noonday Press, 1981.
CP	*The Collected Poems*, William Butler Yeats. London: Macmillan, 1965.
CPP	*The Complete Poems and Plays*, T. S. Eliot. London: Faber, 1969.
D	*Diaries 1910–1923*, Franz Kafka. Trans. Josef Kresh, Berlin: Shocken, 1976.
DID	*Derrida and the Inheritance of Democracy*, Samir Haddad. Bloomington: Indiana University Press, 2013.
DQ	*Don Quixote*, Miguel de Cervantes. Trans. Charles Jarvis. Oxford: Oxford University Press, 1992.
E	*Egoists: A Book of Supermen*, James Huneker. New York: Charles Scribner's Sons, 1909.
EGT	*Early Greek Thinking*. Trans. David Farrel Krell and Frank A. Capuzzi. San Francisco: Harper and Row, 1984.
HLT	*How to Live Together*, Roland Barthes. Trans. Kate Briggs. New York: Columbia University Press, 2013.
HN	*Here and Now, Letters 2008–2011*, Paul Auster and J. M. Coetzee. New York: Viking, 2013.
IGJT	*The Infancy Gospels of James and Thomas*. Trans. Ronald F. Hock. Santa Rosa, CA: Polebridge Press, 1995.

IMH	*Inventions of the March Hare: Poems, 1909–1917*, T. S. Eliot. Ed. Christopher Ricks. New York: Harcourt Brace, 1996.
JOCI	*Oeuvres Complètes*, vol. I, Alfred Jarry. Ed. Michel Arrivé. Paris: Pléiade, 1972.
LI	*The Letters of T. S. Eliot, Volume One: 1898–1922*, T. S. Eliot. Eds. Valerie Eliot and Hugh Haughton. New Haven: Yale University Press, 2011.
LTL	*Living, Thinking, Looking*, Siri Hustvedt. New York: Picador, 2012.
M	*Murphy*, Samuel Beckett. New York: Grove Press, 1957.
MNIR	*Messalina, A Novel of Imperial Rome*, Alfred Jarry. Trans. John Harman. London: Atlas Press, 1985.
N&P	*Nietzsche et la philosophie*, Gilles Deleuze. Paris: Presses Universitaires de France, 1967.
Notebooks	*The Notebooks of Malte Laurids Brigge*, Rainer Maria Rilke. Trans. M. D. Herter Norton. New York: Norton, 1964.
O	*Othello: Texts and Contexts*, William Shakespeare. Ed. Kim F. Hall. New York: Bedford/St. Martins, 2007.
PD	*The Pathos of Distance*, James Huneker. New York: Charles Scribner's sons, 1922.
SA	*The Sorrows of an American*, Siri Hustvedt. New York: Picador, 2008.
SF	*Soul and Form*, Georg Lukács. Eds. John T. Sanders and Katie Terezakis. New York: Columbia University Press, 2010.
SP	*Le Sang d'un Poète, Edition anniversaire*, Jean Cocteau. Paris: Editions du Rocher, 2003.
SR	*The Spirit of Romance*, Ezra Pound. New York: New Directions, 2005.
SW	*The Sacred Wood*, T. S. Eliot. London: Methuen, 1976.
S.X	*Anxiety. The Seminar of Jacques Lacan, Book X*, Jacques Lacan. Trans. A. R. Price. Cambridge: Polity, 2014.
TS	*The Supermale*, Alfred Jarry. Trans. Ralph Gladstone and Barbara Wright. Cambridge: Exact Change, 1999.

U.	*Ulysses*, James Joyce. Ed. H. W. Gabler. New York: Random House, 1986.
VMP	*The Varieties of Metaphysical Poetry*, T. S. Eliot. Ed. Ronald Schuchard. New York: Harcourt, 1993.
WD	*Writing and Difference*, Jacques Derrida. Trans. Alan Bass. Chicago: Chicago University Press, 1978.
WIP	*What Is Philosophy?* Gilles Deleuze and Felix Guattari. Trans. Hugh Tomlinson and Graham Burchell. New York: Columbia University Press, 1994.

Introduction

Formations of Pathos: Nietzsche, Benjamin, Warburg

The idea of this book came to me the day I was fascinated by a writer's fascination. Teaching a class on colors, I had chanced upon *Blue Arabesque: A Search for the Sublime*,[1] Patricia Hampl's captivating memoir. I was struck by the sheer power with which she evokes the shock caused by one painting. She was twenty-six, just out of graduate school, walking through the corridors of the Chicago Art Institute, when her gaze was caught by Henri Matisse's portrait of a woman staring at fish in a bowl. It is called *Woman Before an Aquarium*. Here is her account: "I came to a halt before a large, rather muddy painting in a heavy gold-colored frame, a Matisse labeled *Femme et poissons rouges*... But that's wrong: I didn't halt, didn't stop. I was stopped. Apprehended even. That's how I felt" (BA, 2). Hampl, who was not an art lover, who was not used to visiting museums, galleries or art shows, felt at that moment that she had been forcibly "moved." An "uncanny moment" had touched her to the core. Immediately the picture became an "icon" for her (BA, 4). Soon after, in order to make sense of her obsession, Hampl wrote a poem about the picture, did research on the many portraits of women by Matisse, met one of Matisse's sitters, and finally devoted a memoir to her experience. Her first collection of poems, *Woman Before an Aquarium*, contains an eponymous poem describing her encounter with the picture. Her memoir narrates her quest for one model of Matisse still alive, an old French nun whom she interviews at the end.

What stopped her in her tracks was the rapt intentness with which Matisse's model stares at the fish. Hampl soon perceives new details like the woman's post-Great War bob, how the fish and pinecones, each group almost a reflection of the other, are engaged in parallel lines of force; she interprets a small white rectangle on the table as a notepad, suggesting to her that the woman is a writer (BA, 4). She gathers that the blue screen in the background was brought back to the Nice studio from Morocco. Her description (BA,

4–5) exhausts the painting, catching nuances and formal parallels, like the pairing of the woman's eyes and the fish:

> The woman's head is about the size of the fishbowl and is on its level. Her eyes, though dark, are also fish, a sly parallelism Matisse has imposed. Her steady eyes are the same fish shape, fish size, as the orange strokes she regards from beneath the serene line of her plucked brows. The woman looks at the fish with fixed concentration or somnolent fascination or—what *is* the nature of her fishy gaze that holds in exquisite balance the paradox of passion and detachment, of intimacy and distance? I wonder still.

How many fishes could I see swimming in that shiny bowl? Or was there only one fish I had followed in its downward glide? Why was half the woman's face bathed in the light reflected by the bowl? Under the power of Matisse's brushstrokes, the aquarium turns into a fisheye lens, that is to say a crystal ball: it holds the past and the future in suspension, its magnified distance presses a compulsive intimacy on all viewers.

To avoid getting trapped in my own fascination for Hampl's fascination for a woman gazing at fish that began staring back at me, I had to understand the source of the infectious enthrallment. It seemed to be caused by a baffling combination of distance and proximity—a contradictory tension that explains why the captivated stare of the woman was so catching or contagious. Hampl (BA, 6) analyzes this paradoxical conflation of depth and flatness eloquently:

> What was she? A woman regarding a glass globe: in the fishbowl, several aloof residents, glinting dimly from their distorting medium, hypnotic but of no particular use. This modern woman looks, unblinking, at the impersonal floating world. Detached, private, her integrity steeped not in declarative authority but in an ancient lyric relation to the world. Something of eternity touched her. She was effortless. Or, as the deep language of my old faith would have said, she was *blessed*. Like the English major I was, I had my metaphor. Or at least I had my icon. She existed timelessly, this gazer at the golden fish suspended in their transparent medium. Who she was and what she regarded existed in the same transcendent realm.

The language turns religious, which may have to do with the fact that Hampl, who grew up in Minnesota from Czech parentage, had been educated at a Catholic school. The only way for the memoir to avoid being stuck, halted, entrapped in this uncanny exchange of stares was to find an exterior object—the metonymic aim of the quest displacing a metaphorical freeze. It would have to be a living person, and it turned out to be Matisse's model. Hampl finally meets Sister Jacques-Marie, the woman who had posed for other paintings in 1942, a source of inspiration and renewal for Henri Matisse at the end of his life. The sitter, of course not the woman staring at the fish, was a nun in the South of France who died in 2005. She had chosen to join a contemplative order after having sat for Matisse and helped him through an operation. One of Matisse's last works was the chapel of the Rosary in Vence that he planned and decorated for her in 1949–1951; an atheist creating a jewel of religious art for a Dominican order.

What the portrait brought Hampl was not nostalgia for the lost faith of her youth. Even though the portrait had turned into a sacred relic, its contemplation failed to convert her; her quest replaced the issue of belief with that of meaning. If she wanted to find Matisse's model, it was to hear from her lips what it meant to be in the presence of the artist. However, the old nun kept her mystery. The painting held the key. Its efficacy was to convey the message its medium carries: surprisingly it was not space, as if it was all a painting could bring, but time. In her busy life after university, Hampl had forgotten about looking. Her experience of being stopped in her tracks by a painting made her realize that a gaze not only arrests time, for an instant at least, but also requires time—a lot of time. The portrait acted as a Platonician messenger coming not from the gods but from the essence of time: "I seemed to possess a memory trace, something imprinted not from my own experience but from instinct, of how life *should* be. It should be filled with the clean light of that gaze, uninterrupted. Looking and musing were the job descriptions I sought" (BA, 6–7).

Both Matisse's portrait at the beginning and the wizened Dominican nun at the end teach the same lesson: Hampl is reminded of what disinterested contemplation means. The woman on the flat canvas and the old nun in her cell give her the courage to let time go to waste. One can wait for what comes, expect creativity or not, without caring about daily productivity. Hampl asks the old nun in her convent how she would define contemplative life. She replies with one word: "Leisure" (BA, 9). Sensing Hampl's bafflement, she adds: "It takes time to do this" (BA, 9).

I could not help being reminded of Walter Benjamin's definition of the "aura" as the experience of a distance no matter how close the object may be. Hampl's book shows that such a distance should be understood as temporal too. The aura surges forward when time and space are interwoven in the eerie proximity of distance that we cannot cross. Here is Benjamin's famous definition: "[T]he unique appearance of a distance, no matter how close it may be."[2] I quote the famous passage:

> What, then, is the aura? A strange tissue of space and time: the unique apparition of a distance, however near it may be. To follow with the

eye—while resting on a summer afternoon—a mountain range on the horizon or a branch that casts its shadow on the beholder is to breathe the aura of those mountains, of that branch. In the light of this description, we can readily grasp the social basis of the aura's present decay. It rests on two circumstances, both linked to the increasing emergence of the masses and the growing intensity of their movements. Namely: the desire of the present-day masses to get "closer" to things, and their equally passionate concern for overcoming each thing's uniqueness by assimilating it as a reproduction.[3]

The German terms are precise: "*Die letzere definieren wir als einmalige Erscheinung einer Ferne, so nah as sein mag.*"[4] *Ferne* should not be confused with *Distanz*; it suggests a "distance" in space and time as well as the "remoteness" of a thing however near it seems to be, but not yet the moral or ethical distance between people. Conversely, as Benjamin argues, the modern destruction of the aura brought about by technology begins in the audience's perception with their desire to bring things closer, whether spatially or humanly ("die Dinge räumlich und menschlich *näher* zu bringen").[5] The intractable distance of the aura, on the other hand, remains suspended in a web of time and space to stay uniquely present in the glory of its medium. Hampl evokes the suspension in those terms: "She existed timelessly, this gazer at the golden fish suspended in their transparent medium." Indeed, the medium is not just the water of a fishbowl, or the air separating us from a canvas or a computer screen in which we see a reproduction, but the time it takes to see the painting, which is also the time of a narrative that has been frozen on the canvas. Is the woman a writer, as Hampl surmises in her effort at ekphrasis, or has she just got bad news in the letter left on the table, and meditates sadly, looking into the void? Beyond these infinite speculations, we can simply imagine the time it has taken for a great painter like Matisse to reach that perfect execution.

If we may never penetrate Matisse's motivations no matter how much we read about his life and theories, his time and our time intersect in a timelessness that it would be rash to call "eternity," even though it has something to do with transcendence. This time-medium is also made up of light—after all, time and light travel in waves together. As Mr. Turner says at the end of the eponymous 2014 film by Mike Leigh, when he is on his deathbed: "The sun is god." Similarly, Matisse had decided to leave Paris where he had had a successful career and settle in Nice, because the Southern light of the Riviera reminded him of the rich and warm substance he had discovered in Morocco. Another painter who was born in Nice and found that he had been blessed from birth, Yves Klein, can be seen as the direct heir of Matisse. It was not only the geographical proximity, but because the famously saturated "Yves Klein blue" had been invented by Matisse who used it in later cut-outs.

If we return to Benjamin's definition of the aura, we can note that it first appeared in his "Little History of Photography" (1931), when he discusses the work of Parisian photographer Atget. The "Little History of Photography" contains material reused in the "Work of Art in the Age of its Technical Reproduction." Numerous parallels and discrepancies between the two essays partly account for the notorious conundrum relative to the function of the aura. Was Benjamin nostalgic for the aura whose passing he seems to regret when he discusses Surrealism for instance, or was he pleased to see it wither away in the historical process by which the multiplication of reproductions destroys the fetishism attached to uniqueness and private ownership? Diarmuid Costello gives a nuanced picture when she presents Benjamin's hesitations as marked less by personal ambivalence than by strategic modulations: "Benjamin's attitude is marked not so much by ambivalence as by a double-edged response. He welcomes *and* mourns its passing simultaneously; his remarks about aura manifest both a 'liquidationist' and an 'elegiac' undertow, and which is prominent depends on what dimension of aura as a general category of experience is under discussion."[6] The passing of the aura in the modern period is a phenomenon that is globally positive for Benjamin; thanks to the increased role granted to technology, a new humanity capable of endorsing a socialist or communist revolution should be born; the passing of the aura metamorphosed into innumerable flat surfaces should abolish inner distance, the dungeon of interiority above which traditional bourgeois values have been erected. However, such a withering is never total, besides generating dangerous displacements or regressive mystifications as one witnesses with the "star system" of Hollywood.

The aura keeps a positive value when Benjamin analyzes what attracts him in old photographs by Hill and Nadar. Benjamin's lovingly detailed readings of those ancient portraits testify that their aura evinces no negative connotation whatsoever. Besides, as Richard Shiff suggests, it is likely that Benjamin hit upon the concept of "aura" when translating Proust's *In Search of Lost Time*.[7] The section that he was translating, "Within a Budding Grove," contains a passage in which the narrator goes to the theatre to look at the famous actress Berma (whose model was Sarah Bernhardt) through his grandmother's opera glasses. He wonders whether the technically increased proximity with her face has not produced an artificial distortion: "[W]hen one believes in the reality of things, making them visible by artificial means is not quite the same as feeling that they are close at hand (*près d'elles*)."[8] The narrator has the choice between a simple "image" appearing close enough, and the distance between his eyes and the real Berma, not being sure which to choose. The main analogy is between the charisma emanating from the famous actress and the "aura" surrounding "momentous happenings" like a victory or a defeat signaling the end of a war.[9] This comparison brings the "aura" into contact with the concept of an "event," a radical novelty introducing a break with a previous historical continuum; this path was not taken by Benjamin, even if all the terms mobilized about the work of art are gathered in Proust's one page. In spite of the superficial adoration of the mass responding in a kneejerk manner to pauses in Berma's rapid delivery, and the mediating function of opera glasses, the crowd and the narrator clap at the right time: they grasp that something unexpected and radically new has happened; the Berma's inspiration has functioned as a sudden "*trouvaille*" (a find, a felicitous improvisation) that sends rays ("*rayons*"), vibrations, or radiations immediately perceptible. This is the supreme "aura" hailed by the enthusiastic crowd of viewers. The unique sense of distance facing a sublime performer is perceived thanks to an "aura," even though the mystical rays will soon be swept along by the fluctuating affects of the narrator who remains hesitant, ambivalent, uncertain of what his "feelings" are. He shifts from boredom to admiration; from adoration to disappointment. However, even if the narrator's affects are constrained by a theoretical vise made of technology that abolishes distance but creates artificiality on the one hand, and the contagion of mass hysteria in the infectious proximity of passions on the other, the true aura will always pierce through.

In Benjamin's elaboration, the aura displayed by old photographs was caused by their technical conditions of production: the long immobility of the pose, the props to rest the bodies or heads forced the "subject to grow into the picture," thus allegorize a whole life in an instant. However, by the end of the nineteenth century, photographers recreated the aura by blurring the image or adding artificial halos and retouches. Then came Atget, the artist who announced the experimental art of the Surrealists who had, in fact, rediscovered him. Atget "cleansed" the atmosphere and "killed" the aura;[10] he "disinfected" modern culture and initiated the "emancipation" of the object from aura, sweeping away fake halos, the fetishism of obsolete cultic values, mystifications created by late nineteenth-century aesthetics.

Even if these texts are well known, they still pose many problems. Benjamin hoped that his analysis would prove that the aura was withering because of technological reproducibility. However, the evolution of media such as film and video suggests that the aura has come back in full force. There is a craving for the signature of the artist even when we deal with infinitely reproducible photographs, internet videos or invisible conceptual art. The return of the aura, triumphant in its polymorphous perverse reincarnations staged by capitalism, has brought along the derivative pathos of exacerbated commodification. The artist's signature remains endowed with unique force, even when the work of art has lost any substance, as one has seen with Yves Klein's immaterial works. In fact, the more immaterialist an artwork is, the more it requires the anchoring function of the artist's signature, the last stronghold of fetishistic value. Indeed, all this confirms that the most authentic values are grounded in the phenomenon of distance.

Benjamin's *Ferne* exhibits a troubling proximity with Nietzsche's concept of the *pathos of distance*—a pathos in which Nietzsche saw the root of all true values. My contention is that Benjamin is describing less a historical process than an ethical direction to follow. Verbs like "cleansing" and "emancipating" used for Atget testify to an ethical drift. In that sense, Benjamin would be closer to Nietzsche than is commonly said. James McFarland has devoted a book to the exploration of tantalizing parallels between the lives and concepts of Nietzsche and Benjamin.[11] He stresses the relationship between their philosophies of time, both having been brought to a contemplation of a "now-time" suspended between madness and suicide. Benjamin revisited critically Nietzsche's doctrine of the "eternal return of the same" in the *Arcades Project* and criticized the mythical nature of a doctrine in which he saw the aftermath of a metaphysical and social boredom that permeated the whole nineteenth century. Nevertheless, in the "Theses on the Philosophy of History," Benjamin envisaged a redeemed history in which every fact, instant or detail would find a place as a quotable past. The insight dovetails neatly with Nietzsche's intuition about the need to make every moment count, of subsuming personal history under aeons of endless repetitions. Whereas Nietzsche recycled the myth of the eternal return, assuming that it would usher in the feeling of eternity adhering to each and every moment, Benjamin tapped a messianic hope for redemption. This hope for an open future is linked with his meditation on the age of technology.

Nietzsche's formulation, as we will see in more detail in the first chapter, comes from *Beyond Good and Evil*, a book opposing the "noble" creation of true values to the slave morality whose spurious values derive from resentment. The "pathos of distance" is a recurrent expression whose all-encompassing meaning passes through a broad arc going from the notion that all men living in groups cannot be called "equal," to the idea of a "self-surmounting" or "self-overcoming" (*Selbstüberwindung*) of man, thanks to which one ascends to the higher humanity of the "Overman":

> Without the *pathos of distance*, such as grows out of the incarnated difference of classes, out of the constant outlooking and downlooking of the ruling caste on subordinates and instruments [...] that other more

mysterious pathos could never have arisen, the longing for an ever new widening of distance within the soul itself, the formation of ever higher, rarer, further, more extended, more comprehensive states, in short, just the elevation of the type "man," the continued "self-surmounting of man," to use a moral formula in a supermoral sense.[12]

For Nietzsche, as for followers like Georg Simmel, one moves from a sociological analysis insisting on issues of domination and subordination, the vertical logic of class differentiation being opposed to horizontal group formation, to an aesthetic meaning, in which the aim is to suggest the painful or dangerous, but exalted refinement of the creation of difference within oneself. What unites them is a "pathos": a term that should be understood as "strong affect," "intense emotion involving the whole body," or "exalted passion," and not simply as "emotion." It takes its root in a critique of the origins of morality. An entry in an 1885 notebook states: "[M]oral feeling is first developed with reference to man (starting with classes!); only later is it transferred to actions and characteristics. The *pathos of distance* is at the deepest root of that feeling."[13] Nietzsche's ambivalence facing the double value of this "pathos of distance" calls up Benjamin's ambivalence facing the extinction of the aura. Nietzsche knew that his reverie on noble brutes who created values is a nostalgic fantasy facing a modern age marked by democracy, egalitarianism, and the reign of science. Processing this undeniable evolution, Nietzsche does not take a simply reactionary position, for, like Benjamin, he welcomed the passing of older cultic values, as we can see in the following passage, that followed a meditation on a weakened humanity and diminished values. Nietzsche is seeking for cures in domains like "will, responsibility, self-assurance, the capacity to set goals"; here would be some remedies:

> The *means* would be those taught by history: *isolation* through interests of preservation that are the opposite of the average ones today; learning opposite values by practice; distance as pathos; a free conscience regarding what is most undervalued and forbidden today.
> The *leveling out* of European man is the great process which cannot be impeded: it should be speeded up even further. The necessity of *a chasm opening*, of *distance*, of an *order of rank* is thus given: *not* the necessity of slowing down the process.[14]

A new aristocracy of the mind would bring a solution. A similar idea was developed at the same time by William James, who had come back quite distraught from a week at an adult retreat summer camp in Chautauqua Lake, which was rumored to be "a middle-class paradise."[15] James was aghast at the display of well-meaning, moralizing, meliorist culture and boring sameness. In the essay "What Makes a Life Significant," first given in 1898, James deplores that an "irremediable flatness is coming over the world": "Bourgeoisie and mediocrity, church sociable and teachers' conventions, are taking the place of the old heights and depths."[16] The usually meek and courteous pragmatist was so shocked by middle-class philistinism that he seemed ready to welcome violence, even imagining a massacre of Armenians, just to shake everything up rather than be engulfed in the tide of mediocrity. James was not joking: at the time, Armenians were regularly slaughtered in massive pogroms throughout the Ottoman Empire. This sudden outburst of sadism can be explained by James's revulsion when he discovered the sadism of the moral super-ego. This was what Freud was trying to explain to him in 1909 when they met at Clark University, just before the philosopher's death. Freud failed to convince James—it was too late for pragmatism to be confronted with the Freudian drive. A similar pattern can be observed in Nietzsche: only the most explicit sadism, wielded as a moral hammer by the "immoralist," can be strong enough to fight the covert sadism unleashed by the moral code of the majority. It is because of the general social evolution towards "flatness" in which a leveling of distances seems inevitable that one must consider the roots of the pathos of distance.

To retrieve a sense of distance, intensity, and relevance, a heady combination called "precipitousness" by James in a suggestive conflation of the temporal and local meanings mixing overtones of steepness and precipitation, he points to the novels of Tolstoy: they offer a model because they praise manual labor and probe the inner lives of suffering people.[17] However, difference emerges more sharply when the general context is dominated by sameness. Thus *Distanz* in the intellectual or moral sense compensates for a lack of *Ferne* in the material sense. Pathos as such offers a key—it is not only suffering, although suffering is its most frequent manifestation. Nietzsche also lists extreme joy, passion, distress, disgust, anger, enthusiasm—all these emotional "highs" being accompanied by uncomprehending stares of those who were near him: "Such revolts I experienced, very different in degree but from almost anybody who was close to me. It seems nothing offends more deeply than suddenly letting others feel a distance."[18] At the same time, distance is necessary if only to achieve the serious task of philosophizing: "Considering that in those days I practiced the scholar's craft, and perhaps *knew* something about this craft, the harsh psychology of the scholar that emerges in this essay is of some significance: it expresses the *feeling of distance*, the profound assurance about what could be my *task*."[19]

This untimely task was taken as a point of departure by Aby Warburg in his meditations on art. Warburg had read Nietzsche voraciously and enthusiastically, and then invented a series of concepts that attempted to reconcile tensions and contradictions that he perceived in Nietzsche's pathos; they also make better sense of Benjamin's auratic distance. Warburg not only coined the expression of "*Pathosformel*" but also systematized a theory of thinking via images and symbols that would enact psychic distance (*Distanz*) while redeeming a lost historical distance (*Ferne*). The lecture given by Warburg in Ludwig Binswanger's sanatorium in April 1923 exemplifies this wish. Warburg had felt his sanity vacillate at the end of the war. Because of his growing psychosis, his obsessions with terrifying images of mass killings of the Jews, he was interned in Kreuzlingen between 1921 and 1924.[20] This lecture proved not only that his intellectual capacities were intact, but also that he could provide a conceptual bridge between his studies of Renaissance painting and his anthropological investigations of the Pueblo Indians in New Mexico. Observing similarities in the handling of snakes in certain ritual dances and the expressive gestures in Renaissance paintings, Warburg concluded that there was a universal language of pathos.

The expression of *Pathosformel* ("formula of pathos") combines the expression of strong or violent affects and the idea of a comparative analysis founded on an encyclopedia of forms. Warburg's observations are predicated upon the term of "distance" without which one could not even think, let alone compare different cultural forms. In spite of this syncretic and comparative effort, the essay ends with a rather disabused diagnosis:

> The modern Prometheus and the modern Icarus, Franklin and the Wright brothers, who invented the dirigible airplane, are precisely those ominous destroyers of the sense of distance (*Ferngefühl-Zerstörer*), who threaten to lead the planet back into chaos.
>
> Telegram and telephone destroy the cosmos. Mythical and symbolic thinking strive to form spiritual bonds between humanity and the surrounding world, shaping distance into the space required for devotion and reflection: the distance undone by the instantaneous electric connection.[21]

Against this leveling tendency, Warburg promotes *Distanzierung* (the act of distanciation) as a universal apparatus. "Distance" means first the distance taken with the world, as a subjective space; it is then distance taken with the past of history, for Warburg always insists on the "return" of ancient motifs taken from pagan antiquity into Renaissance art and the modern world; finally this distance constitutes an intermediary "thought-space" in which signs can reverberate and be combined without being reduced to one other. His disciple Gombrich systematized this "intermediary thinking" in the name of distance.²² Such a crucial distance would be rendered visible by hundreds of reproductions of images juxtaposed on an exhibition panel. The panels of his Atlas had to materialize the distance needed to think their connections. Those connections had to be perceived as contributing to a universal language of gesture combining the most archaic and the most modern. The *"Distanzierungsprozess"* makes us inhabit a world of signs and think in it and through it in a process allowing specialists to see the return of "formulas" via gestures culled from the most varied cultural contexts.

Warburg's distance functions both formally and emotionally. The observer compares and situates diverse *Pathosformeln* arranged in subtle or dizzying juxtapositions on the panels of Atlas. As Agamben wrote, the *Pathosformel* is "an indissoluble intertwining of an emotional charge and an iconographic formula in which it is impossible to distinguish between form and content."²³ Therefore it is misleading to translate *Pathosformel* by "emotive formula" as David Britt did when he translated Warburg's *The Renewal of Pagan Antiquity*. The first essay in which the term was introduced dates from 1905. It was devoted to Dürer's classical models, especially his early modern rendering of the "Death of Orpheus" *topos*. The language used by Warburg implies that *"Pathos"* is not reducible to "emotion," no more than *"Formel"* can mean "form" or "formalism": a *Formel* calls up "formulaic" expressions, a matrix of encoded sequences in a specific language. Warburg demonstrates that Dürer borrowed from a universal language of gestures and adapted a formal vocabulary of expressive forms, which led to a process of intensification culminating with the Baroque: "It was a revelation of something that Italians had long sought— and therefore found—in the art of the ancient world: extremes of gestural and physiognomic expression, stylized in tragic sublimity."²⁴ Warburg describes the enthusiasm that "the striking expressiveness of the suffering figures" and concludes: "This was the Vulgar Latin of emotive gesture: an international, indeed a universal language that went straight to the heart of those who chafed at medieval expressive constraints."²⁵

A good example of a *Pathosformel* could be given by Proust, who arrived at similar conclusions about expressive gestures as Warburg's. In the same section of "Within a Budding Grove" I have already quoted, but a little later, we see the narrator explaining to Bergotte, the novelist who is his first literary role-model, how much he admires Berma's performance in *Phèdre*. Bergotte then highlights one single gesture, commenting on her arm raised to the level of her shoulder—this was the moment that had triggered the most resounding applause—which suggested "certain classical figures which quite possibly she had never even seen, a Hesperid carved in the same attitude upon a metope at Olympia, and also the beautiful primitive virgins on the Erechtheum."²⁶ Bergotte speculates that Berma's genius consisted in having reproduced intuitively the universal pathos of such antique gestures: "[S]he's really charming, that little sixth-century Phaedra, the rigidity of the arm, the lock of hair 'frozen into marble,' yes, you know, it's wonderful of her to have discovered all that."[27] Proust confirms the validity of Warburg's theory of *Pathosformeln* by connecting the gesture with his analysis of the actress's "aura." Bergotte even plans to "register" (*repérer* is his favorite verb) whether Berma might not be in the habit of frequenting the Louvre to find inspiration by looking at Greek and Roman statues.

Warburg found the same heightened expressiveness and auratic power in the snake dances and pagan rituals of the Hopi tribes he visited in New Mexico during his trip to the United States, and in the works of the Italian Renaissance that he knew so well. Philippe-Alain Michaud describes Warburg's *Mnemosyne* project as the project of defining an "expressivity without a subject,"[28] which refers to the mute language of expressivity brought to light by eloquent visual juxtapositions, transversal moments of time frozen in pantomimic gestures that have reached the most extreme intensity possible. Georges Didi-Huberman has guided us there, showing how Warburg's thought evolved from that of Nietzsche and Darwin before moving towards that of Freud.[29]

I was tempted to call this book "*Pathosformeln* of modernism," had not the title looked too outlandish, the scope too broad, and the claims too huge. I have preferred to focus on one type of *Pathosformel*, which has to do with distance. My method is similar to that of Warburg when he collected and displayed reproductions of paintings, objects, newspaper cuttings, and other visual aids in the sixty-three panels of the *Image Atlas* (1924–1929) that he called *Mnemosyne* even though I have only nine panels to present. They are limited to "chronotopes,"[30] specific configurations of form and time pertaining to literary genres, selected slices of cultural history all taking modernism as a privileged conceptual attractor.

Peter Sloterdijk has been an important influence here; his book *You Must Change Your Life* helped me understand nuances in Nietzsche's ideology of distance and verticality. In *You Must Change Your Life*, Sloterdijk presents the "pathos of distance" as a "division of asceticisms" following Nietzsche who opposed pathological asceticism to progressive asceticism—the latter offering a road to the "Superman."[31] This division sketches a whole ideology of verticality running through philosophy and ethics from the end of the nineteenth century to the middle of the twentieth century. Michel Foucault succumbed to it, on his reading, when praising Ludwig Binswanger's work, in which a "tragic verticality" played a central role.[32] We saw that Binswanger treated Warburg in his clinic in the twenties. Binswanger's *Daseinsanalyse* parted ways with Freudian psychoanalysis to deploy Warburgian themes:

Binswanger took the power of expression as a positive factor against Freud's reductive determinism; he insisted on the vertical dimension of existence, pointed to a "tragic verticality" perceptible in moments of enthusiasm and self-overcoming: "It is on the vertical axis of existence that the axis of tragic expression is situated."[33] Foucault, who combined expression, tragedy and verticality, saw the "vertical axis" as necessary for a philosophy of "self-overcoming."[34] Binswanger took the example of Solness, Ibsen's hubristic "masterbuilder" to illustrate this dangerous verticality. Solness had a morbid fear of extreme heights yet felt compelled to climb a high steeple, then fell to his death. Foucault himself became a "man of the vertical" even if he avoided the discourses of "transcendence in the Christian-Platonic style" as Sloterdijk puts it.[35] Foucault deployed a "pathos of distance" in the manner of Nietzsche and combined verticality and self-overcoming. Much later, he reformulated the vertical drive as a "care of the self" in which self-shaping efforts would lead to a similar self-overcoming.

This attitude, sketched by Sloterdijk, leads to a philosophy of affects capable of producing a profane self-transcendence.[36] Often, the subject will fall; the higher the aspirations, the more hurtful the collapse. Indeed, the history of twentieth-century art can be schematized as a chronicle of abrupt falls, some with positive outcomes like the Second World War crash of Joseph Beuys's plane in March 1944. His Stuka bomber was shot down in Crimea, and he was saved by Tatar tribesmen who wrapped his wounded body in fat and felt, providing him not only with a personal mythology of salvation, but also with two substances, the material all his work shaped and staged afterwards. Other falls remained sadly literal like that causing Ana Mendieta's death in 1985 when she was only thirty-six, after she was defenestrated in New York by her husband, Carl Andre. In between, we find Yves Klein who launched his public career with a stunt, the famous trick-photograph from 1960 showing him "jumping into the void," and ended it when he had a heart-attack in Cannes, caused when he was watching what he thought would be his triumph, the film *Mondo Cane*, but realized that he was depicted as a conceited buffoon. The shock made him crash from the sublime of his blue monochromes to the ridicule of public derision. This was too much to bear. He died soon after in 1962 at the age of thirty-four.

Such pathetic distance plays against the main vectors of modernity, at least those defined by the Surrealists and Dadaists, or by radical practitioners like Marcel Duchamp and Joseph Beuys: if any mass-produced object can be a work of art, as Duchamp claimed with his "ready-mades," or if, as Beuys stated, anyone can be—and is already—an artist, then the pathos of distance looks terribly reactive, regressive, old-fashioned. Its anxious interrogation revolves around the nagging sense that, in spite of most egalitarian and democratic programs, we are reminded that we cannot all be called "equal," or the worry that we might not all live in the same time, do not share the same history with the same intensity. The exaltation of difference tends to provide less compensation than ways of seeing the positive side in our drift to technological sameness. There is a tension between the hierarchical verticality of the aura in which the fetishistic value of art is condensed, and the wish to address all—viewers and artists as well. The awareness of a contradiction between egalitarianism and elitism cause pain and discomfort felt acutely by the main modernists; it fed again their own pathos of distance.

I will map out its formulations by presenting two privileged observers, James Huneker and Roland Barthes, before tackling a few chronotopes of modernity: the French moderns with Jarry; the Irish moderns with Yeats, Beckett, and Joyce. I will then zoom in on one year, 1910, so as to sketch a tension between ethos and pathos. This will lead to a philosophical conversation opposing pathos of affectivity to the pathos of transgressive jouissance; for this, I will parallel the analyses of Gilles Deleuze and Jacques Lacan. Using Lacan's insights, I will limn the faces of existential despair and sexual anxiety in T. S. Eliot's works and in Jean Cocteau's modernist masterpiece, the film *Blood of a Poet*. The latter work also exemplifies the pregnancy of Warburg's *Pathosformeln*. I will end by tackling the issue of trauma in a novel by Siri Hustvedt, and of the response to a de-pathologized nihilism that Coetzee situates in a future dystopia. These novels suggest that literary and philosophical modernism has not disappeared. It treats more elusive themes like trauma, but trauma also organizes a form of pathos provided it can be narrated, as Hustvedt demonstrates. When Coetzee addresses the disappearance of pathos in the world of Novilla, he shows that this utopia produces another pathology. The pathos of the future carries hope for a renewed hospitality and openness to the other. Finally, Duchamp will allow me to conclude by exemplifying the ghostly return of pathetic distance in the uncanny proximity of one door—the famous door of *Etant Donnés*.

1

"Pathos of Distance"

Huneker and Barthes Reading Nietzsche

In 2006, as I was gathering documentation for my "year book" *1913: The Cradle of Modernism* (2009), I chanced upon a striking title by an author hitherto unknown to me, James Huneker. It was *The Pathos of Distance*,[1] a collection of essays published in 1913. At the time, I tried to read *all* the books in the languages I know published in 1913. Even when I despaired of completing this, the book's title kept mystifying me. What did Huneker mean with this *Pathos of Distance*, a broad heading he used to collect a bunch of earlier essays? I gathered information about the author, born and educated in Philadelphia, and a true cosmopolitan, now all but forgotten. His books are hard to find; however, at the time, in New York, Boston, and Philadelphia, Huneker exerted the same appeal as Susan Sontag for a later generation. For three decades, Huneker was the most influential American cultural *"passeur"*—an unofficial ambassador who kept American students like the young T.S. Eliot informed of cultural developments coming from France, Germany, and England.

At first glance, *The Pathos of Distance* appears too rich and mixed. Huneker moves seamlessly from memories of his bohemian life in Paris in the 1870s and 1880s, vignettes from trips to Germany (mostly Cologne, Kassel, and Frankfurt), to discussions of paintings by Matisse and Picasso, manuscripts by Stendhal and Flaubert, disquisitions on Stirner's anarchism or Bergson's philosophy of time. Abstract considerations are mixed with personal reflections, biographical portraits, and bibliographical advice. Huneker even adds a belated preface for a previous book entitled *Egoists: A Book of Supermen* (1909),[2] with which he assumes his readers are familiar. Writing my *1913* book with other issues, questions or perspectives in mind, I decided to leave this hodge-podge aside for later investigations.

A little later, I met the French artist Camille Henrot in New York. We started exchanging ideas for a show in Philadelphia; at the time, she was planning an exhibition about Roland Barthes whose last seminars, already published in French, were forthcoming in English. She focused on the seminar entitled *How to Live Together*, published in English in 2013.³ Camille Henrot designed an impressive set with a huge bed on which spectators were invited to lie down while listening to Roland Barthes's voice saying in French what my voice repeated in English. I had to impersonate Barthes aurally, which forced me to record the whole seminar *How to Live Together*; the English version read with my French accent kept an echo of Barthes's original intonation. This was shown as an installation displayed at Slought Foundation between January and May 2013.⁴ Reading the seminar for long and at times grueling recording sessions, I stumbled upon the phrase of "pathos of distance." This was when we recorded the session of May 4, 1977. Barthes had written:

> Distance as value. This is not to be considered from the narrowly selfish perspective of plain "reserve," "*quant-à-soi*." Nietzsche makes distance a strong value—a rare value: "[...] the chasm between man and man, between one class and another, the multiplicity of types, the will to be one's self, and to distinguish one's self—that, in fact, I call the *pathos of distance* is proper to all ages (*The Twilight of Idols*, 70).
>
> (HLT, 132)

Reading this, I was brought back to James Huneker's *Pathos of Distance*. I will attempt to connect the first collection and its almost forgotten author with the more recent problematic launched by Barthes with the help of Nietzsche and Deleuze.

The pathos of distance in 1913

Huneker's *Pathos of Distance* collects previously published essays, partly rewritten and updated; the collection is self-importantly subtitled "A Book of a Thousand and One Moments." The author was indeed prolific; there is something fascinating in the exuberant works and personality of James Gibbons Hunker. Living in Philadelphia myself, I can relate to a writer who was born in Philadelphia in 1857, and died in New York in 1921 after having come back to his native city regularly. The life of this American music critic, journalist, and short-story writer was memorialized in two autobiographical volumes *Steeplejack* (1920) and *Painted Veils* (1920). His memory not being totally reliable, it is safe to supplement these with Arnold Schwab's biography, *James Gibbons Huneker: Critic of the Seven Arts*.⁵ Huneker came from a Catholic family of German-Hungarian descent on the father's side, Irish on the mother's side. Huneker married early and went to Paris in 1878 to study the piano under Leopold Doutreleau. In Paris, he audited piano classes given by Chopin's pupil Georges Mathias; he gathered original details about Chopin's career,[6] soon becoming a Chopin expert. Huneker wrote abundantly about Chopin, published *Chopin: The Man and His Music* in 1900, followed by a book on Liszt and countless essays on modern composers.

Huneker returned to America and settled in New York City in 1885. Close to the end of his life, he worked in his hometown Philadelphia as the music critic of *The Press*. An untiring writer of reviews for the most-varied periodicals, Huneker lived by his pen, which explains the journalistic quality of his essays. He was a serious journalist—a specialist who gave detailed analyses of the complete works of Chopin, or perfect assessments of the piano works of Johannes Brahms. Huneker had been the music editor of the *Musical Courier* and the music editor of the New York *Sun*. He contributed to the leading magazines and reviews of the times. He published excellent short stories. Besides his expertise as a musicologist, he was knowledgeable about French, English, and German literature and philosophy. Huneker, a wonderful conveyor of new ideas, familiarized Americans with modern trends in a highly idiosyncratic language full of pyrotechnical metaphors, rhetorical flourishes, and wisecracks. What made him notable was his vivid style, full of jokes, personal anecdotes, funny metaphors, unexpected detours, and witty asides.

Thanks to Huneker's travels to Europe (in his career he went twenty times to Europe, staying from two years to a few months), the American public was kept informed of the "new" in the arts. In January 1913, he reported on Arnold Schoenberg's *Pierrot Lunaire*. Even if he failed to love it, his remarks were perceptive:

> In the welter of tonalities that bruised each other as they passed and repassed, in the preliminary grip of enharmonies that almost made the ears bleed, the eyes water, the scalp to freeze, I could not keep a central grip on myself. It was new music, or new exquisitely horrible sounds, with a vengeance. The very ecstasy of the hideous![7]

Huneker felt that these chords without harmony destroyed his psychological balance, but added that he might be persuaded to like them. Often Huneker used terms such as "ugly" or "hideous" to record the truly new. On the other hand, he appreciated the new work by Richard Strauss that he heard in Stuttgart in 1912. Perceptively, he concluded that Strauss would be remembered because of *Elektra*.[8]

Even though the young T. S. Eliot saw Huneker as an arch modernist (while a Harvard student, he began his review of *Egoists* thus: "Now that Arthur Symons is no longer active in English letters, Mr. James Huneker alone represents modernity in criticism. [...] [H]e is far too alert to be an American; in his style and in his temper he is French"),[9] Huneker was never a principled or doctrinaire modernist like the French poet Guillaume Apollinaire. Apollinaire, to whom we will return, applauded the new, whatever it was and wherever it came from. Huneker resisted it at first, especially when confronted with the more aggressive or cutting-edge innovations in the arts of the 1910s. Because of his verve allied with an unsparing honestly, he became a privileged witness of the emergence of modernism between 1890 and 1920—a modernism that he experienced in the "seven arts," to quote Schwab's biography. Huneker spoke and read French and German fluently; he was knowledgeable in music, literature, philosophy, and the visual arts. In the United States, he was the first to present the work of painters like Gauguin and Van Gogh; philosophers like Nietzsche and Bergson; writers like Henrik Ibsen, Remy de Gourmont, and George Moore. Feeling half-Irish, he supported the Irish Renaissance and promoted Synge, Yeats, and George Moore. Huneker was a brilliant conversationalist who would hold forth on any topic for hours while downing impressive quantities of beer. He was a fierce and uncompromising critic who once wrote that a bad musical was "Art with a capital F."[10] In the last decades of his life, young artists and aspiring writers eager for a quick education in European trends would seek him out.

The two books published by Huneker in 1913 are markedly different. *Old Fogy* pairs an older curmudgeon and a younger musicologist who discuss new "fads" in music; the book collects Huneker's music reviews, and has an axe to grind: it attempts to debunk the cult of Wagner, then at its height. *The Pathos of Distance* is literary and philosophical and collects essays unified by the theme of egoism. The obvious initiator of this concept was Stendhal, who wrote it as "egotism" in dazzling autobiographical notebooks entitled *Souvenirs d'Egotisme*, a book taken by Huneker as a point of departure (PD, 36). Huneker moves on to Karl-Joris Huysmans whose decadentist *Against the Grain* continued Stendhal's program of militant aestheticism. Stendhal and Huysmans repudiated bourgeois morality by exploring their individual psyches. They find place in a pantheon of artists called "Supermen": William Blake, Charles Baudelaire, Gustave Flaubert, Anatole France, Maurice Barrès, Friedrich Nietzsche, Henrik Ibsen, and Max Stirner. The ambition of *The Pathos of Distance* is to propose an alternative survey of the modern movement by taking the exact opposite point of view from Max Nordau's 1892 jeremiad against the moderns, *Degeneration*.

Nordau, a contemporary of Huneker, had provided a sweeping indictment of what he called *Entartung*, "degeneration"—a term encompassing European modernism presented as a disease of the will and the arts. Nordau pilloried the fin-de-siècle in Europe, excoriated Baudelaire, Wilde, Nietzsche, Wagner,

Ibsen, in fact all the "moderns." His attack was mounted in the name of a "health" that he wanted to embody in Zionist dreams of an independent Palestine. Nordau had become Huneker's bête-noire. In 1907, Huneker derided Nordau's pathologization of great men: "Nordau has, despite his varied reading and experience, a petty, provincial, even parochial mind; his soul lives up an alley, he is utterly without imagination. It is his priggish insolence, his filthy insults, leveled at men, living men, whose shoestrings he is not worthy to unlatch that I resent."[11] There was nevertheless a paradoxical effect in Nordau's work: under pretext of providing as many examples of "decadence" as possible and condemning them, in fact Nordau was disseminating the ideas of those he was criticizing, including those of Ibsen and Nietzsche. Sensing an obvious ambivalence in this gesture, Huneker added this humorous aside to a refutation published in the *Musical Courier* in 1895: "Ah, Nordau, Nordau, *du Schlemihl!* You are very human after all; you only quote favorable authorities."[12]

This was the context for the program outlined by Huneker in 1909–1913. It combined original readings of Stendhal, Baudelaire, and Flaubert, whose manuscripts he studied closely (there is even a facsimile of a letter by Flaubert correcting *Madame Bovary*), and a genealogy of philosophical anarchism going from Max Stirner, the radical Left-Hegelian, to Nietzsche, Huneker's favorite philosopher: "Nietzsche is the poet of the doctrine, Stirner is its prophet, or, if you will, its philosopher" (E, 352). In his vague doctrine of "egoism," Huneker offers rhapsodic statements that fundamentally state that we are all egoists or individualists. Since "Supermen" are artists who are so individualistic and idiosyncratic, they cannot be yoked together under a single banner. Huneker had been reproached for his equivocations and vagueness. In 1913, he wanted to condense a general theory that would answer to his readers' queries: was he an anarchist, a fin-de-siècle aesthete, a radical Fenian, a Republican, a Democrat, or a Nietzschean elitist, as Yeats thought he was?

Like Remy de Gourmont, Huneker asserted that he did not believe in "general ideas" but only practiced "dissociations of ideas" (PD, 386). These dissociations gesture in the direction of a philosophy of egoism: Stendhal is a forerunner, Baudelaire its epic poet, Stirner and Nietzsche its prophets. Huneker did not endorse all of Nietzsche's ideas; he objected to the doctrine of the "eternal return of the Same" that he found "sinister" (PD, 389). He observed with irony that Nietzsche, claiming to destroy religious beliefs in transcendent entities, was the strongest believer of all: "[I]n an age that is almost pyrrhonistic Nietzsche at least believed in something, believed that Christianity was on trial and found wanting; whereas his contemporaries in the world of intellect, for the most part, didn't care who ruled, Jove or Jesus, Jehovah or Buddha" (PD, 390). Above all, Huneker endorsed Nietzsche's diatribes against sentimentalism deemed to be the cause of all the evils of the contemporary world: "Rousseau, not Nietzsche, is the real Antichrist, for he invented that lying legend: Liberty, Equality, Fraternity" (PD, 391). As in *Egoists*, Huneker dissociated Max Stirner from organized anarchists and socialists. The heroic individuals whom he praises, those "supermen," worked alone. They were suffering, they often become mad under the strain, hence all their pathos—but ultimately humanity would owe its progress to their contributions.

Huneker's effort was thus doubly Nietzschean: he applied to history itself what Nietzsche said about the creation of values. In his modernist historiography, he presented European literature and culture as shaped by the forceful personalities of the subversive artists he praised. However, some distance was necessary to perceive the value of what they brought: "[The supermen] made history and any one who can run and is not blind may read this history. No doubt when the corridor of time lengthens between them and newer generations the pathos of distance will again operate and fresh critical perspectives form" (PD, 393). The "pathos of distance" works as a tool to analyze creators and also "invent" the historical signs that announce their ideas. Huneker's book ends with an apposite quote by Nietzsche: "Some souls will never be discovered unless they be first invented" (PD, 394).

Distance works spatially and temporally as *Ferne*, while entailing an awareness of the vertical separations between individuals as *Distanz*. The chapter entitled "The Pathos of Distance" harps on Nietzsche's famous phrase, and applies it to very different contexts: "The pathos of distance! It is a memorial phrase. Friedrich Nietzsche is its creator, Nietzsche who wrote of the drama and its origins in a work that is become a classic" (PD, 332). The expression is used to test the difference between a journalist's account of *Twelfth Night* in 1877 and Huneker's memory of the actress who played Viola in 1913. The critic who discussed her in 1877 was missing something: "There was no pathos of distance in his criticism" (PD, 334). The expression is made to fluctuate strategically. Huneker is aware of the original meaning of Nietzsche's expression. As we have seen, Nietzsche uses it to describe the process by which values were created. For Nietzsche, original values were created by the rulers; the "herd-instinct of the masses" made them forget or erase that original creative force. The analysis of *Genealogy of Morality* recurs in *Beyond Good and Evil* in the section "What is noble?" already quoted. The "pathos of distance"[13] asserts that no original judgment of value ever came out of "altruistic" motives; values only derive from the "egoistic" motivations of the noble leaders of the past.[14] However, Huneker, also took the phrase in a different sense, as alluding to nostalgia, even when he refused the sentimental lure of nostalgia about the past: "Distance lends pathos, bathes in rosy enchantments the simplest events of a mean past; is the painter, in a word, who with skillful, consoling touches disguises all that was sordid in our youth, all the once mortified or disgusted, and bridges the inequality of man and man" (PD, 332). At first glance, the "equalizing" property of memory stands in opposition to Nietzsche's meaning, insofar as it depends upon a theory of a radical inequality presiding over the birth of values. Huneker, who knew Nietzsche well, distorted the original meaning deliberately, and often used it metaphorically, which testifies to the elasticity of meanings deployed in the spectrum going from fin-de-siècle aestheticism to modernist Nietzscheism.

As a first-generation American Nietzschean, Huneker was conflicted in his wish to be "modern" and often voiced his indecision:

The last plays of a Hauptmann or a Maeterlinck give me more of a thrill than all the musty memories of the days that are no more, and of the dust on forgotten tombs. To-day is more than a million yesterdays or tomorrows! Let the theatrical dead bury the theatrical dead! Yet here I am circling about the past like a fat moth in a lean flame. The pathos of distance!

(PD, 336)

Tender reminiscences of the old days in Philadelphia cannot be erased because the "pathos of distance" reminds him of the ghosts of the past that will not be laid to rest. Distance adds a halo to banal moments and places of the past. Huneker relived the co-existence of places like Philadelphia and New-York or Berlin, and makes room for nostalgia, which appears most in romantic evocations of old Kassel that he visited several times (PD, 161–71).

However, one city would be singled out to allegorize the sheer novelty of the modern: New York—a city to which he gives a vibrant and impassioned homage because it reconciles the radically new with its own vertical "pathos of distance." Huneker writes:

New York is not beautiful in the old order of aesthetics. Its beauty often savours of the monstrous, for the scale is epical. Too many of our buildings are glorified chimneys. But what a picture of titanic energy, of cyclopean ambition, there it is if you look over Manhattan from Washington Heights. The wilderness of flat roofs of London, the winning profile of Paris, the fascination of Rome from Trinita dei Monti, of Buda from across the Danube at Pesth: these are not more startling or dramatic than New York; especially when the chambers of the West are filled by the tremulous opal of a dying day, or a lyric moonrise paves a path of silver across the hospitable sea we call our harbour.

(PD, 1888–9)

Such a modernism remains aware that the traditional canons of beauty remain in the background, even if they have been superseded.

Huneker perceived that what was at stake for the new art was not a quest for beauty or novelty, but an ethical search for freedom of expression: "There is no absolute in beauty; expression, not beauty, is the aim of art. All the rest is mere illustration. Beauty is relative" (PD, 132). Huneker took position about Matisse and Picasso. Having missed the Armory show, since at the time he was in Berlin, he left his two friends, John Quinn and Frederick James Gregg, to defend the values of the new in New York.[15] Just before the war, the three men, united by common Irish family ties, were often called the "Three Musketeers."[16] The American taste for modern art was spurred by the wealth and energy of John Quinn, a refined collector of Matisse, Picabia, and Picasso who also bought manuscripts by Pound and Joyce. Quinn had been advised by Huneker first, and then Pound took over and helped him choose rare items in his ever-expanding collection.

The Pathos of Distance evokes regular visits to Berlin and Paris galleries, and in anticipation of a dichotomy later developed by Gertrude Stein, it sets up an early opposition between Matisse and Picasso: "Matisse, Picasso, and others" documents a period that goes from 1910 to 1912, while discussing the "Post-Impressionism" presented by Fry at the Grafton Galleries in London. As we will see, this exhibition struck Virginia Woolf so strongly that she declared that "human character" changed on that date. Huneker reviews the 1912 Autumn Salon in Paris and mentions visits to Stieglitz's 291 gallery, where Matisse was exhibited in 1908 and 1910. Huneker appears knowledgeable about the Cubists, Futurists, Post-Impressionists; he places Cézanne as the undisputed master behind all the efforts of the younger artists, but his judgment is less assured when it comes to Picasso and Cubism. He was still craving for representation, even if he realized that the aim of the Cubists was "not to represent, but interpret" (PD, 151). Huneker could not resist an easy dig when praising Matisse, who, he said, had a great talent because "you can always tell a human figure of his from a cow, and the same can't be said of the extraordinary productions of Picasso or Picabia" (PD, 150). When there was representation, he pretended to be shocked: "Matisse is at his best—also at his most terrific. One nude sits on a chair drying herself with a bath-towel. You look another way. Degas at his frankest never revealed so much. Nothing occult here. All plain sailing for the man in the street" (PD, 155). The tone is not far from the desultory and prosaic remarks made by amateur urban *flâneurs* like Leopold Bloom in *Ulysses* . . .

Quite often, Huneker praises Matisse and attacks Picasso for the wrong reasons: he loves the line in Matisse who, he thinks, will remain a "classic," whereas he sees only nihilism and destruction in Picasso. And he is not above getting an easy laugh: "The Woman and the Mustard Pot is emotional enough, for the unhappy creature is weeping, no doubt, because of the mustard in her eyes; certainly because of the mustard smeared over her dress. A pungent design, indeed" (PD, 155). This attitude shows the level of resistance met by modernist painters in the United States; indeed, Huneker was not Fry or Gregg, who had more sympathy for Picasso and understood what Duchamp and Picabia were up to. What matters most is that Huneker repeated that novelty in the arts derived from a new aesthetics whose main ambition was pathetic, hence ethical. The pathos of distance would give birth to the pathos of the new; a birth accompanied by as much pain, horror, and stupefaction as joy and satisfaction.

This ethical pathos was a theme treated by Max Stirner, one of the philosophers that Huneker had read attentively. Several times, Huneker summed up *The Ego and His Own*. Stirner's attack on abstract value systems that commanded his "ego" led to a general rejection of any source of value but the ego. Huneker distinguished Proudhon's anarchism from Stirner's egoism:

> Unlike his great contemporary, Joseph Proudhon, Stirner is not a constructive philosopher. Indeed, he is no philosopher. A moralist (or immoralist), an *Ethiker*, his book is a defense of Egoism, of the submerged rights of the Ego. [...] His doctrine is the Fourth Dimension of ethics. That his book will be more dangerous than a million bombs, if misapprehended, is no reason why it should not be read.
>
> (E, 359)

This new ethics was indistinguishable from immoralism, as Gide was to understand as well. In Huneker's view, early modernism was conflicted; there was a serious egotism deriving from Baudelaire and late Symbolism, a more ironic Egoism owing its cynical barbs to Stirner and Nietzsche, and a feminist modernism for which the impact of Meredith's *The Egoist* was not negligible, as Huneker notes.[17]

Huneker's impact on the reception of modernism in America should be better acknowledged. As we have seen, when T. S. Eliot reviewed Huneker's *Egoists* for the *Harvard Advocate* in 1909, he praised the relaxed style of the celebrated conversationalist, whose capacious culture he admired. Eliot later admitted that he had learned more from lists of names dropped by the critic than by the accuracy of his analyses.[18] It was in this discursive and digressive manner that Huneker managed single-handedly to bridge a cultural gap between modernist Europe and the new world. His choice of *Egoists* as a title would not be forgotten—it was not a total coincidence that Eliot became the editor of *The Egoist* in London, relaying Pound and Dora Marsden.[19] Marsden embodied the move from feminism and Suffragism to Stirnerian anarchism. The review became more an arts journal, without for all that losing its radical edge. It is to *The Egoist* that we owe the publication of the first novels by James Joyce and Wyndham Lewis. Its pages welcomed the avant-garde poetry sponsored by Pound. Huneker was the missing link in that complex chronicle of individualist modernism; his doctrine of egoism presented a living bridge between the nineteenth-century lineage of Stendhal, Stirner, Baudelaire, Huysmans, Nietzsche, and the culture of the younger generation also influenced by Frazer, Bergson, Rimbaud, Mallarmé, and Gide. It ushered in what we know best, the high modernism of Ezra Pound's London just before and after the First World War.

The pathos of distance in 1977

It may come as a surprise to see Roland Barthes echo and redouble Huneker's theses. I will try to point out similarities in their positions. When Barthes praised the "pathos of distance" as an "excellent expression," he added: "What is desired is a distance that won't destroy affect" (HLT, 132). Let us go back one more to Nietzsche's text, this time paragraph 37 of *Twilight of the Idols*:

> We are likewise too old, too belated, to be capable of indifference—also a form of strength: our morality of sympathy, against which I was the first to warn, that which one might call *l'impressionisme moral*, is one more expression of the physiological over-excitability pertaining to everything *décadent*. [...] Strong ages, *noble* cultures, see in pity, in "love of one's neighbor," in a lack of self and self-reliance, something contemptible.— Ages have to be assessed by their *positive forces*—and by this assessment the age of the Renaissance, so prodigal and so fateful, appears as the last *great* age; and we, we moderns, with our anxious care for ourselves and love of our neighbor, with our virtues of work, of unpretentiousness, of fair play, of scientificality—acquisitive, economical, machine-minded— appear as a *weak* age ... Our virtues are conditional on, are *demanded* by our weaknesses.... "Equality," a certain actual rendering similar of which the theory of "equal rights" is only an expression, belongs essentially to decline: the chasm between man and man, class and class, the multiplicity of types, the will to be oneself, to stand out—that which I call *pathos of distance*—characterizes every *strong* age. The tension, the range between the extremes is today growing less and less—the extremes themselves are finally obliterated to the point of similarity.[20]

Why is there pathos just because there is an ethical distance? This question had been glimpsed and posed but never fully resolved by Huneker; it is not entirely answered by Barthes either. Barthes keeps the two terms coupled, but somewhat unsteadily. Indeed, if there is a logic of distance next to a logic of pathos, it is not immediately clear how both are connected. In order to progress in this question, Barthes devotes a whole entry of his subjective encyclopedia to "Distance." In that sub-section, Barthes develops the idea that "living together implies an ethics (or a physics) of distance between cohabiting subjects" (HLT, 72). He adds that this is a fundamental problem; his whole seminar hinges around it, with all its marvelous examples, its aporetic juxtaposition of texts, periods, concepts. Why do we find a qualification after "ethics": "(or a physics)"?

The theme of distance posits a neutral space thanks to which Barthes can talk of "bodies" whether in rest or motion as they interact (or not) together. He calculates moves in a physics of distance in which intervals and ratios, speeds and minimal differences like the fine line separating touching and brushing against can be accounted for. We will see later that this corresponds to what Marcel Duchamp called the "infra-thin." Barthes examines the libidinal component of such a physics of small differences, as when he mentions "the threshold between anaclitism and erotic pleasure: the mother caring for her newborn baby [...] the strategic play of distances (always keeping the other at an arm's length) ≠ all the strategies of furtive contact (cf. *Werther*). => A veritable manual of the pleasures of contact, of brushing up against" (HLT, 74). Duchamp added that only a new physics of allegories could describe these quasi imperceptible phenomena that obey the skewed laws of infra-thin distances (*l'infra-mince*).[21] I will return to the infra-thin in the Conclusion.

When Barthes discusses the wonderful passage about Aunt Leonie and Françoise in *Swann's Way*, the term of "anacliticism" brought another discourse, the Freudian analysis of attachment. In his essay on Narcissism, Freud discusses anaclitic attachments, for instance, to the woman who feeds a person, or to a man who acts as a protector.[22] Both are substitutes for the mother. The anaclitic type is opposed to those homosexuals or perverts who take as a model of love-object not their mothers but themselves.[23] This psychoanalytic worry underpins most of the "calculations" of Barthes's physics. The "pathos of distance" is generated by his own situation, a gay man living with his mother who ignores his real sexuality, and whose constant presence and care entails delicate maneuvers with proximity, desire, and indifference. Too close, and one risks incest; too far, and the danger of narcissistic indifference reappears.

Without falling into the trap of biographical fallacy, one may recall a few dates. On January 7, 1977, Barthes gave his inaugural "lesson" at the Collège de France. In the Spring of 1977, he published *A Lover's Discourse*, soon a best seller making Barthes a public intellectual all of a sudden. In the summer of 1977, his mother Henriette became sick; she died on October 25, 1977. These dates bracket the seminar, which both looks backward to *A Lover's Discourse* and forward to *Camera Lucida* and *Mourning Diary*. *How to Live Together* was the last seminar given while Barthes's mother was still alive.

In *How to Live Together*, Barthes lists the reasons why an ethics of distance is needed. What the rules of Saint Pachomius, Saint Benedict, and other founders of religious communities had in common was a regulation of distance and affect. Hence the interesting idea that monks or nuns should wash themselves fully clothed. There could no better prohibition, since it is at the same time a call for self-erotic indulgence. As Lacan showed to Barthes, the prohibition of the Law is indispensable to sustain desire. The justification for an ethics of distance is that it is an ethics of desire, a thesis consistent with what Freud, Winnicott, Lacan, and Reich (the latter quoted 74–75 about the body's armor) all bring to Barthes. The seminar then sketches a chain of reasons that follow the logic of the "bathmology" analyzed by Pierre Force[24]:

(1) I see other people's bodies and because I desire them, I engage in the exhausting strategies of desire.

(2) I conclude that the only way to avoid confusion is to opt for *hesuchia*, a vacancy without desire, or affective equanimity.

(3) I look for a set of rules about the proper distance that will allow me to reach the wished for equanimity.

(4) If I go too far into asceticism and extinguish the desire for other bodies, I also extinguish the desire to live.

(I sum up HLT, 72–73)

Reaching level four, one wants to return to level one, and the whole cycle starts again. This is why most monastic rules stop at level three. This analysis proves the need for a clear positioning of pathos on a scale of gradations. We now understand why pathos—an intense feeling that is often painful—is generated by an ethics of distance. Such pathos, closer to bliss, painful ecstasy, and extreme jouissance than milder pleasures, to use another Barthesian distinction, was revealed to Barthes by Nietzsche. The "pathos of distance" offers all at once a fundamental maxim of non-moral morality, a principle of feeling and a method of philosophy allowing one to rethink philosophy subjectively.

The seminar *How to Live Together* begins and ends with Nietzsche. In the session of January 12, 1977, Nietzsche is adduced to introduce an antihumanist notion of culture as a play of forces generating differences. Culture should be understood as "dispatching" an eccentric array of subjective forces

(HLT, 4). Barthes alludes here to a particular Nietzsche: the Nietzsche rethought by Deleuze. The first pages of *Nietzsche and Philosophy* point in the same direction. Deleuze begins with the concept of "genealogy" and explains that the term means not simply "origin or birth" but also "difference or distance at the origin": "Genealogy means as well nobility and lowness, nobility and the vile, nobility and decadence at the origin."[25] The differential element, based upon the passage from *Genealogy of Morals* quoted earlier, entails the loss of any foundation allied with a strong *feeling* of distance of difference as the key affective position. Any *meaning* will have to derive from this intense feeling that we can agree to call simply "pathos."

Deleuze explains why genealogy implies the emergence of pathos by comparing Nietzsche with Spinoza, whose *Ethics* states that to any force there corresponds a power to be affected: "The same obtains with Nietzsche: the power to be affected does not mean necessarily passivity but affectivity, sensibility, sensation. It is in this sense that Nietzsche, even before having elaborated the concept of will to power and having endowed it with all its signification, talked already about a *feeling of power*" (N&P, 70). The allusion sends us back to Deleuze's 1968 book *Expressionism in Philosophy: Spinoza*.[26] The previous analysis of Expressionism in Spinoza's *Ethics* had distinguished between suffering, passion, feelings, affection, and affect; above all, Deleuze reiterated Spinoza's question: "What can a body do?"

What bodies do best is express—for expression is always embodied, all the while implying a certain idea of the infinite. Spinoza defines his main affects as joy and sadness. Spinoza is grafted onto Nietzsche so as to establish a bridge between pathos as affection and the will to power; this new composite deflates the few pronouncements that sounded quasi neo-Nazi in Nietzsche's original conception. The main point is to argue that power entails a differential sensibility and not just the wish to invade Poland because one has listened too much to Wagner, as Woody Allen quipped. Power is first of all a power to be affected.

When Barthes's lecture ended with a last allusion to Nietzsche (HLT, 133), one could verify that he had indeed followed a Deleuzian trajectory. In his alphabetical encyclopedia of distance, Barthes moved in a non-linear manner from force to force, from affect to affect, from radiant node to radiant node, according to a "non-method" in which he presented the lineaments of a new ethics (HLT, 137). The seminar concluded by opening avenues for further research: Barthes announced either a new pragmatics or a new philology: "a New Philology or an Active Philology, the kind Nietzsche wanted: philology of the *who*, not of the *what*" (HLT, 170). The last insight brings us back to the beginning: "The dis-cursive is therefore not of the order of demonstration, persuasion (it's not a matter of setting out an argument, of convincing someone of a belief, a position)—but of a 'dramatic' order, in the Nietzschean manner: *who*, rather than *what*" (HLT, 19). Deleuze had opposed Plato's fundamental ontological question ("What is this ...?") to the Nietzschean question: "Who?" Thus "We are led to essence only via the question of the meaning and value of the thing" (N&P, 87). Here would lie the root of Nietzsche's perspectivism, which rejects the question "What is that?" because it imposes meaning from an essentialist viewpoint. Nietzsche asserted: "'Essence,' the 'essential nature,' is something perspective and already presupposes a multiplicity. At the bottom of it there always lies 'what is that for *me*?' (for us, for all that lives, etc.)."[27] Here is the point of departure for Barthes's "philology of forces, differences, intensities" (HLT, 107). This sketches an "active philology of discourse" (HLT, 168), which suggests that "active" is synonymous with "affective."

On this affective path, Nietzsche had always accompanied Barthes. Barthes had been introduced to Nietzsche by André Gide. Barthes owes a lot to Gide's admiration for a philosopher who exerted such a deep influence on him as a young man. More precisely, it is in Gide's journal that Barthes discovered Nietzsche. One sees this in one of Barthes's earliest pieces, "On Gide and His Journal," from 1942. A passage sketches a program that has remained valid for Barthes's entire career: "Nietzsche writes: 'Far from being superficial, a great Frenchman has his superficies to the extreme degrees, a natural envelope which surrounds his depths.' (*Dawn*, aphorism 192)."[28] The superficies of the Journal would limn Gide's textual surface while uniting its extremes—which is why Gide could write: "Extremes move me"—an epigraph chosen by Gide for an anthology of his texts *Morceaux Choisis*, a collection that he put together in 1921. The sentence distorts Pascal's famous *Les extrêmes se touchent* to add a Nietzschean twist; Gide asks indeed: for whom are these extremes? (In French: "*Les extrêmes me touchent*.") Such a sentence could be Barthes's own motto.

A second passage refers to Gide's novels, at the time dismissed by Barthes because he assumed that Gide was undermining them by showing the process of creation itself: "This is because we have realized that art is a game, a technique (this dates from the French invention of the formula *l'Art pour l'Art*. See Nietzsche's *Beyond Good and Evil*, aphorism 254.)"[29] In this aphorism, which comes just before the analysis of the "pathos of distance" already quoted, Nietzsche praises the taste, intelligence, and refinement of French culture. He criticizes German boorishness along with the new craze for Wagner in Paris. His forerunner is indeed Stendhal, who condenses French virtues such as sharpness of psychological analysis, boundless curiosity, and a mastery of *tempo* in the writing.

The sentence that attracted Barthes's attention is: "[T]he capacity for artistic emotion, for devotion to 'form,' for which the expression, *l'art pour l'art*, along with numerous others, has been invented—such capacity has not been lacking in France for three centuries."[30] It may be surprising to see Barthes quote Nietzsche in order to defend *l'art pour l'art* in 1942; however, because they pave the way to a new *pathos of distance*, those sentences could have been written by James Huneker in 1913.

For Roland Barthes, Gide's highly ironical *Paludes* was the most influential and successful book in the writer's abundant corpus. This parody of the symbolist literary milieu was a lever that helped André Gide put a distance between the Parisian aesthetes and the vitalism that he developed under the combined influence of Nietzsche's philosophy and of Dostoevsky's novels. The same pathetic Nietzscheism led Gide to adopt the notion of "immoralism" in a novel, *The Immoralist*, whose hero Michel discovers sensual health, whereas his religious and repressed wife dies. However, Michel did not shake off the specters of religion and morality for Gide's "Preface" highlighted his "neutrality" close to "indecision."[31]

Gide's true heir was Roland Barthes, who began his career as a critic in 1942 by meditating on Gide's Journal. Gide was relayed by Albert Camus, and then by the Nouveau Roman, both of whom enabled him to define the notion of "writing degree zero," a literature of non-literature, a "blank" style rejecting Proust's superb architecture of convoluted metaphors. At the other opposite, Gide stands there, an always young writer: "Gide is ageless; he is always young, always mature; he is always sage, always fervent."[32]

Pathos as poetry and distance

Given this "fervor," a recurrent Gidean term, the Nietzschean question one is tempted to ask of Barthes himself is whether his Seminar aimed at producing knowledge and inventing concepts, or whether he saw himself as an artist motivated by a wish to create new affects. When reviewing the sequence of the three seminars given at the Collège de France by Barthes between 1977 and 1980, Antoine Compagnon discovered a common feature linking them. To understand the later Barthes, he argued, one should see him as an "antimodern" who finally found the courage to confess publicly that he was a traditionalist.[33] It is undeniable that Barthes had felt hijacked or taken hostage by his avant-gardist friends at *Tel Quel*. He was moving in a different direction when he imagined writing a Proustian novel, or when he launched an ethics combining Dante's *Vita Nuova* and a Deleuzian theory of affects. Compagnon, who knew Barthes personally, insists on the theme of poetry as a focal point, more so than the autobiographical novel that Barthes planned to be writing one day. The Japanese haiku emerged as a new fantasy of escape, an easier and lighter counterpart to the unwritten Proustian novel: sadly, Barthes died on March 25, 1980, just as he was planning a major change in his life and career.

What is at stake is the role played by poetry as a formal negotiation with distance. When, much earlier, Barthes had tackled the issue of poetry in *Writing Degree Zero*, he argued then that poetry could never reach a "degree zero," because it was too "vertical." Barthes had quoted René Char before concluding firmly that there was no poetic "writing," but only poetic "styles":

> The explosion of the poetic word institutes then an absolute object; Nature becomes a succession of verticalities; the object suddenly stands erect, filled with all its possibles: it can only be a landmark in an unfulfilled and thereby terrible world. [. . .] [T]hese poetic words exclude men: there is no poetic humanism of modernity: this erect discourse is full of terror, that is to say, it relates man not to other men, but to the most inhuman images in Nature: heaven, hell, the sacred, childhood, madness, pure matter, etc.[34]

The assessment had sounded terribly negative at the time. Twenty years later, the same verticality acquired a Nietzschean ring that led directly to the pathos endorsed by Barthes.

A similar post-Nietzschean model was provided by Georges Bataille, who also hesitated between poetry, novels, essays, and aphorisms. In 1972, Barthes discussed Bataille's essay on "The Big Toe" for a Cerisy conference in which he read Bataille via Nietzsche.[35] Here again, Nietzsche was adduced to criticize the loss of distance and the flattening of modern values. In that context, Barthes provided a Bataille lexicon, with entries in alphabetical order such as "Flattening of Values," "Beginning," "Playing Out" (*Déjouer*), "What and Who?" These are found next to "Codes of Knowledge," "Dressed," "Idiomatic," "Paradigm," or "Vocables"—terms corresponding more to a classically semiological or poetological analysis.

These entries offered less close readings of one text as Barthes had done earlier with *Story of the Eye*, explicated as a network of intertwined metaphors creating an original prose poetry, than a continuation of Bataille's materialist anthropology. Barthes moved from echoes of Lacanian psychoanalysis when analyzing the "big toe" as a phallic excrescence, to a philosophical lineage in which Deleuze's reading of Nietzsche was applied. Once more the pathos of distance was brought to bear on the French writer. An entry entitled "What and Who?" illustrates this strategy:

> Knowledge says of each thing: 'What is it?' What is the big toe? What is this text? Who is Bataille? But value, according to the Nietzschean

watchword, prolongs the question: *What is it for me?* In a Nietzschean way, Bataille's text answers the question: *What is the big toe for me, Bataille?* And by displacement: What is this text, *for me, the reader?* (Answer: It is the text I would want to write.)[36]

As we have seen, the constant reference to Deleuze's *Nietzsche and Philosophy* allowed Barthes to deploy his philology of forces, differences, and intensities (HLT, 107). In this case, philology generated less a *poesis* than a *poeien*, an active verb, a "making." Barthes continued the creative work begun by Bataille in a mimetic manner and expanded the zany classifications of *Documents*. In the section entitled "*Habillé*" ("Dressed"), Barthes listed new items and drew on his personal culture to discuss habits like those "of certain hustlers who remove every garment except their socks."[37] Bataille had concluded his "The Big Toe" essay from 1929 with a caveat against any idealization, specifically of the poetic type.[38] He was attacking the idealism that he regularly denounced in Breton and other surrealists.

Barthes's essay may be the double in length of Bataille's text on the big toe; it nevertheless elides the materialist program or the anthropology of feet. "Codes of Knowledge" thus begins with remarks in which we can measure the impact of the "Pathos of Distance": In Bataille's text, there are many "poetic" codes: thematic (high/low, noble/ignoble, light/muddy), amphibological (the word *erection*, for instance), metaphorical ("man is a tree")."[39] Treating the amphibology of "erection"—most of Bataille's essay rests on the double meaning of man who "stands upright" thanks to a magical toe unavailable to apes, and the sexual sense of erection—as "poetic" may be justified (I will return to Jarry's poetics of erection later), whereas the decision to treat the couples "high / low" and "noble / ignoble" as "poetic" sounds more surprising. Even if Bataille's thinking is structured by couples of opposites, his theory can hardly be called a "poetic" mode of thinking, unless he is supposed to think through Aristotle's *Poetics*, with the discussion of "high" characters fit for Tragedy and "low" characters fit for Comedy. In fact, as we will see later with Jarry, Bataille's notion of "poetry" is to condense distance by performing literary erections.

Subsequent discussions of the same dichotomies place them under the heading of ethics—an ethics underpinning fragmented or scattered codes: "Thus, Bataille assures the baffling (*truquage*) of knowledge by a fragmentation of the codes, but more particularly by an outburst of value (*noble* and *ignoble*, *seductive* and *deflated*). The role of value is not a role of destruction, nor yet of dialectization, nor even of subjectivization, it is perhaps, quite simply, a role of *rest*."[40] This paradoxical rest can be equated with jouissance and heterology. Another passage in "Outcomes of the Text" situates heterology within a Nietzschean paradigm. Whereas Nietzsche has two terms only, *noble* and *base*, (this should qualify for a poetic logic), Bataille would articulate three terms: *noble / ignoble / low*. The *low* will be represented by spittle, mud, blood streaming, fury, terrors, and obsessions, the violent discord of the organs, the bellowing viscera.[41] Barthes analyzes a non-dialectical dialectics for which the third term is not neutral but is an added value doubling as an independent, eccentric, and irreducible factor. A double pathos is at play: what matters for Nietzsche is the vertical distance between the high and the low; a distance that will not allow reversals transforming the high into the low and conversely. To this Bataille adds another pathos—the pathos of desperate laughter, the laughter of the low.

By endorsing this lowness, Barthes confesses his proximity with Bataille in whom he refused to see a mystic, the inventor of an anti-theology or a gnostic system, as Sartre had famously argued. Barthes steers away from these anti-theological niceties to stress the "third" term:

> [A] third term appears: *Laughter*, which baffles Modesty, the *meaning* of Modesty; and on the other hand, language itself is audaciously distended: *low* (*bas*) is used as a positive, approbative value ("the low materialism of gnosis"), but its correlative adverb, which according to language should have the same value as the original adjective, is employed negatively, disparagingly ("the *basely* idealistic orientation of Surrealism").[42]

Nietzschean re-evaluation is brought to light in this heterology. Rebelling against any "Flattening of Values," the "Pathos of Distance" invokes the verticality and dehiscence so well balanced and combined in *How to Live Together*.

Deleuze had given to Barthes the theme of a joyful pathos related to aesthetics; this comes to the fore in a passage devoted to *The Birth of Tragedy*. *The Birth of Tragedy* was not one Barthes's favorites earlier on. In "Powers of Ancient Tragedy" from 1953, Barthes takes Nietzsche to task for having reduced Greek tragedy to Wagner's drama[43]—a theme already developed by Huneker in his strictures on Wagner. It was only after reading Deleuze in the 1970s that Barthes was reconciled with Nietzsche's views on tragedy. Tragedy can bring joy, into which negative affects like terror or pity will be transmuted. Deleuze praises Dionysos, the god of tragedy, because he affirms that everything that appears in the world, even the most painful or horrible things, brings joy. Joy corresponds to an affirmation of what is, and its pathos is so strong that it impels us to wish that all should be repeated eternally. In his *gaya scienza*, Dionysos asserts a knowledge akin to the tragic "pathos mathos" (we learn when we suffer) that we find in Aeschylus's *Agamemnon* as Deleuze states in *Nietzsche and Philosophy* (N&P, 19).

The example of Nietzsche explains why Barthes in his later years appeared as an artist or a poet more than a critic or philosopher. Barthes's last seminars were underpinned by lyrical, anguished or ecstatic questions touching upon his body. The ethics of distance to be deduced from those pages is an ethics that anyone can elaborate with their bodies, persons, and private lives. In parallel, the Nietzsche who emerged for Barthes in the last years hesitated between the figure of the distraught lover writing to Cosima Wagner: "Ariadne, I love you," quoted in *How to Live Together* (92), and the mad philosopher who embraced a horse in a Turin street before collapsing, as Barthes reminisced in *Camera Lucida*. Watching a few moving photographs, he could enter "crazily into the spectacle, into the image, taking into my arms what is dead, what is going to die, as Nietzsche did when, as Podach tells us, on January 3, 1889, he threw himself in tears on the neck of a beaten horse: gone mad for Pity's sake."[44] Here, the pathos of distance has reached a paroxysm, caught up between Maurice Blanchot's *Writing of the Disaster* and D. W. Winnicott's last, posthumous, paper, "Fear of Breakdown."[45] Barthes has translated Bataille's erotic excess into his own pathos, revolving around the anxious expectation of a catastrophe.

This pathos adheres to every powerful photograph and turns each of them into a lyrical poem touching a nerve in the subject: "I shudder, like Winnicott's psychotic patient, *over a catastrophe which has already happened*" (CL, 96). Barthes was meditating on his own catastrophe at the time, his mother's recent death. The tragedy was condensed by a photograph of the mother when she was five, which functioned like a private haiku. However, many other photographs shown in *Camera Lucida* keep alive the future death of the subjects who posed for them, as with Lewis Payne in Alexander Garner's 1865 portrait, because he was awaiting his execution. He is both dead and going to die, for ever, which exemplifies a perfectly Nietzschean "eternal return of the same." Barthes generalizes: "Whether or not the subject is already dead, every photograph is this catastrophe" (CL, 96)—an insight that reintroduces a forceful pathos into his images and his personal network of associations.

These poignant and moving images, flickering as beacons in an endless labyrinth, all offer pathetic metaphors. Unspeakably private, they nevertheless testify to the possibility of a communal grieving. *How to Live Together* presents Barthes's version of the impossible or "unavowable" community called for by Bataille. Bataille sensed in Nietzsche a "desire for a community," but felt that he was doomed to isolation in the private world of lyricism, for him almost a form of madness if it was not underpinned by the "sacred":

> Literature (fiction) took the place of what had formerly been the spiritual life; poetry (the disorder of words) that of real states of trance. Art

constituted a small free domain, outside action: to gain freedom it had to renounce the real world. [...] Nietzsche is far from having resolved the difficulty. Zarathustra is also a poet, and a literary fiction at that![46]

Under the influence of Jacques Derrida's aggressive reading of Bataille in *Writing and Difference*, Barthes had started taking a distance that was less pathetic than theoretical facing Nietzschean and Bataillean pathos. Derrida had come down hard on Bataille in *Writing and Difference*; Barthes mentions this critical discussion several times without endorsing Derrida's questioning heterology as a misguided anti-Hegelianism. However, in a 1980 "Preface for an Album of Photographs by Lucien Clergue," we find a conflation of Bataille's term of "excess" allied with a specifically Derridean concept (the supplement). Barthes writes: "When a work exceeds (*déborde*) the meaning that it seems to have posed, this means that the Poetic (*le Poétique*) is in it: the Poetic is one way or the other the supplement of meaning."[47] This echoes what Bataille wrote about poetry in *Guilty* ("Poetry that is not engaged in an experience exceeding poetry (distinct from it) is not the movement but the residue left by the turbulence"),[48] while combining "excess" with Derrida's "supplement."

Barthes's critique remained Nietzschean facing Bataille, but his Nietzscheism became muffled, muted, tempered by deconstruction. Derrida demonstrated that Bataille, like Sartre, had misunderstood the issue of language when reading philosophy, getting sidetracked when he tried to grapple with Hegel and Nietzsche. Cunningly, Derrida pinpointed the impossibility of Bataille's theory of the Impossible as Poetry. If poetry appears whenever a text disobeys its own program and opens itself to the loss of meaning, then poetry is indistinguishable from pathos. Bataille defines poetry as a "play without rules" avoiding any domestication in a Nietzschean affirmation of sovereignty; but, as Derrida notes, this leads to "an admirable, untenable formulation which could serve as the heading for everything we are attempting to reassemble here as the form and torment of his writing, 'the commentary on its absence of meaning.'"[49] (WD, 261). Bataille's life-long confrontation with Breton's Surrealism and with Hegel had generated a poetic pathos that became grist to Derrida's debunking machine. The outcome is a demonstration that such a subjective and lyrical position could not avoid being caught up in Hegelian dialectics, therefore in the mechanism of philosophy as such. The affect of pathos would ultimately be subsumed by the concept. If the concept returns, it dominates everything, and Nietzsche cannot guide us out of the maze. Pathos paints itself in a corner because it thrives upon a loss of meaning that ends up attributing a meaning to the absence of meaning. In that sense, the best exemplification of the pathos of distance would be the famous photograph of Barthes's mother in the Winter garden when she was five—a family photograph that he glosses lovingly but that he wisely refused to display for our voyeuristic gazes in *Camera Lucida*.

This ethical refusal of reproduction in the age of its banalization was a sure way of retrieving the aura for this trivial, but unique, private and beloved image. We can only imagine it, as some artists have done in recent years. This calls up what Walter Benjamin has to say about a Victorian portrait of Karl Dauthendey, the father of a famous German poet and painter, seen with his fiancée who would much later commit suicide in Moscow. While the man "seems to be holding her" in fact, she is already elsewhere, for "her gaze passes him by, absorbed in an ominous distance."[50] This is the impassable distance of death, madness, and suicide. Sketching in advance the program of *Camera Lucida*, Benjamin's analysis gives a rationale for Barthes's refusal to show his mother's picture:

> No matter how artful the photographer, no matter how carefully posed his subject, the beholder feels an irresistible compulsion to search such a picture for the tiny spark of contingency, the here and now, with which reality as, so to speak, seared through the image-character of the photograph, to find the inconspicuous place where, within the suchness of that long-past minute, the future still nests today—and so eloquently, that we, looking back, may rediscover it.[51]

2

"Hard" Modernism

Alfred Jarry

No one has done more to promote the interaction between theory and the cultural historiography of the modern moment seen from the point of view of its "now-time" (as the previous quote confirms) than Walter Benjamin. His essays have provided original, cogent, and intelligent definitions of modernism. Benjamin's effort in his unfinished compendium of *The Arcades Project* was to delineate the fault-lines between modernity and modernism. He was not deluded by the shrill claims of artists who insisted that they had to be "absolutely modern," a task that Rimbaud had argued would loom larger at the end of the nineteenth century.[1] Benjamin noted wryly that each epoch believes itself to be in the vanguard of the modern: "Each age unavoidably seems to itself a new age. The "modern" (*das "Moderne"*) however, is as varied in its meaning as the different aspects of one and the same kaleidoscope."[2]

Das Moderne / die Moderne : Modernismus

The image of the kaleidoscope evokes less the constant reshuffling of moving elements caught up in a huge cultural machine than it echoes Baudelaire, who compared the subject of modernity to a "kaleidoscope gifted with consciousness." Baudelaire was defining the rapture engulfing the subject of modernity who was a new "man of the crowd," as Poe saw him, but also a "lover of universal life" able to penetrate the mass of urban passersby in order to tap this "immense reservoir of electrical energy."[3] Benjamin meditated at length on Baudelaire's concept of modernity, and brought it into connection with the two important philosophies of history of the nineteenth century, those of Hegel and Marx.

In the same passage of *Arcades*, Benjamin quoted Roger Caillois, who had alluded to Paris as a "modern myth." For Caillois, modernity entailed the "elevation of urban life to the level of myth" (AP, 555); a feature that we tend to associate with Joyce, Eliot, and Pound, and that was obviously a determining factor for Baudelaire. Benjamin wondered whether Baudelaire's *modernité* could have generated *modernism* in a simple historical development, by a rupture or as a weakening of the first wave. This led to a simple question: "How does modernism become *Jugendstil*?" (AP, 561). The word that the translators correctly render as "modernism" is not a neutral as before (*das Moderne*) but feminine: *die Moderne*. Benjamin often uses the term *Neuheit* (translated as "Novelty"), or the "New," but this is the first occurrence of a feminine word as a parallel to the masculine term of *Modernismus*. Beyond arbitrary grammatical rules (in French, we have the feminine *la modernité* and the masculine *le modernisme*, but mythical qualities like the hardness of the masculine and the softness of femininity have been exchanged), one may ask pointedly what the "gender of modernism"[4] might be.

There was a shared sense that "high modernism" had to be masculine, hence "hard," aggressive, ferocious even, against an effeminate culture of decadence, or even worse, the production of mass culture for a dominantly feminine audience, allegedly the consumers of popular novels, as we will see with Ezra Pound. Even within the field of modernist theory, authors like Peter Bürger have argued that modernism as such had kept elements of the "soft" aestheticizing touch, whereas the real revolution in the arts and everyday life was to be found only in the "historical" avant-gardes. Indeed, not so long ago, as influential a critic as Hugh Kenner refused to grant the epithet of "modernist" to Virginia Woolf, deemed too "soft" and not experimental enough. Kenner reserved the term for the group animated by Ezra Pound.[5] Gertrude Stein could state forcibly that geniuses were all men—which included her as well! In all these discussions, gender and politics seem inextricably confused.

Benjamin's use of a feminine term (*die Moderne*) should be referred back to the "*Jugendstil*" moment, a movement often rendered in English as "art nouveau." It corresponded to the post-symbolist generation of 1890–1910, and could be sketched as a loose lineage linking Baudelaire to Mallarmé, Laforgue, Wilde, Jarry, and the younger Gide and Yeats. Odilon Redon and Beardsley would be its main artists. Needless to say, Benjamin, who embraced the material, technological, and ideological acceleration of modernity, could not but reject the legacy of the *Jugendstil*, a movement that he always associated with the decadent poetry of Stefan George, with whom he had fought at the beginning of his career. Sexual perversion and fake mysticism are the ways in which *Jugendstil* would attempt to bring back a lost aura: "Jugendstil forces the auratic" (AP, 557). In other words, Benjamin points to possible links between modernism, the "aura" and regressive aestheticism leading to stillborn productions, bad art, or simply put, Kitsch. Modernism since Clement Greenberg's time at least has been haunted by an always possible transformation of the aura into Kitsch.

In order to avoid such a degradation, Pound's modernism, like that of Yeats, was characterized by a masculine "hardness"—a term that he found operative when surveying the history of French poetry. Pound saw it split in a bifurcation between a "hard" school going from Villon to Gautier and a "soft" school flourishing with Mallarmé and the *Unanimistes*. Here is how these terms are defined: "By 'hardness' I mean a quality which is in poetry nearly always a virtue—I can think of no case where it is not. By softness I mean an opposite quality which is not always a fault."[6] It would be a mistake to identify these qualities with gendered terms referring to their authors; Pound believed that Mallarmé was soft, while his old friend H. D. (Hilda Doolittle) stood firmly on the side of "hardness." Pound prodded his Irish mentor Yeats to get rid of the softness of his initial Celtic Twilight touch. Pound's concept of modernity cannot be reduced to an obsession for hardness, but this feature was always a plus for him. The concept helped Eliot "modernize" *The Waste Land*.

Wayne Koestenbaum has attracted our attention to the collaboration of the two American poets whose co-editing process made a great poem shift from a bisexual confession doubling as a poetic autobiography to a more masculine text then taken to embody the essence of high modernism: "Eliot's poem—semiotic, negative, riddled with absences—is 'feminine' not because women always sound like *The Waste Land* but because, in 1922, its style might have seemed more recognizably a hysterical woman's than a male poet."[7] Pound not only excised the "femininity" of the poem, but he forced Eliot to frame its bisexual elements within a mythical discourse. The famous beginning of the poem ("April is the cruelest month …") spoken by an anonymous voice, a "we" floating in the void, ushers in feminine modulations with countess Marie Larisch's story.

Controlling such sexual modulations was a main incentive for Pound's editing of the draft given to him by Eliot. Pound reduced it by half, deleted the opening section about a night out in Boston, canceled the genteel hesitations, muted autobiographical asides, cut most pastiches of classical genres. Pound wanted to eliminate anything "wobbly," "hesitant" or reminiscent of the tone of "Prufrock." Pound, impatient with Tiresias as a central figure, went as far as write: "make up yr. mind you Tiresias if you know know damn well or else you don't" (*sic*) in the margin.[8] On this point, Eliot remained firm: Pound never made Eliot modify the character of the bisexual seer. What annoyed Pound was Eliot's indulgence for psychological ambivalence, stylistic ambiguity, and his dramatic representation of sexual unease. If Tiresias is the "most important figure" of the poem, as stated in Eliot's endnote, it is because Tiresias embodies the hysterical bisexuality that was haunting Eliot at the time. The Tiresias paradigm provided Eliot with a fantasy of ecstatic gender-crossing well expressed in "The Death of Saint Narcissus," which culminates with a transsexual fantasy:

> Then he had been a young girl
> Caught in the woods by a drunken old man,
> Knowing at the end the taste of her own whiteness
> The horror of her own smoothness,
> And he felt drunken and old.[9]

The rape of a girl by an old man, a violation whose taste lingers in the speaker's memory, gives poignancy to metamorphoses experienced through a Keatsian "negative capability." The troubling fantasy corresponds to what Pound wished to eliminate. On the whole, Pound's cuts were positive: they forced *The Waste Land* to become tighter, more intense, less of a sprawling adolescent autobiography, offering a more mature statement. An example of this effort towards mythical cleanliness is observable in the scene of love-making when we are privy to Tiresias's disgust as he witnesses the sexual encounter between the typist and the young clerk. The original quatrain had:

> I Tiresias, old Man with wrinkled dugs,
> Perceived the scene, and foretold the rest
> Knowing the manner of these crawling bugs,
> I too awaited the expected guest.[10]

Pound crossed out the third line, adding: "Too easy." The consequence of this editorial change is that "dugs" remained without its rhyme, thus sounding more ominous, whereas Tiresias's revulsion was muted to bleak compassion. Then Pound wrote "Echt" facing Tiresias's recapitulation ("And I Tiresias . . ."). Pound's annotations attempted to expunge the lurking hysteria in the poem, a hysteria climaxing at the end when the voices cannot stabilize themselves in one single idiom and madness seems to triumph over order. Before returning to Eliot in Chapters 5 and 6, I will first engage with French modernism and apply to an early practitioner the concepts of "hard" and "soft" laid out by Pound.

The French context

"Modernism" is a loaded word when understood in a French context, whereas its meaning is relatively clear in an Anglo-Saxon context: one adds Ezra Pound, Gertrude Stein, T. S. Eliot, James Joyce, William Carlos Williams, and

Virginia Woolf, and states that all combined stylistic experimentation with an effort to restate ancient cultural themes. It may not be so easy with the French context. Thus, when she had to describe French literary modernism in a comprehensive collection of essays devoted to international modernism, Kimberley Healey began by asserting that French modernism did not exist.[11] This caveat was less paradoxical than it sounds, for indeed one can entertain doubts about the universalism of "modernism." The concept of modernism was invented for an Anglo-Saxon corpus in a promotion by academics for academics; this took place in the 1950s and was retroactively applied to works from the 1920s. Such a periodization is not relevant if we consider the French cultural scene or its Spanish counterpart. However, the concept of modernism has begun to be used by French literary critics. If an influential review in English speaking counties is *Modernism/Modernity*, its French equivalent is simply called *Modernités*. As we have seen with Benjamin, the term that was felt to be more relevant was that of "modernity"—a *modernité* encompassing a tradition of the new taking Baudelaire, Mallarmé, Lautréamont, and Jarry as its beacons. If we agree that there is room for a specific French modernism, I would like to explore how it displays a specific pathos of distance as opposed to proximity. I will take as my point of departure the literary and stylistic revolution performed by Symbolism, with Mallarmé as leader and chief experimenter, as it invaded the genre of prose.

In the last decade of the nineteenth century, Marcel Proust evoked the "power of the novelist" with a startling image: "We stand in front of the novelist as slaves in front of the Emperor: with one word, he can set us free (*il peut nous affranchir*)."[12] In Proust's analysis, if we follow novelists and move into their fictional universes, we become someone else, general, weaver, singer, peasant. Experiencing their lives by proxy, we leave our cares and selves behind in a giddy superabundance of freedom. Proust's words evoke another freedom, often discussed at the time—the freedom of the artist who feels liberated from stylistic constraints, as exemplified by symbolist poets who had discovered "free verse." Mallarmé defined this moment as a "crisis in verse," which corresponded to the moment when the tyranny of the alexandrine had been destroyed. When in 1897 Mallarmé observed that "literature is here undergoing an exquisite and fundamental crisis,"[13] his choice of the word "literature" evoked poetry above all. Thus, on his reading it was Victor Hugo who had confiscated verse and swallowed it in his larger-than-life personality; meanwhile, a "very modern taste"[14] praised by Mallarmé had led to the practice of "free verse," which meant abandoning the codes, rules, and guidelines that had determined French versification for centuries. Proust pointed out in a similar manner that this escape from formal shackles, abundantly displayed by French poets after Rimbaud, Lautréamont, Verlaine, and Mallarmé, had in fact created a new conformism, not the poetic freedom that would change "literature" and modernize it once and for all.

I have tried to show that the modernist school in France had started with Paul Verlaine, who used the term in 1871 as the melodious double of Rimbaud.[15] French modernism found a new lyrical and ironical voice with the poems of Jules Laforgue, and continued with Guillaume Apollinaire as a softer version of Alfred Jarry's proto-futurism. Finally, it flowered with Valery Larbaud, a cosmopolitan author who had translated countless contemporaries and lost precursors, and who discovered in Joyce's *Ulysses* the realization of his own literary program. Hence, French modernism existed historically; at least insofar as several writers have exemplified the main characteristics of the Anglo-Saxon regrouping. French modernism was exemplified both by authors who wrote in the wake of symbolism, like Edouard Dujardin, Jules Laforgue, the younger André Gide, and Guillaume Apollinaire, and by authors coming from different horizons, like Jules Romains, Valery Larbaud, and the younger Marcel Proust.[16] In order to combine a historical perspective and a theoretical angle, French modernism can be framed by critical discussions from the period. These were not disagreements so much as moments of blindness or incomprehension registering the novelty of certain initiatives later identified with modernism and indicating the complexity of this evolving consciousness.

A first discussion opposed Marcel Proust and Stéphane Mallarmé. In 1896, Proust published "Against Obscurity"[17] in the symbolist *Revue Blanche*, a scathing attack on the style of Symbolism. Investing the literary organ of the movement, Proust took to task the devotees of the new school for their habit of writing incomprehensibly. He dismissed the idea that obscurity was condoned by the themes treated. Hugo and Racine had been accused of being obscure in their times, which had little to do with stylistic obfuscation and circumlocution found everywhere in poems written by members of the French *Symboliste* school. *Symboliste* obscurity did not stem from the depth of thought, as with Heraclitus or Hegel: a poet stuffing poems with philosophical reflections errs; this was the wrong genre. Obviously, this reminder about generic borders was not heeded by Proust two decades later when he composed his own magnum opus as a medieval "Summa" doubling as a "philosophical novel." Debunking the wish of symbolist poets to reach the Absolute in verse, Proust opposed to their convoluted prose or verse the unaffected simplicity of a prose writer like Anatole France, the model of Bergotte.[18] France's elegant prose and linear plots kept alive a sense of fiction that symbolist poets had forgotten: universal truths must first be embodied in the particularities of characters or situations.

Stung by a criticism that looked like an "aggression," Mallarmé replied that his contemporaries had forgotten how to read.[19] "Obscurity," taken as an insult, made it easy for readers who "didn't have to understand."[20] Such a debate, a landmark for the turn of the century, did not boil down to a clash between poetry and the novel, or between experimental writing and realism. It betrays more than a generational divide; Proust was attacking less Mallarmé, whom he respected, than his younger epigones. The debate impacted prose fiction written in French in the last decade of the nineteenth century and the first two decades of the twentieth century and remains crucial for our understanding of international modernism. Proust was wondering how to continue writing readable novels after the experiments with syntax and imagery lushly deployed by Rimbaud, Lautréamont, and Mallarmé.

Jarry: Holding hard to the drive

The most visible experimenter in French modernism was Alfred Jarry, one of the first exuberant avant-gardists who had been touched by the spirit of Nietzsche. Jarry's main invention was to transform Nietzsche's ethical energies in the sexual domain, rewriting Zarathustra's Supermen as a phallic Supermale. Some of Nietzsche's rhetoric of violence finds its way into Jarry's plays. In the artistic domain, he grafted late Symbolism onto his specific variation of anarchism. I will focus on the novel *The Supermale*, since it contains most of the seeds of subsequent French modernism.

Jarry had been lucky with his teachers, and he never forgot them, not even the unfortunate "Père Hébert," the ridiculous and rotund science teacher monumentalized in the savage parody of Père Ubu. In Paris, it was Henri Bergson himself who introduced Jarry to his philosophy of time and intuition in 1893. Earlier, while still at Rennes in 1889, Jarry was introduced to the thought of Nietzsche by Benjamin Bourdon, then just back from Germany. Bourdon had worked with Wilhelm Wundt on experimental psychology and would soon complete his dissertation entitled *The Expression of Emotions and Tendencies in Language*.[21] Bourdon followed Wundt in linking Darwinian expressive universals visible in animals and humans, and a "popular psychology" stressing features of simplicity, intensity, stylization, and emotional empathy.[22] Wundt's psychology insisted on the pregnancy of formulaic creation when discussing gestures: gestures would be constructed from an initial emotion into a "formula," a term that helped Aby Warburg coin the expression *Pathosformel* (formula of pathos).

Jarry's creation of Ubu as a terrifying puppet, a schoolboy's bogey condensing the laughable power of adults, their omnipotence experienced as random and pathetic outbursts of violent sadism by children, owes a lot to Wundt and Bourdon's psychology of emotions. The barely caricatured figure of Bourdon appears as Ubu's "Conscience"—easily identifiable because of his mannerism, the regular interjection of "*et ainsi de suite*" in all his sentences—in *Ubu Cocu*. It is astonishing to think that Bourdon introduced French high-school students to un-translated works of Nietzsche eleven years before the philosopher's demise. Bourdon would "explain" Nietzsche, as Jarry writes in memories of his youth.[23] In 1893, the future poet Léon-Paul Fargue, Jarry's close friend, one-time lover, and soon bitter enemy, wrote to Jarry from Germany, confessing that he wished that Bergson could talk more about Nietzsche; if he did, his lectures would truly be beyond good and evil![24] Soon, Jarry blended Nietzsche's self-proclaimed persona of the "Anti-Christ" with Bergson's theory of Intuition in his "pataphysical" or "anarchist" version of "César-Antechrist." King Ubu appears for the first time in *César-Antechrist*, published in several installments in 1894.[25]

Besides being a cultural anarchist tending to nihilism and a gifted literary provocateur, Jarry was a fervent disciple of Mallarmé. Mallarmé congratulated him on the success of *Ubu Roi*, and then wrote to the very young writer several times. When Mallarmé died in 1898, Jarry attended the funeral. His moving obituary evoked the "island of Ptyx" as a homage to the most esoteric and obscure sonnet in "X."[26] Jarry was a living bridge between late Symbolism and early Futurism. Marinetti, a futurist rarely linked to symbolism, was impressed by the Ubu plays. He met Jarry several times. In 1906, Jarry thanked Marinetti, who had sent him *Roi Bombance*, a proto-futurist play inspired by the Ubu cycle.[27] I will focus on two novels by Jarry, *Messaline, Roman de l'ancienne Rome* (1901) and *Le Surmâle, Roman moderne* (1902). While the former novel takes imperial Rome as its setting, the latter is situated in the future: it takes place, by a neat inversion, in 1920. If we notice the subtle ways in which the future and the past are intertwined, we can conclude that the conditions are gathered for the creation of French modernism.

However, what has not been translated in the English version, strangely, is the subtitle of the second novel: "*The Supermale: A Modern Novel*"[28] flaunts its modernity, a condition manifested by heaping up real and fantastic machines, bicycles, locomotives, fast cars, phonographs, and dynamos. At the end, a terrifying machine-to-inspire-love explodes and kills the hero. The *Supermale*'s plot is similar to that of *Messalina*: in both novels, a character seeks a paroxystic sexual pleasure and dies after having beaten world records in sex-making. The feminine half of the diptych is situated in the histories of the debaucheries of the Roman emperors, whose piquant vignettes had been narrated by Suetonius and Tacitus. The future of 1920 is marked by American inventors, and above all by delirious machines. Jarry's central conceit presupposes an almost total identification of technology and sexuality. In both novels, sexual excess leads to new wisdom, but it flirts so much with the Absolute that it leads to an explosive and apocalyptic demise.

Jarry's modernism was constituted by the splicing of the "modern" text of *The Supermale* with *Messalina*, a historical novel evoking more Flaubert's *Salammbô* than the *Ubu* plays. Both novels display narrative techniques that are daringly innovative; this is perhaps more visible in *The Supermale*. The two main "events" of the plot—a bicycle race of ten-thousand-miles won by the hero, André Marcueil, against a racing locomotive and a team of five cyclists fueled by "perpetual-motion-food," and the sexual contest in which Marcueil, disguised as an Indian, has sex for a whole day before making his partner reach eighty-two orgasms—are narrated by several filters like the voice of a journalistic report, the account provided by a doctor records the sexual prowess while speculating on God and "pataphysics," the pseudo-science invented by Fautsroll, another character of Jarry. *The Supermale* is a modernist novel because it splices the present and the past seamlessly. Even though it is shot through with science-fiction speculations about a futurist intermixing of men and machines, it keeps harking back to the past. Marcueil's wish to make love indefinitely is based upon his reading of a Latin poem. His curiosity is woken up when he reads about Messalina in Juvenal's satire that describes how when the Emperor Claudius was asleep, Messalina, disguised, would go to a brothel and sell herself to the clients; she would be the last to leave reluctantly, and with "her taut sex still burning, inflamed with lust," she would return to the Emperor's bed.[29]

Marcueil is both a super-athlete and a fine Latinist. The point of departure for his sexual fantasies is the word "rigidae" used by Juvenal to depict the Empress Messalina's insatiable appetite (TS, 30):

adhuc ardens rigidae tentigine vulvae,
Et lassata viris nec dum satiate recessit.[30]

The epigraph for *Messalina*[31] is not translated—those who do not know Latin need to follow Marcueil's gloss in the third chapter of *The Supermale* (TS, 29–31). Marcueil explains to the doctor and the general that lines 128–30 of Juvenal's sixth satire present us a woman "still ardent," but he refuses to translate more. A Latinist can reconstruct the sense. Messalina leaves her "cell" in the "House of Happiness," her brothel in Suburra, feeling "still ardent with the tension of her rigid vulva, and tired of men but not satiated yet." The events evoked in the first chapter of *Messalina* become the object of a heated discussion in *The Supermale*.

The doctor reduces Messalina to a pathological case of nymphomania, to which he adds hysteria, priapism, and satyriasis (TS, 32). Defending her, Marcueil states, "The only real women are Messalinas" (TS, 30), and assures his listeners that her case proves that women can also experience what men know, that is, ithyphallicism: "There is no reason why there should not be produced in men, once a certain figure is reached, the very same physiological phenomenon as in Messalina" (TS, 31). In short, men and women are entitled to experiencing shattering, absolute, and overwhelming paroxysms of sexual jouissance. When the doctor expresses skepticism facing this literalist interpretation of "*rigidi tentigo veretri*" (the rigid tension of the penis), Marcueil complicates his position by asserting that the line was an interpolation that he retranslates: "still ardent or kept ardent by the tension of her rigid vulva" (TS, 30).

The sexual vertigo experienced by Marcueil hinges around classical texts, numbers, and infinite series: he is as fascinated by the fact that women carry all their ova in their organs (eighteen million), as by the fact that the repeated sexual congress should induce the state of sexual rigidity. The conceit of the novel is that "this manifestation becomes permanent, and even more pronounced, as one moves beyond the limits of human strength toward numerical infinity; and that it is consequently advantageous to pass beyond as rapidly as is possible, or if you prefer, as is conceivable" (TS, 31). Here is the ithyphallic fantasy of the novel—by playing on infinite numbers, one reaches immortality beyond all excess, because excess has become the norm. Marcueil asserts: "[I]t is possible that a man capable of making love indefinitely might experience no difficulty in doing anything else indefinitely" (TS, 34). The absurd boast that would transform the "Supermale" into a literal "Spermale" triggers the ire of the doctor, who accuses him of not being scientific, of wallowing "in the department of the impossible" (TS, 34). Against common sense, Marcueil asserts that sexual excess leads to a superhuman transformation of women and men into rigid, turgid, ever-ready phalluses. He gladly endorses his station in the department of the Impossible. Bataille has his predecessor.

This futurist fantasy is the counterpart of Messalina's quest. Her deepest wish is to be united with Phales, the god of erect phalluses. Phales, she thinks, has fled her brothel, to her immense despair. "A sputtering: Messalina saw, quite distinctly, the flight of the god in a strident clatter of unfurled wings" (MNIR, 13). She keeps invoking the god of phalluses, Pan, Priapus, Phallus, Phales, Love—the various names of her multifaceted god. A passage describes its emblem in a way that would have attracted Freud's attention, precisely because he was writing about the "Thing" (*das Ding*) in his unpublished "Project for a Scientific Psychology." Freud attempted to pinpoint the irreducible exteriority or intractable otherness of libidinal objects that cannot be processed by consciousness.[32] In the novel, this is also called, quite symptomatically, the "Thing" (*Chose*): "But the Thing is more monstrous, strange and enticing, for it has meaning. / This divine emblem, the great Phallus carved from a fig-tree, is nailed to the lintel like a night-owl to a barn-door, or a god to the pediment of a temple" (MNIR, 10). If one could only catch and keep the priapic "Thing," one would feel an endless immersion in love. This outpouring of jouissance is compared to the union of the Emperor and his whore: "A man is the husband of Messalina during the moment of love, and then for as long as he is able to live an uninterrupted series of such moments" (MNIR, 10–11). This sentence generates the entire narrative and the first sentence of *The Supermale*: "The act of love is of no importance, since it can be performed indefinitely" (TS, 3). In the end, what happens is the reverse: the act of love is of supreme importance because it can be performed indefinitely.

Why this parallel debasement and exaltation? *Messalina* provides a clue of what is at stake by showing one of the rare positive characters is Claudius. Although he is weak, a cuckold, and a stutterer, he keeps on writing poetry and playing with dice, with repeated allusions to Mallarmé's "ancient master" losing himself in abstruse calculations in *Un Coup de dés* . . . Indeed, when by a curious bigamy Messalina marries her lover, the virile Silius, a Roman consul, the only obstacle to their sexual bliss comes when he discovers one of Claudius's dice in the bed where they just had sex: "Silius searched, fumbled feverishly [. . .] and captured what was it that was causing his discomfort—had an insect bitten him? Livid, angular, crystalline, sharp, senile, obscene, naked to the bone. A die" (MNIR, 56–7). The diminutive die is "that thing" (MNIR, 57) preventing Messalina from loving him "absolutely." Because of this obstacle, Silius will never possess the phallic "Thing." When he grasps this, he screams all of a sudden, quite surprisingly: "MESSALINA IS VIRGIN!" (MNIR, 57). How can this be, given her record of more than twenty-five lovers per night? It all becomes clearer if we see Messalina as a Mallarméan heroine like Hérodiade, who in *Igitur* stands for Salome, a name evoking castration or beheading. However, a Christian Virgin is not far.

Hérodiade obtained the decapitation of the prophet John in the same way as Messalina manipulates Claudius who forces Asiaticus to commit suicide whereas he is innocent. The impure Messalina announces the Christian Saint Messalina mentioned in the fanciful Almanach of Père Ubu for the month of January 1901. Next to *"Décervelage"* ("Debraining," the punishment meted out to the nobles under King Ubu's despotic rule), given for January 1st, we find "Saint Messalina" as the patron saint for January 23 (JOCI, 575). The Christian meaning of "real presence" refers to the Eucharist, a symbol endowed with the reality of divine presence in Catholic rituals at least. In conformity with the logic elaborated at the end of *L'Amour Absolu*, and the Mallarméan logic of abolition, the divine absolute kills whoever experiences it. The only chance of an encounter with excessive jouissance will have to be mediated through art.

The outcome of Messalina's relentless quest for the "real presence" of a phallic god will, of course, cause her death, which comes at the end, once Claudius has seen her for what she is. While he reluctantly condemns her to death, she welcomes the centurion's sword, for in her delirium she mistakes it for an ivory phallus. She wants to be penetrated by it. She falls in front of the soldier. When he plunges the weapon into her naked breast, she exclaims: "O how you are a god, PHALES! Phalès, I knew nothing of love; I knew all men but you are the first Immortal I have loved! Phalès, at last, and so late!" (MNIR, 69). The centurion has to assert that his sword is a blade, not his penis, she keeps asking Phalès to take her away, and thus dies—of love. As she dies, the god Phalès vanishes for good: the great Pan of phallicism has gone.

In this fin de siècle fantasy of *Liebe und Tod*, the ithyphallicism sought by Messalina and Marcueil betrays a hyperbolic fantasy of bisexual enjoyment. Jarry's pataphysics depicts men and women as having the possibility of attaining a superhuman energy and sexual bliss, even if their ultimate erection always spells out death. At the last minute, Messalina gazes at her own reflection in the sword that will dispatch her. The phallus is a mirror but also a sharp stake, as those used for impalement. By a loaded Latin pun, the *phallus* turns into *palus*, an association made explicit in *Cesar-Antichrist*:

> The Templar: Uprooted phallus, do not bounce around so much.
>
> Fasce: Tail [*pal*] or head [Jarry puns on "*Pile ou face*"], reflection of my master, in you I gaze at my reflection. [...] Phallus perpendicular to the smile of the Ithyphallic in your laterality.
>
> (JOCI, 289)

Jarry's own ithyphallicism was not devoid of humor. When Apollinaire visited the small apartment in which Jarry lived (the rooms had been cut in two, and only a small man like Jarry could stand upright in it), he saw a huge stone phallus made in Japan, a gift of the painter Félicien Rops. As all the objects in the room looked diminutive, Jarry retorted to a visiting lady who had asked playfully whether the object was a plaster cast of his organ: "No, this is a reduction."[33]

Jarry's mixture of laughter and tragedy, of heresy and saintliness, tapped an old doctrine that Joyce would apply to *Finnegans Wake*, the doctrine of the unity of the opposites. Joy and Sadness combine to heighten each other. Fasce continues:

> Axiom and principle of identical contraries, the pataphysician, clinging to your ears and retractable wings, flying fish, is the dwarf climax of the giant, beyond all metaphysics; thanks to you, it is the Antichrist and God

too, horse of the Spirit, Less-in-More, Less-that-is-More, cinematics of the zero remaining in the eyes, infinite polyhedron. [...] You are the owl, Sex and Spirit, hermaphrodite, you create and destroy.

(JOCI, 289–90)

A similar pun on a lethal *phallus* underpins several scenes in *Messalina*. At one point, Messalina wonders why she cannot find any "lingam or ithyphallus silhouetting its tall pale" (MNIR, 32) when she visits the stately garden of Asiaticus. The recurrent phallicization of the objects of desire derives from an obvious wish to compensate for the wobbly nature of emotions. Feminine sexuality is bounded with a hard and rigid pole. It is from such a vantage-point that one can then jump into infinity, as we see at the end of *Absolute Love*, when we are introduced to "The right to lie." The sex or gender of lies is feminine, we learn (JOCI, 949). Truth is to be found in a masculine God; however, God would prostitute Himself if He gave access to the truth He embodies. The way out of this contradiction is to affirm human desire:

Human truth is what man wants: a *desire*.
The Truth of God is what he *creates*.
When one is neither one nor the other—Emmanuel—*one's* Truth is *the creation of one's desire*.

(JOCI, 950)

Jarry agreed with Freud's contention that libido, all libido, is male; if a feminine pole is necessary for the transmutation into an infinite power to affect, this pole will be firmly controlled. The love scenes between Marcueil and the young passionaria Ellen in *The Supermale* are curiously fraught with tension, marked by aggression. After Marcueil's exertions make Ellen reach the fatidic number of eighty-two orgasms, she feels mostly hostile to Marcueil and comments dryly: "That wasn't the least bit funny." Then, instead of being thankful, she tries to blind him with her hatpin, so that he has to hypnotize her to prevent this (TS, 104–5). When he believes (wrongly, it turns out) that Ellen, exhausted, is dead, Marcueil expresses immense tenderness conveyed in a love poem that he recites on her inert body, concluding with "I adore her." In fact, she has just passed out; the lyrical profession of love was triggered by a "love machine," which explodes and kills Marcueil. With these anarchic and self-destructive machines, we enter the world of futurist modernism. Jarry singlehandedly invented both Italian Futurism and the desiring (and bachelor) machines popularized by Deleuze and Guattari.

It is no coincidence that the best essay on Jarry's philosophy was written by Gilles Deleuze, who understood the links between Jarry's anarchism and

Heidegger's meditation on the disappearance of Being and the domination of technology. Technology is the modern danger, but a form of salvation can come from it: "The bicycle is not a simple machine, but the simplest model of a Machine appropriate to the times. [...] The Bicycle, with its chains and its gears, is the essence of technology: it envelops and develops, it brings about the great turning of the earth. The bicycle is the frame, like Heidegger's 'fourfold.'"[34] What Deleuze did not say because he was reluctant to use Freudian terms is that Jarry's textual and allegorical Bicycle connects desiring subjects with the ontology of the drive. Jarry calls up the specific Freudian term of *Trieb*, a term that should not be confused with "instinct" even under its form of "death drive." Freud saw in the drive a general force accounting for the upsurge of erotic energy in human beings. He defined it in 1915 according to its force, source, object, and aim. Jarry anticipated Freud's later invention of the "death drive" as Thanatos, an ultimate allegory in which Lacan saw the model for the structure of all drives. Jarry's particular hardness, intensity, and eccentricity derive from his intimate familiarity with a death drive whose increased speed he was hoping to harness and that he magnified until it reached infinity.

The same symbol of infinity is also hidden in the speeding bicycle drafted by Marcel Duchamp in 1914. His mysteriously titled "Having the apprentice in the sun" ("*Avoir l'apprenti dans le soleil*") represents a man pedaling up a slope towards the sun, sketched on yellowing paper music. Inverting the common expression of "*Avoir le soleil dans l'oeil*" ("To be blinded by the sun"), Duchamp evokes Jarry's cyclist, Marcueil. His title also puns on "*à voir: l'empreinte dans le sol*" and "*avoir la pente dans le soleil*" ("To be seen: the imprint in the ground," and "To have the slope in the sun"). A speeding "apprentice," a learner sublimely fighting against a Sun blinding him, was Duchamp's oblique homage to Jarry, a notoriously fierce cyclist: we learn in our *apprentissage* by toiling upward and fighting against a paternal and domineering Sun. Thus, like the wheels of a bicycle, Jarry's novels form a diptych of sexual excess. The "novel of ancient Rome" and the "modern novel" combine like two wheels spinning together; by reading, re-reading, and pedaling, readers create a lemniscate, the symbol of infinity; if sexual excess leads to a superhuman transformation of women and men into rigid phalluses, textual excess ushers in the pathos of the new. The frantic ithyphallicism sought by Messalina and Marcueil recycles Nietzsche's religious parody in *Zarathustra* while pointing to the future, heralding Bataille's orgiastic and lethal "accursed share" that exceeds even modernism.

3

The Birth of Irish Modernism from the Spirit of Nietzscheanism (Yeats, Joyce, and Beckett)

What captures best Irish modernism is its Nietzschean quality, which does not only allude to the influence of Nietzsche's thought on writers such as Yeats and Joyce,[1] but describes specific features displayed by the Irish moderns. Irish modernism, caught in a Nietzschean moment, triggered an array of manifestations that were very different from their French counterpart. The Irish Nietzscheans evinced a fundamental discordance in their groups, programs, ideas, genres, and ideologies. Irish modernism absorbed quickly various influences without unifying them. The creativity of its main actors and authors was spurred by a contrarian impulse that brought forward inner strife rather than ecumenical attempts at defining a common platform.

What has been called "high modernism" in the context of Anglo-American modernism was a retrospective program that brought together different individualities under a single banner. Instead of staking its assets on the cohesion of a movement, Irish modernism tended to be at war against itself and against the world, especially if the world was embodied by British imperialism and colonialism. Early on, its evolution was caught up in centrifugal patterns; it thrived on controversies and conflict that in turn generated fissiparous offshoots, tensions that were productive although impossible to channel into a single goal. Two chroniclers of the movement, George Moore and Oliver St. John Gogarty, produced books deemed libelous—and for good reasons. *Hail and Farewell: Ave, Salve and Vale* (1911–14) and *As I Was Going Down Sackville Street: A Phantasy in Fact* (1937), both retrospective constructions, kept vivid traces of the spirit of contentious mockery and ad hominem satire that pervaded the exchanges among the main proponents of an Irish modernism. As Joyce would put it, the Irish were a "brood of mockers"—this included him, along with his friend Gogarty, the original of Buck Mulligan. Even religious allegiances were unstable: Moore publicized his conversion to Protestantism in 1903, whereas Maud Gonne converted to Catholicism the same year.

If the modernist impulse in Ireland was marked by sectarian intrigue and malicious satire, dynamic change emerged from inner dialogism. Internal strife transmuted the Irish renaissance into a modernism that became at once local and global. Its international visibility is still attested by the busloads of American and Japanese tourists doing the rounds of Dublin armed with *Ulysses* or trekking in pilgrimage to Sligo with Yeats's poems in hand. As soon as major achievements had been accomplished, that is by the 1920s, Irish modernism entered its golden phase; its late flowering produced the somewhat overblown syntheses of Yeats's *A Vision* (1925) and Joyce's *Finnegans Wake* (1939), both *summae poeticae* quoting each other with distant respect. Nonconformism returned with the young Beckett's querulous admonitions to his elders, which included a critique of the revival's parochialism in the name of an internationalism of Irish modernism. Even then, this late modernism did not avoid a certain Nietzscheism, but it was a Nietzsche working against himself: it felt affinities with Nietzsche's eternal return of the Same when dealing in mythological patterns presenting universal history as a cyclical scheme, or engaged with a radical questioning of the value of value, as the young Beckett did.

To make sense of such a permanent cultural war, one needs to go back to the main European intellectual trends in which Nietzsche appeared as the privileged catalyst for intellectual and cultural reawakening, much more than a prophet of doom. If the fin de siècle Nietzsche who was invoked in most debates on aesthetics and politics that shaped European modernism was an offshoot of "decadence,"[2] he also embodied an energetic rebirth of the spirit. Focusing on three main figures—Yeats, Joyce, and Beckett, and their attempts at becoming modern—I will start from modernist reviews to grasp how new ideas were disseminated. I will begin with Yeats: before Pound, Yeats initiated his own modernization when he took the thought of Nietzsche as a weapon against the vagueness of fin-de-siècle aestheticism. For Joyce, fashionable Nietzscheism became a stage prop in a deliberate dramatization of his farewell to Dublin: it presented both what he rejected in his fellow Dubliners and a figure of lofty exile. Joyce would work satirically, taking Nietzsche as a straw man useful to expose the limitations of an earlier egotistic posturing still dominant in the juvenile drafts of *Stephen Hero*. As for the young Beckett, Nietzsche would be relayed early on by two other figures, Schopenhauer and Geulincx.

"Neiche [*sic*] is not Celtic"[3]

Yeats had known of Nietzsche's thought as early as 1896, when *The Savoy* published a series of detailed and substantial articles on him by Havelock

Ellis.[4] Ellis knew Nietzsche well and was the first to point out the parallels between Nietzsche and the philosophies of William Blake, which would be a recurrent theme for Yeats. *The Savoy* can be taken as a useful point of departure: it exhibited a rare mixture of decadent thought, post-symbolist writing, and new "modernist" ideas. Its eight issues from January to December 1896 were published by Leonard Smithers, a notorious libertine and pornographer. Its intellectual content was in the charge of Arthur Symons, also a libertine who specialized in "decadence." His survey *The Symbolist Movement In Literature* (1899) would soon leave a huge mark on English literature—and it was dedicated to W. B. Yeats. Aubrey Beardsley had chosen the name of the review, thinking a new London hotel would evoke ideas of luxury and modernity. He also provided the covers as well as numerous illustrations. The group gathered by *The Savoy* was associated with Oscar Wilde, whose recent trials (in 1895) added to the sulfurous reputation of the magazine. Thus, the first accounts of Nietzsche's thought to catch the eye of Yeats were associated with decadence. Yeats knew Ellis's essays on Nietzsche, since he contributed prose regularly to *The Savoy*: "Rosa Alchemica" was published in the third issue, and "The Tables of the Law" in the seventh. He also published his essay "William Blake and His Illustrations to *The Divine Comedy*" in *The Savoy*.

When Yeats revised the essay in 1924, he included a reference to Nietzsche. Discussing Blake's suspicion of government in general and his dalliance with all sorts of revolutionary thought, Yeats wrote: "One is reminded of Shelley, who was the next to take up the cry, though with a less abundant philosophic faculty, but still more of Nietzsche, whose thought flows always, though with an even more violent current, in the bed Blake's thought has worn."[5] This was a later addition; the original *Savoy* essay had begun with a comparison between Blake and French symbolism that sounded very much like Symons: "The recoil from scientific naturalism has created in our day the movement the French call *symboliste*, which, beginning with the memorable 'Axel' by Villiers de l'Isle Adam, has added to drama a new kind of romance, at once ecstatic and picturesque, in the works of M. Maeterlinck."[6] Yeats mentions Edward Burne-Jones and Mallarmé, for indeed, the pages of *The Savoy* were given over to symbolists of all types. They were the French models, first Verlaine and Mallarmé whose prose poem "The Future Phenomenon" was translated, then Dante Gabriel Rossetti, Ernest Dowson, and less-classifiable writers such as Max Beerbohm, Edward Carpenter (who would resurface in the pages of *The New Freewoman* and *The Egoist* twenty years later), and Yeats's lover, Olivia Shakespear. The Nietzsche whom Yeats discovered in 1896 was filtered by the discourse of a symbolism still in thrall to the "mystery" contained in poetry, still operating with deliberate vagueness, calculated indirection and evocative suggestion. The remainders of Pater-inflected aestheticism first blocked Yeats's comprehension of Nietzsche's revolutionary theses.

There are as many "Nietzsches" as readers, but the fin-de-siècle Nietzsche was not amenable to a workable program of self-modernization. It is the same Nietzscheism that startled the young André Gide and led him to launch the notion of "immoralism." Wilde had introduced Gide to Nietzsche, along with other decadent pursuits; both Wilde and Nietzsche denounced the repressive structure of Christian morality. For Gide, however, the full impact of Nietzsche would be deferred, which explains why the same character, Menalcas, is a pre-Nietzschean in *Les Nourritures Terrestres* (1895) and a post-Nietzschean in *The Immoralist* (1902).[7] Gide found in Nietzsche a logic of liberation that allowed him to understand how his Protestant roots, that were very close to Nietzsche's own, brought about its own negation. Here was a self-undoing that would unleash a new sexual freedom. What had helped Gide progress in the sexual domain would help Yeats take place in the political domain: instead of freeing a new hedonist gospel of instant enjoyment, Yeats's Nietzsche allowed him to combine late symbolist aesthetics and a nationalist doctrine, as Louis MacNeice observed.[8] This "aestheticization of Irish nationalist politics," as Walter Benjamin would put it, indeed also entailed a "revolution," or perhaps simply a "re-evaluation" of all values, similar to that undergone by Gide, but with different effects.

Propitiously, Yeats's interest in Nietzsche was reawakened by his American friend, the New York lawyer John Quinn. In September 1902, Quinn sent him copies of *Thus Spake Zarathustra*, *The Case of Wagner*, and *On the Genealogy of Morals*. Soon after, Yeats acknowledged his fascination in a letter to Lady Gregory: "You have a rival in Nietzsche, that strong enchanter. [. . .] Nietzsche completes Blake and has the same roots—I have not read anything with so much excitement since I got to love Morris's stories which have the same curious astringent joy."[9] Yeats also worked closely on Thomas Common's *Nietzsche as Critic, Philosopher, Poet and Prophet* (1901), a collection of passages from the main works in which he underlined or annotated passages from *On the Genealogy of Morals*, *Beyond Good and Evil*, and *Thus Spake Zarathustra*. As well as these, Yeats's library contained *The Case of Wagner*, *The Dawn of Day*, *The Birth of Tragedy*, and *Thoughts out of Season*. Several critics have documented Yeats's sustained immersion in Nietzsche's writings, listing points of convergence and pointing out the importance of Yeats's marginal annotations on Common's book.[10] Yeats remained engaged in a productive albeit critical dialogue with his German mentor.

Above all, Yeats learned from Nietzsche a new "hardness" and a new masculinity. In his dealings with people, he became more imperious, less passive, and would often impose his ideas, as shown by the complex history of the founding and handling of the Abbey Theatre. The new attitude led him to change his style; he repudiated the fuzzy magic and the ineffable mysteries of the Celtic twilight. The trembling of the veil turned into a rending of the veil, while the Celtic twilight paved the way to a Twilight of the Idols. At first, Nietzsche's philosophy appeared compatible with an older aestheticism based on Pater's ideas. Nietzsche wanted a renaissance, after all, just like Pater, who in *The Renaissance* (1873) portrayed the mind as a whirlpool, a supreme subjectivity fluctuating uncontrollably between moods and impressions that were flickering and inconstant. Subjectivity was a "perpetual weaving and unweaving of ourselves," a process evoked by Stephen Dedalus in *Ulysses* in the name of the goddess Dana. Yeats's aesthetic catechism had taught him to burn with a hard, gem-like flame, as Pater wanted it. If the object of the quest remained the same, the diction and the underlying gestures had changed. It was from Nietzsche's revisions of his texts and selves that Yeats adopted the practice of self-remaking. He expressed this in 1908, stating that when he rewrote earlier versions of his poems or plays, it was "myself that I remake." The new self-fashioning did not simply entail the creation of a "mask" but of an anti-self; thus Yeats learned to wield power as when he had to deal with the Abbey Theatre. "The fascination of what's difficult" deplores that the "theater business" and the "management of men"[11] impinged on his free time, yet in the end he proved remarkably successful in his business transactions.

The plays written by Yeats in the first decade of the twentieth century hum with Nietzschean echoes. In *The King's Threshold* (1903), the dying words of the poet Seanchan, who has started a hunger strike the day he has been expelled from the King's counsel, convey defiance not only facing earthly powers but also facing the mirage of a god in heaven:

> I need no help.
> He needs no help that joy has lifted up
> Like some miraculous beast out of Ezekiel.
> The man that dies has the chief part in the story,
> And I will mock and mock that image yonder,
> That evil picture in the sky—no, no!
> I have all my strength again, I will outface it.[12]

This climax of a "joy before death," later sung vociferously by Bataille in his Nietzschean journal *Acéphale*, conflates a metaphysical gesture of defiance with a political posture: in 1922, when Yeats revised his play and gave it a tragic ending, he noted that at the time "neither suffragette nor patriot had adopted the hunger strike," hinting that he may have invented its use as a "political weapon."¹³ In a similar way, Cuchulain, the violent king who fights against the higher king Conchubar in *On Baile's Strand* (1903), offers a perfectly Nietzschean definition of love. For the Irish hero, love has to be considered in all its fundamental ambivalence, and the poet knows that true love ought to make room for hate:

> I never have known love but as a kiss
> In the mid-battle, and a difficult truce
> Of oil and water, candles and dark night,
> Hillside and hollow, the hot-footed sun,
> And the cold sliding, slippery-footed moon –
> A brief forgiveness between opposites
> That have been hatreds for three times the age
> Of this long-'stablished ground.¹⁴

Such ambivalent feelings were inspired by a frustratingly diffident but tantalizing Maud Gonne. Gonne, who had not read Nietzsche and did not like him, had good grounds to object to his influence on "Willie." Indeed, she had a point when she failed to see any Celtic note in what she took for the ravings of a mad protestant. Gonne, let us not forget, was a Francophile who had adapted for Irish nationalists aims that Zeev Sternhell has called "French fascism."¹⁵ Sternhell has shown how the combination of populist Boulangisme from the late 1880s and Sorel's concept of revolutionary violence produced a blueprint for Mussolini's fascist doctrine. Gonne's association with Lucien Millevoye, a staunch Boulangist, situates her in the camp of a nascent European fascism. When she announced to Yeats that she was in a French convent, about to convert to Catholicism so as to marry Millevoye, she wrote those famous words: "I have always told you I am the voice, the soul of the crowd."¹⁶ Her reactionary populism justified a half-hearted conversion, since she was joining the Catholic majority of the Irish. Her involvement with extreme-right figures set a dangerous example followed by her daughter who married the notorious Nazi Francis Stuart.

What saved Yeats from the temptation of joining this emergent Irish fascism was, paradoxically, a topos that he found in Nietzsche, namely the elitism he associated with the doctrine of Zarathustra's *Übermensch*. This explains his wish to invent an ideal and eternal Irish peasant, the natural ally of the no less ideal aristocrat embodying the values of the Anglo-Irish ascendancy. This group was "healthier" because it shrank from the excess and the vociferousness of a Catholic populace. Yeats was saved by a decision to be both "timely" and "untimely" in his self-willed aristocratic heroism. In this he proved, like Nietzsche, that he was, if not always "modern," at least a true modernist. Nietzsche had written in a notebook, "If I once wrote the word 'untimely' on my books, how much youth, inexperience, peculiarity that word expressed! Today I realize it was precisely the kind of complaint, enthusiasm and dissatisfaction that made one of the most modern of the moderns."[17] This led to "Attempt at Self-Criticism," which introduced the new edition of *The Birth of Tragedy*, an introduction in which Nietzsche satirized the "excesses" of a book that he saw retrospectively tainted by Schopenhauer's pessimism, "enervated" by Indian Buddhism. To avoid the positivist belief in science as a cure for all the ills of humanity, one should find a balance between art, science, and life. For Nietzsche as for Yeats, the point was to transform radically the whole of life.

If Nietzsche's first book was badly written, the injunction to write better underpinned any effort at self-modernization. This modernization entailed a rigorous imperative to re-read oneself so as to erase all the remnants of juvenile enthusiasm and romantic illusions. The ultimate value would finally rest with "Life"—a life freed from its shackles by the claim that "God is dead," a claim leaving the power to create to the humans. Since the humans have created God, they will also create like God, but are therefore all the more responsible for their creations. Yeats summarized this cryptically with the famous motto: "In dreams begin responsibility" (C, 112). A heightened awareness of the "responsibility of form" as Roland Barthes would say, turned into an ethical impetus, which would sustain Yeats throughout his career:

> Grant me an old man's frenzy,
> Myself must I remake
> Till I am Timon and Lear
> Or that William Blake
> Who beat upon the wall
> Till Truth obeyed his call
>
> (CP, 347)

The Blake quoted in *Last Poems* (1938–39) has swallowed Nietzsche, who, in *A Vision*, appears both as seer and madman. Symptomatically, the first notes for *A Vision* conflate Nietzsche with Pound, the other great modernizer: "I am more interested at 12 where Neitzsche [*sic*] emerges & all men discover their super man, though there are also more violent among whom I would be sorry to include types like <your friend Mr Pound of whom> your enemy Mr Pound."[18] The impact of Pound on Yeats, and his crucial role in forcing the older poet to become harder, sparer, and more direct, have been well documented.[19] What is revealing in the first typescript of *A Vision* is the hesitation between "friend" and "enemy," a hesitation all the more telling that in the final version, Wyndham Lewis, the arch "enemy," is listed next to Pound and Joyce, just after Nietzsche.[20] Joyce is praised as having given to the "vulgarity of a single day prolonged through 700 pages" the dignity of myth— yet he also exemplifies the moment when "the intellect turns against itself."[21]

Joyce, Yeats, and Magee: Sparring partners

There have been as many accounts of the famous meeting between Joyce and Yeats in 1902 as of the encounter between Joyce and Marcel Proust in 1922. What stands out for certain is that Yeats was generous with Joyce, who indirectly owed him the contact with Pound, which in turn connected him with a powerful network leading to the publication of his major works. What paved the way for the meeting had been Joyce's critique of his elder's position in the essay "The Day of the Rabblement" (1901), where Joyce wonders whether Yeats has genius or not (later he would say that Yeats incarnated poetic genius). Joyce praises *The Wind Among the Reeds* (1899) as "poetry of the highest order," and notes that the best Russian writers could have written "The Adoration of the Magi," (1897) texts that show what Yeats "can do when he breaks with the half gods."[22] The following sentence is cruel: "But an aesthete has a floating will, and Mr. Yeats's treacherous instinct of adaptability must be blamed for his recent association with a platform from which even self-respect should have urged him to refrain."[23] These are severe words from a nineteen-year-old student. Joyce had identified the symptom of weakness if not of impotence as a wavering of the will. This was what Yeats himself identified as his main limitation: an uncertain willpower, a failing that Yeats resolved to compensate by opting for the "masculine" virtues of constancy and direction. He would increase the "direction of the will," to quote Pound's motto. In 1901, Joyce pierced through the regressive backsliding of the Irish Literary Theatre, whose mistake was to "cut itself adrift from the line of advancement" by a reactionary "surrender to the trolls."[24] The ironical allusion to Yeats's belief in fairies and Celtic folklore contrasts with the Truth embodied by "the old master" in Christiana, Henrik Ibsen. Ibsen's true heir is not Yeats but the German playwright Gerhard Hauptmann, who was almost Yeats's age.

Joyce's generation was that of John Millington Synge, but Joyce proved less pliant and did not heed any advice from Yeats. For Joyce, there was one path to follow: to measure oneself with European models. Yeats hesitated on this issue. He betrays his wish to appeal to international modernism in a comment made to *The San Francisco Examiner* on January 30, 1904: "Your theatre will not be doing good modern work till you can write after a performance, 'It is as great as Tolstoy, it is as great as Balzac!' – not till then."[25] At this moment, Yeats agreed with Joyce's internationalist position: the Irish renaissance had to come up to international standards. It was not a pure coincidence that Yeats, for once, sounded like a modernist committed to internationalism in 1904: 1904 was the year chosen by Joyce when he placed the action of *Ulysses* in June 16, 1904.

Ulysses presents a contrarian version of Irish modernism, mostly of the Irish revival, which is not flattering. Some of its actors are gathered in the library to hear Stephen lecture on *Hamlet*. The last to arrive is the most Nietzschean: it is Buck Mulligan, who sounds the note of parody and irreverence in the first page. He has nicknamed Stephen "Kinch the superman"[26] and speaks of "hyperboreans" (U. 1: 92), which marks him out as a disciple of Nietzsche. His reliance on blasphemy facing religious rituals evokes Zarathustra, whose gospel inverts the teachings of Christ. Mulligan's parody takes to task Yeats, Synge, and Lady Gregory. He imitates Synge's fake Irish brogue to devastating effect and mocks Yeats's pretensions and flattery. He upbraids Stephen for not having displayed "the Yeats touch," which means kowtowing to Lady Gregory and extravagantly praising her limited literary means. He takes off Yeats's personal style: "He went on and down, mopping, chanting with waving graceful arms: – The most beautiful book that has come out of our country in my time. One thinks of Homer." (U. 9: 1163–6), adding that Shakespeare must be "the chap that writes like Synge" (U. 9: 510–11). Indeed, these were easy targets for the Dublin wits in 1904.

Stephen appears closer in spirit to Mulligan than to the others, but even if his audience dwindles when Russell leaves the debate early, annoyed by Stephen's pedantic display of biographical details, he faces an impressive group of intellectuals. What stands out is the fact that an Irish renaissance is happening in Dublin and that he is not welcome in it. He is not invited to the gatherings and parties celebrating new magazines and collections. One of the three librarians, Richard Irvine Best, had translated Arbois de Jubainville's book on Celtic mythology and was a disciple of Mallarmé. Best mentions forthcoming local publications, but Stephen is painfully aware that he will not be included. The most important critic of Ireland at the time according to Yeats, William Magee, is among the listeners. A renowned essayist who dominated intellectually the scene of the Irish literary revival, Magee could quote Novalis and Goethe in German, knew the Vedas, and had a sharply critical mind. In the episode, he resists Stephen's sophistic reasoning. In May 1904, Magee had just launched with Fred Ryan the new little review, *Dana*, which survived only one year. Joyce had submitted the eight pages of his first version of *A Portrait of the Artist as a Young Man*, which were rejected by Magee, who found them unreadable. Stephen quotes Magee's recent collection

Pebbles from a Brook (1901), seemingly to flatter him, also because he respects his opinions, even if they lead Magee to question why Stephen would publish a Shakespearean theory in which he pretends not to believe.

Yeats had shown a similar deference: he chose Magee as a sparring partner several times, as when he campaigned for an Irish national theater. He and Magee exchanged opinions in *The Express* in the autumn of 1898, when Magee accused Yeats of distorting the Irish legends he was adapting without understanding them. Magee's position was that of a cosmopolitan intellectual who rejected Yeats's glib and sentimental appropriation of Celtic mythologies as passing fads. He objected to the idea of the "peasant plays" that Lady Gregory and Yeats were promoting as the best subjects for a national drama. His position was therefore not far from that of Joyce, which is why their confusion in "Scylla and Charybdis" is so important. In fact, even the title of the episode appears in *Pebbles from a Brook*: "In spite of the Scylla and Charybdis of sensuality and ennui, the human soul is enamored of the ideal."[27] It would be unfair to reduce Magee's position as a critic to this idealist thesis. In the library scene, Stephen's suspicion of Magee's religious leanings is based on his awareness that Magee was the son of a Presbyterian minister. For all that, he was also a solid intellectual, even if his rejection of Joyce's youthful and, to be fair, not-so-easy-to-read autobiographical essay was motivated by his disapproval of the sexual confession it contained. On the other hand, Magee accepted one poem by Joyce, "My Love in Light Attire."[28] It was published in the fourth issue of *Dana* as "Song." Happily, Magee never suspected that the "light attire" of the loved one has been "lifted up" so as to reveal an erotic posture that delighted Joyce: he was ogling a urinating female form.

Magee helped create a different Irish modernism that was less sectarian and more open. *Dana* embodied a spirit of fairness and balanced critical evaluation. From the start, *Dana* juxtaposed two versions of modernism, the recent controversy in the Catholic Church opposing Abbé Loisy, leading to a stubborn refusal of the hierarchy to discuss Darwin, and Nietzsche's notion of the "death of God." Curiously, the philosophical debate about theological "modernism" was summarized by no less than Edouard Dujardin in the first issue of *Dana*.[29] Dujardin, the inventor of interior monologue, had been a recent discovery for Joyce. In *Dana*, Dujardin outlined the theses of the followers of Loisy; obviously, he sympathized with them, and concluded that the Church has made a mistake when deciding that Aristotle was a better guide than Darwin.[30] Even though this meaning of "modernism" has been muted today, it would then reverberate in Dublin's literary circles, especially at University College with its doctrinal emphasis on neo-Thomism.

The debate on modernism framed the confrontation with Nietzsche in Irish intellectual circles. It reappeared in the sixth issue of *Dana* with an essay by Magee, "A way of understanding Nietzsche."[31] Magee began by addressing what Catholics found objectionable in Nietzsche, the proclamation that "God is dead." Facing this apparent provocation, Magee evinced a remarkable equanimity. He ironized about the Dublin bourgeois who expected to find God always there and never worried long about his existence: "The ordinary citizen does not like the doctrine of God to be challenged: he likes to think of God being there, as he likes to think of a limitless supply of coal in the bowels of Great Britain."[32] Nietzsche criticized such "moral cowardice," but then became as dogmatic as the Church. In fact, his teachings went in the opposite direction; they did not so much "kill" God as attempt to redress a worse temptation, backsliding into pessimism or nihilism.

For Magee, Nietzsche had been more courageous than Schopenhauer, who took refuge in pessimism and treated hopelessness as the fate of suffering humanity. Magee quotes Goethe's observation that "man never knows how anthropomorphic he is."[33] By contrast, Nietzsche affirmed a wholly non-anthropomorphic Life. He was an optimist, a lover of fate, or a "yea-saying man."[34] What he rejected, perhaps perversely, was "the ideal." Here is where Magee perceived a contradiction in the writings of Nietzsche. On the one hand, Nietzsche praised power as it has manifested itself in history; on the other hand, he appeared on the side of those who "confront the might of the world with the might of the idea."[35] How could he extol men like Cesare Borgia who terrorized crowds in the spirit of "masters," when he refused the domination of the state?[36] If he denounced Christianity as a perversion stemming from a "slave morality," was he not on the side of the excluded, the heretics, and the revolutionaries? Finally, the very doctrine of the Superman seems "a little crazy" to Magee.[37] Was this a Romantic cult of the genius? Nietzsche, who rejected idealism in the name of "physiology," would acknowledge greatness only of historical heroes, lords, and kings, who could hardly be taken as role-models for an ethics of self-overcoming; Magee asserts: "Undoubtedly all civilizations culminate in a period during which a privileged few appear to subsist at the expense of the rest of mankind. Refinement, wealth, beauty, learning, leisure, amusement, all these things are necessary for art; but we must not therefore conclude that civilization exists for the sake of the few."[38]

These serious and cogent questions point to a weakness in Yeats, since this critical exposition is obliquely aimed at Yeats's recent Nietzschean posturing. Magee demonstrates the possibility of a "softer" Irish version of modernism, a modernism that has not cut all ties with religion, even if it is suspicious of Catholic dogmatism and of archaic paganism. It does not postulate a radical break with the past, but keeps a connection with the spirit of Romanticism. This Romanticism was not just that of Blake and Shelley (as Yeats understood it), for it included Wordsworth, Coleridge, and beyond them the philosophies of Kant, Schiller, and Novalis. A similarly syncretic modernism would underpin Eugene Jolas's "revolution of the word" manifestos when he founded the journal *transition* in the 1920s; "transition" aptly defines the main effort of *Dana* twenty years earlier, and *transition* became the official organ for Joyce's later productions.

However, Stephen Dedalus, insofar as he can be taken as a spokesman for Joyce in 1904, espouses a different philosophy. In fact, Stephen is more radical: he refuses both Catholic modernism with its attempt at blending Darwinism and the Bible, and Nietzsche's joyous affirmation of a free life devoid of *ressentiment*. He has opted for a "perverted" religiosity without God, which makes him negotiate ceaselessly between Berkeley and Blake, between Aristotle and the anarchists, between Dante and Shelley. In matters of cultural politics, Stephen inverts the foundation of Irish modernism, its deep link with a mythified nation, when he tells Bloom late in the night "Ireland must be important because it belongs to me" (U. 16: 1164–5). Stephen adopts the philosophy of the Left Hegelian Max Stirner, often considered to be a precursor of Nietzsche, the Stirner taken as a guide by Huneker. Stirner's central concept of "ownership" underpinned his vehement refusal to be "owned" by God, the Spirit, the Nation, the State, or even by Love. Owning oneself became the motto of a program of self-liberation that informed the modernism of *The Egoist* in London.

In *Ulysses*, a Nietzschean Buck Mulligan is defeated by a Stirnerian Stephen, whereas the Blooms stand close to Spinoza's monism. Joyce knew that the last word of his novel had to be given to Penelope, whom he presents as a "*Weib*" in a famous letter.[39] This "amoral" and "indifferent" woman presents a more positive version of the *Frauenzimmer* evoked by Stephen when he walks along the sea in the Proteus episode. This loaded term of *Frauenzimmer* recurs in Nietzsche, appearing significantly when Truth is allegorized as a woman. Nietzsche portrays Truth both as *Weib* (hence Molly will be a *Weib*) and as *Frauenzimmer*, a disparaging collective word referring to the midwives Stephen imagines walking along on Sandymount strand, carrying "a misbirth with a traveling navelcord," (U. 3: 36). Here is the famous beginning of *Beyond Good and Evil*: "Vorausgesetzt, dass die Wahrheit ein *Weib* ist—, wie? ist der Verdacht nicht gegründet, dass alle Philosophen, sofern sie Dogmatiker waren, sich schlecht auf Weiber verstanden? dass der schauerliche Ernst, die linkische Zudringlichkeit, mit der sie bisher auf die Wahrheit zuzugehen pflegten, ungeschickte und unschickliche Mittel waren, um gerade ein *Frauenzimmer* für sich einzunehmen?"[40] ("If we assume that

Truth is a woman—what then? Is there not ground for suspecting that all philosophers, because they were too dogmatic, failed to understand women—that the terrible seriousness, the clumsy importunity with which they used to address Truth have proved unskilled and unseemly methods for winning a woman?)"

For Joyce, one may say that Truth erupts fully as Woman at the end of *Ulysses*: this woman, more Gea-Tellus than Molly ruminating on the events of the day, will not let herself be possessed—the link between Maud Gonne and Molly Bloom should be clear. Joyce's rejection of Nietzscheism was not only a belated feminism but it also agreed with the theoretical and ethical worries expressed by Magee. Joyce refused the heroic posture of the male hero who uses women for his aesthetic ends. This is why his truth is more modest, and begins *in medias res*, with Molly and Leopold Bloom engaged in dialogue as a married couple, albeit with their share of marital problems. For Joyce, it was logical that Vico should relay Nietzsche. Vico became Joyce's main philosophical reference with a *Scienza Nuova* (1725) focusing on the human family, all the while postulating that the age of the gods has been followed by that of the heroes, and then by the reign of the people. Heroic efforts at individual overcoming and self-fashioning only have to pave the way for the triumph of a democratic crowd, a happily inebriated "rabblement" whose raucous and polyphonic cacophony fills the pages of *Finnegans Wake*. The universal "hero," "Here Comes Everybody," includes us all, for we are all invited to his funeral wake: B.Y.O.B., which means: Bring your own body.

Beckett's Nietzschean occasionalism

Beckett had demonstrated the importance of Vico for Joyce in his first effort at literary criticism after he had arrived in Paris. His 1929 essay "Dante .... Bruno. Vico .. Joyce" defended Joyce's method from any imputation of obscurity and showed its reliance on Vico's philosophy of language. Beckett's essay is still an excellent introduction to Joyce's later work because it highlights the complexity of the links between language and history. Taking the example of the meanings of *lex* in Latin, which evolved from a gathering of acorns to the Law, Beckett pointed to the new "religion" of language, returning to Vico's *religio*, understood as a collective "gathering" of etymologies. Giordano Bruno's identification of contraries, Vico's poetic wisdom, and Dante's divine comedy converge and blend in the new linguistic universe created by Joyce. The process was "purgatorial" for Beckett, who provided his own variation on the theme of a cyclical history: "This inner elemental vitality and corruption of expression imparts a furious restlessness to the form, which is admirably suited to the purgatorial aspect of the work."[41] Beckett's meditation on universal history presented time as flux and metamorphic language. If Vico had anticipated Nietzsche about metaphors and the historicity of language, as one verifies in Nietzsche's theory of metaphorical language, "On Truth and Lies in a Nonmoral Sense" (1873), what mattered above all was to be faithful to the process triggering the "restlessness of the form."

In 1930, Beckett returned to Trinity College, where he lectured, soon to be disillusioned with academia. He resigned in 1931, followed Joyce's heroic example and became an "Artist" himself. His last effort at academic publication was his monograph on Proust, published in 1931. His *Proust* presents the French author as Schopenhauerian from beginning to end. *In Search of Lost Time* was thus a novelization of *The World as Will and Representation*. Proust's pessimism entails a non-moral position reminiscent of Nietzsche. Beckett observes that Proust forces his readers to plunge into spirals of perversion and inversion. After Sodom and Gomorrah have been destroyed, no valid ethical system remains; only art can provide salvation: "Here, as always, Proust is completely detached from all moral considerations. There is no right and wrong in Proust nor in his world."[42] Artistic transcendence operates beyond Good and Evil.

Beckett had immersed himself in Schopenhauer in the summer of 1930 as he worked on his *Proust*, to the amusement of his *normalien* friends for whom Schopenhauer was *passé*. Beckett did not mind:

> I am reading Schopenhauer. Everyone laughs at that. Beaufret & Alfy etc. But I am not reading philosophy, nor caring whether he is right or wrong or a good or worthless metaphysician. An intellectual justification of unhappiness—the greatest that has been attempted—is worth the examination of one who is interested in Leopardi & Proust rather than in Carducci & Barrès.[43]

Schopenhauer's pessimistic view of life offered an antidote to the chauvinism or exacerbated Romantic nationalism of Barrès. Barrès's populism was in line with the Boulangiste doctrine mentioned in relation to Gonne.

Schopenhauer was a launching pad for a new nihilism, which hesitated between linguistic skepticism and an a-theology of passivity. Reading Schopenhauer led to the discovery of other marginal thinkers: first the skeptic Fritz Mauthner, who had invented *Sprachkritik* often discussed with Joyce; then Arnold Geulincx, the Occasionalist who subverted Descartes's foundational *cogito ergo sum* by rephrasing it as *nescio ergo sum* (I don't know therefore I am), a sentence echoing throughout Beckett's works, and which took its full relevance after the psychoanalysis with Wilfred Ruprecht Bion.

The outcome of the two-year therapy in London was the publication of *Murphy*. When the eponymous hero's mind is described, the model of his psyche is similar to Freud's topology. Murphy decides to work and live next to psychotic patients in a mental hospital because he prefers the "little world" of the hospital, the restricted life of patients confined in their delusional safety because they live in their minds only, to the "big world," the site of social and erotic failure: "How should he tolerate, let alone cultivate, the occasions of fiasco, having once beheld the beatific idols of his cave? In the beautiful Belgo-Latin of Arnold Geulincx: *Ubi nhil vales, ibi nihil velis*."[44] The text develops the arcane Latin quote and translates it: "But it was not enough to want nothing where he was worth nothing, nor even to take the further step of renouncing all that lay outside the intellectual love in which alone he could love himself, because there alone he is lovable" (M, 179). Thus *Murphy* presents a negative Cartesian cogito as a yardstick measuring the pathos of distance.

The motto, "*Ubi nihil vales, ibi nihil velis*," which can be rendered as "Where you have no power, you will have no desire,"[45] derives from Geulincx's *Ethics*. Geulincx sums up his "observation of the self" and introduces his doctrine of radical humility: "The axiom, *Wherein I have no power, therein I do not will*, embraces both parts of Humility: *I have no power* denotes Inspection of Oneself, *I do not will* denotes Disregard of Oneself."[46] For Geulincx, if we do not have a clear idea of how our muscles or nerves move our limbs, we cannot claim that the action originates in us. This is what happens when we contemplate the beauties of the world and realize that we have created nothing. If we do not understand how our nerves connect with our muscles, it is because we did not "make" that motion—only God can make things happen. And we do walk better when we are not self-conscious. We watch a stupid or interesting show: "Thus, I am a mere spectator of a machine whose workings I can neither adjust nor readjust. I neither construct nor demolish anything here: the whole thing is someone else's affair."[47]

The consequence is utter passivity, from which one can gain a paradoxical conflation of aesthetics and ethics: if we are merely the privileged spectators of our radical impotence, the result can be beautiful. Nietzsche understood the logic of this reversal in his discussion of Geulincx. In *On the Genealogy of Morality*, he presents Geulincx as a self-despiser, an extreme case of moralistic self-contempt. Geulincx would be the epitome of the "ascetic will" displayed by the priests. However, these priests are allied to the noble creators of values; they promote a pathos of subjective dispossession because there is something to gain: "With the growth of the community, a new interest is kindled for individuals as well, which often enough will lift him up of the most personal elements in his discontent, his aversion to himself (Geulincx's '*despectio sui*")."[48] Like the ascetic priests, Geulincx generates a "debauch" or a "riot of feeling" (*Gefühls-Ausschweifung*). This erotic surplus of pathos, an excess of emotive power, will then lead to enthusiasm, to rapture, and why not to mystical ecstasy. A higher form of possession can be reached by sheer impotence: in a dizzying movement, the soul has been plunged into an abyss to reemerge lighter, purified, and closer to God.[49]

The grace gained by this hyperbolic humility displaces the centrality granted to human subjects: in thrall to the Other, we all turn into puppets of God; however, such grace tends to the purely material and gets rids of its excess of spirituality. The original title of Geulincx's Ethics was *Gnôthi Seautòn, sive Geulincx Ethica* in the 1675 edition, which states that Socratic "knowing oneself" will lead less to irony than to an ethics of impotence, ignorance, and humility. We gain access to a world in which human life is a miracle willed by God. In his garret next to the psychotics, Murphy overcomes his previous avoidance of human proximity (the "*plaisir de rompre*" in which he saw "the rationale of social contacts" (M, 48)) and begins to learn distance, psychotic distance it is true, a first step on the ladder to his "failing better." Here was the self-defeating task Irish modernists imposed on themselves in a last-ditch attempt to overcome their limitations. Beckett took the road leading from the exalted "Pathos of Distance" rewritten by Geulincx to a "Bathos of Experience" that he found in Kant's philosophy. He quotes Kant's "*Bathos der Erfahrung*" (the lowness of experience) in the addenda to *Watt*, his last novel written in English for a while—the choice of the French language then allowed him to play with a new instrument, the bathetic idiom of the ordinary.[50]

Beckett's occasionalism required as its complement the philosophy of the unconscious emerging in the nineteenth century with Hegel and Schelling first, relayed by Schopenhauer, Nietzsche, von Hartmann, and Freud. Geulincx's occasionalism directly announced Schopenhauer, who rewrote in a post-Kantian vocabulary what Geulincx posited in a post-Cartesian idiom. Schopenhauer did not need a Cartesian God to argue that Nature was a sound basis on which one could posit a dualism of "Will" and "Representation," but when he made "Will", by a calculated misnomer, the carrier of the Unconscious spirit of the World, he actualized a philosophy of non-knowing. Will meant in fact Will-lessness, and Nature provided the blind instinct to which Kant's formalist teleology had been reduced. What saved humanity from the pathos of universal pain was artistic contemplation. The "*nihil velis*" had taken care of the question of the "will" that had obsessed Nietzsche and Yeats. Beckett would agree with Martin Heidegger's strictures on Nietzsche. Heidegger debunked Nietzsche's pretension to overcome metaphysics by staking his all on the "will to power."[51] As he observed, Will is the most metaphysical concept; Nietzsche unwittingly marked the culmination of the metaphysics he wanted to destroy with his hammer. Thus when Beckett praised the "un-will to power" leading to radical impotence as the solution to the world's quandaries, he was ushering in a different Irish modernism. It was a later modernism that owed a lot to artists like the two brothers Yeats, both abundantly celebrated and quoted by Beckett. This sends us back to the beginning—but this is another cycle, another bicycle, why not, and altogether another story.

4

Ethos vs. *Pathos* of the New in 1910

Beckett chose Geulincx's motto of "*Ubi nihil vales, ibi nihil velis*" as a way of connecting values and the will, but he was also saying "Vale," that is "Good-bye," to his literary past, hoping to find a new health via ignorance and impotence, new attitudes that took on a French accent. Health is partly a matter of character. We can recall that for Aristotle, *The Art of Rhetoric* bears not only on types of discourses, *logos*, or the logical composition of an argument, but also on *pathos*, the passions or emotive disposition of the audience, and on *ethos*, the character of the speaker.[1] *Ethos* calls up the trustworthiness, the credibility one can grant to a given orator or author. Pathos means the emotional appeal of an argument addressing not the rational faculties but appealing to subjective empathy, captivating emotions, passions or strong feelings, whether positive or negative. Aristotle discusses in detail emotions such as anger, fear, and sympathy.[2] Pathos always keeps the sense that one can share a pain in imagination, or suffer with the narrator. This factor is essential for Aristotle, since one can win a discussion by a low appeal to basic passions.

In that sense, ethos brings about a limit to pathos—character triggers less an ethical impulse than a personal relation with issues of form. The link between character and form remained central for Beckett all his life. The point was well seen and expressed by the young Georg Lukács: "Form is the highest judge of life. Form-giving is a judging force, an ethic; there is a value-judgment in everything that has been given form. Every kind of form-giving, every literary form, is a step in the hierarchy of life-possibilities."[3] Using the insights of Lukács, I will sketch a brief history of value in modernism. It will be underpinned by a sense that the new would entail both pathos and a redefinition of human character. My double point of departure will be taken first with Ezra Pound, and then with Virginia Woolf, all the while focusing on a chronotope, a slice of history, the year 1910.

Modernism, history, and value

A first point of departure will be once more provided by Ezra Pound's invention of comparative literature. Throughout his career, Pound worked by a series of displacements, amalgams, and translations. He first operated vertically in time, going back to Homer, the Greek tragedians, Dante, and the Troubadours, at a time when he felt that all ages were "contemporaneous," a loaded statement that we will interrogate. He then operated horizontally by broadening the field of his comparisons, including India, via Tagore and Yeats, Japan, via Yeats and Fenollosa, China, via Confucius and later the Jesuit histories of China, and Africa thanks to the work of Leo Frobenius whom he pioneered, and finally Australian aboriginal legends that crop up in the *Pisan Cantos*. After WWII, he returned to Greek texts and also explored China differently, taking his cue from Joseph Rock's accounts of the non-Confucian myths and legends of the Naxi. The vertical dimension had established the main tools of the investigation, a series of "rock drill" probes capable of penetrating the dense strata of an European past; the horizontal explorations had extended the map so as to include at least three other continents, Asia, Africa, Australia, next to Europe and the United States. The recantation of the final years put an end to the project of a unified synthesis. After his return to Venice in the 1960s, Pound felt such a strong remorse at having believed so eagerly in fascist myths of a return to Roman ideals of imperialist conquest that he decided to remain silent; the silence that marked his last decade is a perfect embodiment of his version of the "pathos of distance." Pound could have reassured himself if only he had realized that the dangerous fascist myths to which he clung for so long, would be inevitably debunked or exploded by the mass of texts and documents that he had managed to bring together.

The passage from *Spirit of Romance* that I have mentioned condenses the pathos of distance of high modernism:

> It is dawn at Jerusalem while midnight hovers above the pillars of Hercules. All ages are contemporaneous. It is B.C., let us say, in Morocco. The Middle Ages are in Russia. The future stirs already in the minds of the few. This is especially true of literature, where the real time is independent of the apparent, and where many dead men are our grandchildren's contemporaries, while many of our contemporaries have been already gathered into Abraham's bosom, or some more fitting receptacle.[4]

Pound did not choose his locales at random. The Pillars of Hercules are the straits of Gibraltar marking the Western limit of the Mediterranean world. Gibraltar, which Pound had visited and knew well, guards the coast. Morocco is a few miles away, an invitation to explore another continent, a gateway to dark Africa behind. Jerusalem stands for the antithesis of Athens in Pound's view of the Classical world, and one may agree that most of Russia in 1910 evoked a medieval society, with a majority of poor *mujiks* treated as slaves by a minority of rich and Westernized noble families.

Pound's statement that "All ages are contemporaneous" should not be taken to mean that time does not count in history. On the contrary, the sentence suggests the reverse; namely that we all live in different times and periods even when we share the same birthdate. Pound's sense resembles what Adolf Loos had written two years before in a provocative essay, "Ornament and Crime." By comparing ornaments with the tattoos worn by criminals, Loos was pleading for a new culture founded upon clean, pure, and spare lines. His modernity would not be totalitarian, for he knew that in Austria in 1908 there were Tyrolian peasants who loved ornaments on their shoes and houses. These simply did not live in the same historical moment. Loos admits that it would be absurd to make these contemporaries reject their beloved kitschy ornaments. His modernist manifesto from 1908 takes into account the uneven development of culture:

> I live in the year 1908, but my neighbor lives approximately in the year 1900, and one over there lives in the year 1880. It is a misfortune for any government, if the culture of its people is dominated by the past. The farmer from Kals lives in the twelfth century, and on the occasion of the jubilee Procession, tribes walked past which even during the period of mass migration were thought to be backward.[5]

Pound's view of universal literature led him to propose a globalized history, which did not entail that he negated historical time. If he aimed at recreating "myths," helped in this restoration by a belief in the return of Greek gods, such "myths" had to be historicized in a "new" moment that included the past. This is not exactly what Stein, Eliot, and Joyce believed at that time. When Joyce described the structure of *Finnegans Wake* as an a-temporal circle, he proclaimed that his last work presented "no past, no future" and that everything in it should "flow in an eternal present."[6] Pound's contemporaneous "present" implied a trickier and different critical task; it had nothing to do with freezing of history according to mythical patterns of historical returns. Pound's "present" was the time it takes to make discriminations and distinctions. These distinctions cross over long periods of time, and multiply rather than erase differences.

This idea was illustrated by Pound's assertion that we need a "literary scholarship" capable of weighing "Theocritus and Yeats with one balance" (SR, 6). Few professors, whether teaching Classics, Comparative Literature or English, would feel up to the task; it looks daunting. How to establish a "balance" that would measure these poets' respective merits, how to weigh style, versification, common themes, and images, also taking into account the respective impacts of the poets on their ambient cultures, their political ideologies, the reasons why they still think that they have produced "news that stays news," and so on? The "balance" should be attuned to translation issues, which presupposes our ability to understand the distance between Greek metrics and Yeats's lighter Celtic touch. Pound's point does not, of course, boil down to a study of influence; he does not assume a lineage linking Theocritus, the inventor of Greek idylls and bucolic poetry, with Yeats, his friend and mentor, an Irish poet echoing ancient folklore in a modern idiom. As we have seen, *Ulysses* made fun of Yeats's habit of comparing contemporary Irish writers to Homer or Sappho, but here, Pound argues for something different—he requires the elaboration of precise poetological measures, the establishment of complex formal or ideological bridges capable of connecting different cultures and periods. One needs to multiply levels of relevance and technical definitions in order to establish criteria that cannot be reduced to formalist formulas.

To make the point more accurately, I will adduce Virginia Woolf's famous but baffling statement that "in or about December 1910 human character changed."[7] The loaded term is "character" here, a term one might be at a loss to define precisely. Woolf gives a precious hint when she contrasts the Victorian cook, who had lived invisibly in the depths of the house, with the Georgian cook, who suddenly turned into a creature of "sunshine and fresh air." The opposition established is between traditional bourgeois slavery and a more recent emancipation doubling as patronizing camaraderie: a "modern" cook will enter into the family drawing room, she will not hesitate to borrow the daily newspaper or ask the house's lady for advice about fashion. What has changed, then, is the relation between the "high" and the "low." A redistribution of these values has taken place, which does not mean that the class structure has been abolished. "Character" works as a marker of this redistribution. In a first approximation, the concept of "character" sketched by Woolf corresponds to what Hegel calls *Sittlichkeit*, an "ethical substance" which defines the shared values of a whole period. In the *Phenomenology of Spirit*, this term comes into play after self-consciousness reaches an awareness of its "others" before moving on to perceive the global unity made up by individuals and society. *Sittlichkeit* defines the community of a polity, for there, no distinction between private interests and a collective ethos holds.[8]

This should not be confused with morality in general, either with a moral law dear to Kant, or with the values of the "higher" nobles that were the first to be posited according to Nietzsche.

In Hegel's formulation, *Sittlichkeit*, "ethicality," will also encompass the relations between sexes; initially, these relations are immediate and do not suffer any conflict. This *ethicality* underpins another opposition leading to a clash between human laws and divine laws. Antigone, for example, manifests by her stubborn opposition to the human laws that there is another set of transcendent values; finally, Antigone's aggressive irony precipitates a division of the ethical substance itself. This reference helps us understand why Woolf mentions in same sentence *Agamemnon* and the dismal married life of Thomas Carlyle. Hence the famous words: "All human relations have shifted—those between masters and servants, husbands and wives, parents and children. And when human relations change there is at the same time a change in religion, conduct, politics and literature. Let us agree to place one of these changes about the year 1910."[9] This chimes in with Hegel's analysis of *Antigone:* a change in human relationships has brought about a political crisis. It was in those terms that Woolf defined the new *Sittlichkeit* of a modern spirit born in the last month of 1910.

Far from me the wish to try and prove that Woolf was a covert Hegelian! Ann Banfield's *The Phantom Table*[10] has shown that the epistemology of high modernism, at least in its Bloomsbury version, constituted itself *against* Hegelianism. However, these terms are useful to probe the ethical impulse that brought about modernism, which I could define provisionally as a more daring and experimental practice of literature, the arts, and philosophy, aiming at a radical change of life. I will proceed by sticking to a simultaneous cross-cut impacted by Eliot's "historical sense." All the texts I consider in this chapter date from 1910, if not just December 1910. There is of course one exception: Woolf's essay, because it is retrospective in its assessment and dates from 1923. However, if we look closer to the momentous date, Woolf's letters exhibit traces of the shift. The ethical change appears in a letter written to Clive Bell on December 29, 1910:

> As for my writing—you will have to wait for Mel(ymbrosia) to see what has become of it. The Lit. Supt. doesn't print my single review; and the *Guardian*'s Womans Supt. I take to be dead, and giving off odours. I should say that my great change was in the way of courage, or conceit; and that I had given up adventuring after other people's forms, as I used. But I expect that I am really less sensitive to style then you are, and so seem more steadfast.[11]

Melymbrosia was the first title of *The Voyage Out*, only completed in 1912 then published in 1915. What stands out in this admission of fears of being half-dead is the realization that what matters is her struggle to find her own voice without following models. This entails a surprising disregard for form or "style," understood here as the decorum of literary language.

Woolf's 1910 letter confirms that to be modern in 1910 implied less inventing forms than struggling with old values, with the nuance that the system of values that was rejected underpinned a whole architecture of forms. One often hears that modernism was based upon a rejection of a previous generation's style, which entailed a break with ancient forms. Here, Woolf's disregard for style is exemplary. Her issue will be to usher in a new vision of life as a whole: this vision includes a new morality, a new idea of love, new colors, and so on. In other words, what counts is less art than the impact it has on everyday life. Life can be changed by a moral revolution ushered in via a new pathos or new affects.

A similar claim is perceptible in a letter to Violet Dickinson, when Woolf mentions the post-impressionist show at the Grafton Galleries, which is often invoked to justify the choice of December 1910 as the date of the irruption of the new. At first, Woolf was not enthusiastic about the modern painters gathered by Fry. She even tends to put them down:

> I suppose you have been going everywhere—to the Grafton Galleries, and the Bernard Shaw play. Now that Clive is in the van of aesthetic opinion, I hear a great deal about pictures. I don't think them so good as books. But why all the Duchesses are insulted by the post-impressionism, a modest sample set of painters, innocent even of indecency, I cant [sic] conceive. However, one mustn't say that they are like other pictures, only better, because that makes everyone angry.[12]

At first skeptical, Woolf was aware of the shock caused by the paintings by Cézanne, Gauguin, Van Gogh, Picasso, Matisse, and others exhibited by her friend Fry. A positive payoff for her work was soon acknowledged, for she adds: "You will be glad to hear that I am seething with fragments of love, morals, ethics, comedy tragedy, and so on; and every morning pour them out into a manuscript book."[13] Thus post-impressionists led the way in the arts, and modified for good the ethos of 1910 encapsulated here by "love, morals, and ethics."

Lukács and Gide about Bubu

When foregrounding "love, morals, and ethics," Woolf grants "soul" more importance than style or form. These terms had been coupled strategically in a book written by Georg Lukács, *Soul and Form* (*Lélek és a formák*, in Hungarian in 1910, in German *Die Seele und die Formen*, published in 1911). Lukács's brilliant collection gathering earlier essays rests upon a dialectical coupling of "soul" and "form." In a manner similar to Woolf's, Lukács explains that his main concern is not style: he will not strive to write well; his anarchic "denial of form" will be justified if he can outline a new vision of life.[14] Like Woolf, Lukács believes that "destiny" (the ultimate questions about the motivation of life) should determine form, not the reverse. Form is necessary insofar as it puts a limit to abstractions (SF, 23). Hence, a true essayist tackles the main problems of life even when apparently discussing pictures or books (SF, 25).

Lukács's dialectics of form and life finds a good exemplification with Kierkegaard. Lukács focuses on the turning point in the Danish philosopher's career, when Kierkegaard broke off his engagement with his fiancée Regine Olsen in 1841. Kierkegaard appeared as a vile "seducer" in the eyes of his community and the decision changed his life by giving it a final form. Such a gesture cannot be explained by reductive interpretive systems, it was meant to remain as opaque as it was final. The gesture posited a fixed point in a life that is by definition mobile and fluctuating. It was upon this gesture that Kierkegaard founded his philosophy, as we see in *Either/Or* with the tiered succession of the esthetic, the ethical, and the religious. He made a leap from the mixture of meaning and meaninglessness that constitutes everyday life, so as to re-found it. The gesture enabled Kierkegaard "to see the absolute in life, without any petty compromise" (SF, 48). In the end, the dialectic reversed itself: the "gesture" ended up not being a "gesture" because it was so fully justified that it had become life itself. Kierkegaard's painful, torturing decision to break up with Regine may have been the only form of love he was capable of. If the posture could not avoid appearing slightly ridiculous to other men and women, making him both a social outcast and an object of ridicule, this sacrifice was a gesture that expressed the totality of life absolutely.

To express life, Kierkegaard had to withdraw from life. Gesture meant less "form" than an ethical decision, if by ethics we understand the emergence of a pathetic gesture following generic *Pathosformeln* that cannot be identified with a single form. Lukács captures here a founding moment of early modernism, for as we will see with Siri Hustvedt, Kierkegaard's genius consisted in multiplying contradictory forms. Lukács would later attack modernists like Woolf or Kafka for their nihilism and petty-bourgeois individualism, but *Soul and Form*, blending trends coming from Kant and Hegel, German Romanticism, Platonism, and Expressionism, impressed Benjamin, who found a bridge to the later *History and Class Consciousness*.[15]

Lukács's essay about Charles-Louis Philippe entitled "Longing and Form" defines more precisely the form taken by modernist pathos. Charles-Louis Philippe, one of the first proletarian writers in France, had died in December 1909 at the young age of thirty-five. His masterpiece *Bubu de Montparnasse* (1901) was the first French novel exploring the Parisian underworld of pimps and prostitutes. When T. S. Eliot read it in 1910, he was struck by the phrase "mixing memory and desire" and used it in *The Waste Land*. He also developed Philippe's critique of modern civilization that scrutinized its symptom, prostitution. It was not just that civilization was "syphilization," but that debased sexual morality had impacted people's values and behavior. Lukács summarized the plot in one sentence: a pimp and a naïve student fight over a prostitute (SF, 115). For a while, the student lives happily with Berthe, although he has caught syphilis from her. Her pimp is in jail. When the pimp is set free, he comes at night and takes Berthe with him. She accepts her fate without resistance, which leaves the student alone and in despair.

Presenting Philippe as a "poet of poverty" Lukács added that the structure of infinite longing he staged derived from economic circumstances: its main cause is poverty. Poverty prevents Philippe's characters from enjoying happiness or even from reaching for it when it seems to be at hand. He concludes: "Their social position has become a state of longing" (SF, 120). The proletarian pathos Philippe became known for is condensed in this sentence. Lukács insists less on a Marxist analysis of class than on the role of ethics in Philippe's vision:

> Philippe wanted to get away from his world of gentle pity. He aspired to a harder, more rigorous world, and the ways which led him there were to be ethics and work. His ethical sense was always very strong; even the abject Bubu is a product of it. Bubu learns that his mistress is infected and sick and he is about to abandon her, but his friend, another pimp, tells him that this behavior would be dishonorable. Lukács admires his words: "... *on ne lâche pas une femme parce qu'elle a la vérole.*"
>
> (SF, 122–3, tr. modified)

Here is the basic law of pimping: one doesn't cast aside a woman because she has the pox. A code of honor regulates sexual commerce; the true hero is not the sentimental student, who doesn't do much to save his romantic love, crushed as he is by the superior stare of the pimp, or the poor Berthe, trapped in her passivity, but Bubu. Bubu is a "free man," he can walk up and down the boulevards fearlessly, nothing intimidates him, he is not afraid of gang fights, the police or syphilis.

While Philippe insists on a physiological basis for human emotions, he is not a naturalist like Emile Zola. His vision is less clinical than lyrical, but his lyricism is borne by a collective subject. The first scene evokes festivities following the national day parade of July 14. Pierre Hardy, the student, is affected by these desires, but the subject introduced is anonymous: "A man who walks carries all the things of life and revolves them in his head. A vision awakes them, another excites them. Our flesh has kept all our memories and we mix them up with our desires. We traverse the present time with this luggage, move on feeling complete at each instant."[16] However, at the end, one person, Bubu, towers above all the rest, like Herr Peeperkorn swaying over the other characters at the close of Thomas Mann's *Magic Mountain*. Lukács concludes his essay by praising a new novelistic mode that buried Flaubert's cult of the perfect form. Collective lyricism emerges from the conflation of symbolism and realism, and ushers in its dominant pathos, longing, but insofar as longing creates a new form: "Philippe's longing truly dissolved itself into form" (SF, 126–7).

Soul and Form's last essay reiterates the dialectic of form and ethics: "[O]nly a form which has been purified until it has become ethical can, without becoming blind and poverty-stricken as a result of it, forget the existence of everything problematic an banish it forever from its realm" (SF, 198). The idea of a form purified until it becomes ethical will be developed by Jacques Lacan in a reading of *Antigone* to which we will return, and it was shared by Osip Mandelstam, who applied it to François Villon in a pre-Acmeist essay from 1910. Mandelstam points out that, like Charles-Louis Philippe, Villon experienced directly the sordid lives of pimps and prostitutes in the Paris of the fifteenth century. He, too, was longing for possessions that he would never obtain; he was the first modern poet:

> Villon was exceptionally conscious of the abyss between subject and object, but he understood it as the impossibility of ownership. The moon and other such neutral "objects" were completely excluded from his poetic usage. On the other hand, he livened up immediately whenever the discussion centered on roast duck or on eternal bliss, objects which he never quite lost hope of acquiring.[17]

Mandelstam, who was soon going to sing the stones of the gothic age, saw in their hardness a model for his carefully crafted sonnets. The same hardness defines Villon's strength, which derived from a rejection of dominant medieval ideologies. The French poet felt above all values and laws: "Gothic stability and morality were completely alien to him. On the other hand, greatly attracted by its dynamics, he elevated the Gothic to the heights of amoralism."[18] Villon's "dry and rational mysticism" made him to experiment with form. He cast a cold stare on life but expressed both its baseness and its splendor. Like Pound, who took Villon as the paradigm of French "hardness," Mandelstam defines with his usual incisiveness the link between a new form and the ethical convulsions deriving from the transition between an old and a new *Sittlichkeit*.

When André Gide read his homage to Charles-Louis Philippe on November 5, 1910, this was an important cultural event that T. S. Eliot, in Paris at the time, attended.[19] Gide would echo both Lukács and Mandelstam: for him, quite simply, Philippe was a French Dostoevsky. Like the Russian writer, Philippe never created a perfect artistic form. On the other hand, his ethical simplicity, the qualities of his heart, his gushing compassion for the poor and the humble, were authentic—he was an exception in the French literary scene, but also heralded a new generation, the "barbarians."[20] Here was a French Dostoevsky who belonged to the lower classes and was deprived of symbolic capital. He was in a better position to capture the changes that modernity was bringing about when new categories of disenfranchised populations were moving into big cities. Social alienation, sexual humiliation, and capitalistic exploitation, along with the strategies of survival among the louche demi-monde, allied with the experience of raw suffering, were the main themes of Philippe's novels. A pathetic counterpoint came from tender feelings for his mother and a redeeming love for fallen women. Later, Philippe discovered Nietzsche and renounced this sentimentalism. Gide saw in the glorification of the pimp Bubu the lineaments of a Nietzschean ideology. A weak hero accepts his humiliation; he admires the strength of Bubu, in whom he recognizes the superior man. Bubu was a Nietzschean Übermensch.

Croquignole, Philippe's last novel (1906), hesitates between a claim for social justice and an admiration for the strong man embodying the joy of living above the laws. The setting is restricted to bickering clerks in a stifling and petty atmosphere. Felicien, a weak moralist, clashes with Croquignole, a Nietzschean hero who has too much blood, sperm, and verve in his body to be capable of any thought. A first tragedy unfolds when Croquignole tops his social triumphs by negligently seducing a young woman with whom Claude, a friend of the narrator, another timid person, was passionately but silently in love. Croquignole boasts about his conquest. Subdued, cowed even, Claude keeps silent but breaks up with the young woman; heartbroken, she commits suicide. This plot evokes Ettore Schmitz's 1898 *Senilita* (aka Italo Svevo's *Emilio's Carnival*), in which Emilio's sister, who has remained unseen, spurned and finally delusional, is the victim of the clash between the weak and sensitive hero and the strong and domineering Nietzschean artist, his friend the sculptor.

Gide praised Philippe in November 1910, but then grew critical. Writing another homage to Charles-Louis Philippe in 1935, Gide aligned himself with the strictures of the middle-aged Lukács: "I hold for certain that, today, Philippe would be a fascist [. . .] as a reaction to his earlier books that were all about pity, he would now think: woe betide the weak!"[21] The pathos of pity would yield to the pathos of distance; then the "harder" values define a new

Sittlichkeit. A different shift also appears in a novel that takes the Paris of the impoverished middle-class as the site of a disquieting and estranging modernity, Rilke's *Notebooks of Malte Laurids Brigge*.

Rilke's things and Kafka's desk

Based on Rilke's extended stays in Paris in 1902–1903 and in 1906–1909, the *Notebooks of Malte Laurids Brigge* were published in the Summer of 1910. The book documents the growing alienation of a fictional alter-ego, Malte Laurids Brigge, whose diaries alternate between imagistic evocations of sordid Paris locales and distant memories of his stately but lugubrious country estate in Denmark: "The trams rattle jangling through my room. Automobiles drive through me. A door slams. Somewhere a window smashes; I hear the laughter of the large shards and the sniggering of the splinters. Then suddenly a thudding, muffled noise from the other direction, inside the house. [...] People are running overtaking each other."[22] The French capital is evoked as a hellish place full of noise, violence, and exploitation; it combines speeding engines and lost souls. Rilke endows the scenes with pervasive melancholy. Urban pathos culminates in the haunting description of a gutted building, in which we observe that the "stubborn life of these rooms had not let itself be trampled out" (*Notebooks*, 47). Human life has no more substance than old water-pipes, rusty nails, torn wall-paper still adhering to the wall, peeling paint on patches of wood. There we sense the fetid breath of time, and thingly remanence of gone lives. The wall is a stubborn ruin that embodies the essence of life as resistance to the erosion of time.

This passage had impressed Heidegger, who quoted it entire in his 1927 seminar, because Rilke had evoked so concretely what it meant to be "in the world."[23] The mute life of discarded things allegorizes a "being-in-the-world" aware of the life that leaps at humans from things. The passage of the exposed walls was less a screen for the imagination than as an elucidation of what "is" means when we talk about abandoned objects.[24] Heidegger's analysis of a reflexive understanding of our existence through things gives birth to a minimalist ethics. Any self-understanding proceeds ethically by being "authentic," that is based upon an analysis of the ecstatic structure of a future leading to unavoidable death. Rilke demonstrates sensually how urban things help bear life once they have been truly perceived.

Things become more than things when they turn into faces, in a dialectical reversal to which I will return via Duchamp in my Conclusion. The exposed interior of a destroyed and gutted house becomes a face that haunts us because we can recognize ourselves in it: "I swear I broke into a run the moment I recognized that wall. For that is what is terrible (*das Schrekliche*): I recognize everything here, and that is why it enters into me so readily: it is at home with me (*es ist zu Hause in mir*)."25 The Terror is recognized (*erkannt*): the objects that trigger it are already "at home," "in the house," and they dwell in us. This announces the famous Terror marking the apparition of angels in the first lines of the *Duino Elegies*.

The death that inhabits us entails a loaded relation to ethics. The narrator suffers the fates of those anonymous Parisians just by looking at their things; the urban tissue is, as Benjamin wrote about Naples, Berlin, and Paris, porous. The inside of a street is also an outside into which dreams and nightmares are projected: their phantasmagoria has already been enacted there, as Benjamin understood with Parisian arcades. Heidegger's inspired reading highlights the need for an ethics of authenticity linking *Dasein* (existence) with a new awareness of temporality.

Then a poetic manifesto is grafted onto the chronicle of Parisian alienation. What comes across as the dominant idea is a modernist plea for change allied with an unanimist awareness of the unity of human experience—we are all "one" in language—even though we face the singularity of our individual deaths. The past has to be understood dialectically. It encompasses our ancestors, and long sections of the *Notebooks* evoke Brigge's childhood, before defining the artist's task, which points to the future: "This young foreigner of no consequence, Brigge, will have to sit himself down, five flights up, and write, day and night: yes, that is what it will come to—he will have to write" (*Notebooks*, 16–17). Brigge writes to "save his soul" by discovering love in exceptional feminine figures: mystics like Mechthild von Magdburg, Teresa of Avila, and Rose of Lima. His writing bridges the gap between sordid urban experiences and an older but half-forgotten culture. It heals him, brings about convalescence, grants him in the end "*la patience de supporter une âme*" (*Notebooks*, 166), "patience to endure one's soul."

The effort to heal oneself through writing was a concern for another writer also born in Prague, Franz Kafka. Kafka began his diary in 1910, recording dreams, anxieties, fantasies, projects, jottings of plots that became stories and novels. Most entries read like sketches, fragments of dreams interspersed with observations, musings, and even erotic vignettes. A passage in which he tries to describe the "harm" done to him by his education was rewritten six times, four successive versions expanding from a few lines to a few pages, before reverting to condensed formulations. Kafka sensed the need to be modern in 1910, precisely because he had then despaired of reaching the perfect form à la Flaubert that he coveted. Identically, the injunction to modernize himself was couched in the terms of an ethics of courage and conceit. Writing was both the disease and the cure, for it provided a diagnosis while generating a sort of mania, stronger than life. The passion for writing generated its own pathos, which prevented Kafka from living normally, hence marrying and having children. An entry from December 1910 looks like a continuation of Rilke's *tableaux parisiens*:

> When I sit down at the desk I feel no better than someone who falls and breaks both legs in the middle of the traffic on the Place de L'Opéra. All the carriages, despite their noise, press silently from all directions in all directions, but that man's pain keeps better order than the police, it closes his eyes and empties the Place and the streets without the carriages having to turn about. The great commotion hurts him, for he is really an obstruction to traffic, but the emptiness is no less sad, for it unshackles his real pain.[26]

This dream-like passage presents a blueprint for the tragic ending of "The Judgment," its last word referring ambiguously to traffic and sexual relations (*Verkehr*) at the moment when the hero jumps to his death from a bridge in Prague. The somewhat lighter mood is due to a Paris emblematized by heavy traffic on Place de l'Opéra. Kafka had not been a happy tourist there, for a sordid episode in a brothel made him flee the French capital in disgust after just nine days. In the diary entry, pain empties the world of "traffic," which leaves the writing subject in terrifying emptiness, agonizing over debts and commitments. Writing nevertheless provides the only cure; it even generates moments of bliss:

> 16 December 1910. I won't give up the diary again. I must hold here, it is the only place I can.
>
> I would gladly explain the feeling of happiness, which, like now, I have within me from time to time. It is really something effervescent that fills me completely with a light, pleasant quiver and that persuades me of the existence of abilities of whose non-existence I can convince myself with complete certainty at any moment, even now.
>
> (D, 29)

As the year 1910 came to a close, Kafka introduced order in his writing implements, which gave an opportunity for a detailed description of his chaotic desk (D, 32–3). Kafka observed its contents then broke off in the middle of a sentence:

> It is midnight, but since I have slept very well, that is an excuse only to the extent that by day I would have written nothing. The burning electric

light, the silent house, the darkness outside, the last waking moments, they give me the right to write even if it be the most miserable stuff. And this right I use hurriedly.

(D, 33)

The struggle never ended. Kafka had abandoned the draft of *Descriptions of a Struggle* begun in 1904, a lack of courage confirmed on December 27, 1910: "My strength no longer suffices for another sentence. Yes, if it were a question of words, if it were sufficient to set down one word and one could turn away in the calm consciousness of having entirely filled this word with oneself" (D, 34). The sentence was left unfinished, hope dangling in an anacoluthon.

Happily, the New Year brought the changes Kafka had wished for; it unleashed energies that allowed him to write "The Judgment" and "Metamorphosis." Besides in 1911, Kafka embraced the cause of the Yiddish theater, started to learn Yiddish and Hebrew, in order to come to terms with his Jewishness. The process did not offer a miraculous solution, no more than the radical vegetarianism that he embraced, as an entry from January 8, 1914, makes clear: "What have I in common with Jews? I have hardly anything in common with myself and should stand very quietly in a corner, content that I can breathe" (D, 252). This sentence would be true of Apollinaire's position as a modernist writer who felt both Jewish and French, although he never had the patience to sit in a corner.

Ethos vs. pathos of the new

Apollinaire is a test case if one wants to study the clash between the ethos of the new and the pathos of the new. His collection of stories *The Heresiarch & Co.* was published in 1910. It gathered stories published in symbolist reviews like *La Revue Blanche* and *Messidor*; their titles give away the overarching theme: "The Wandering Jew," "The Latin Jew", "The Heresiarch," "Infallibility," "Three Stories of Divine Punishment," "Simon Magus," and so on.[27] The first story brings us back to Rilke's and Kafka's Prague; in "Le Passant de Prague," we meet the Wandering Jew, whose name is Laquedem. Laquedem has lived two thousand years and is quite lusty despite his years; he has sex with a prostitute, but never stops walking during his exertions; he crosses the Jewish ghetto of Prague while making love. He dies every hundred years of a fake death, and he survives for an illusory afterlife. His tale would have been told to "Chrysostom Daedalus"—shades of *Ulysses!*—in a book published in 1564.

Laquedem embodies the plight of modern man that Kafka encapsulates as the impossibility of dying, a fate rendered with poignant fatalism in "The

Hunter Gracchus." Modern man cannot be even born because a true death is no longer available. To express this, Apollinaire invents a new proto-surrealist prose, an adequate medium for stories ranging between obscure theological fantasies and neo-Dadaist extravaganzas. In one story, the narrator follows a rag-picker, collects trash, and finds in it a curious ring with a pale stone in the middle. He puts it on, later learning that this was the gallstone taken from a rich-man's bladder. He had it given to his mistress as a token of his love. Hearing that his gift had been trashed like rubbish, the old man dies suddenly; then the narrator leaves the relic on a church altar. Erudition is abused and perverted as in the metaphysical *ficciones* by Borges. Apollinaire saw himself as Jarry's heir, and on their first meeting they spent a whole night discussing heresies.[28] The tales unfold like the dreams of a perverted theologian who happens be a poet; his pathos is combined with the Uncanny while promoting a supreme jouissance beyond good and evil.

Surprisingly, the last stories proved prophetic for the author who mentions the death of Edward VII, which shows that the writing was finished in May 1910. "The False Amphion, or the Stories and Adventures of Baron d'Ormessan" presents six vignettes about this character, all tall tales based on the adventures of a certain Géry Pierdet, a con artist from Belgium who had befriended Apollinaire in 1905. Fleeing the police, Pierdet spent several years in the United States; he came back to Paris in 1911 after the publication of *The Heresiarch & Co.* Apollinaire hired him as his secretary. In May 1911, Pierdet stole objects from the Louvre and hid them in Apollinaire's apartment. When the Mona Lisa was stolen from the Louvre in August 1911, Apollinaire brought back those stolen pieces, which attracted the attention of the police. He ended up in jail for a week because of the exactions of the real-life model for baron d'Ormessan. Pierdet denounced himself but Apollinaire felt the blow: he lost the love of Marie Laurencin and never recovered his peace of mind afterward. D'Ormessan the con-man and artist was another avatar of the Wandering Jew—a false messiah reappearing under many reincarnations in the collection.

In one story, Baron is in America during the gold rush; the winter comes, food is scarce, they are starving and decide to commit suicide. He alone avoids killing himself and then survives by eating the body of his girlfriend. In the end, he projects his own image via multiple film screens so as to be shown everywhere at once. This new false messiah has a sadistic imagination. The story "A Good Film" shows d'Ormessan launching the International Cinematographic Company that enacts murders for the delight of rich viewers. He forces a man to shoot his beloved in front of the camera. An innocent is condemned and executed; this is filmed as well. Apollinaire's take on modernism was a mixture of technology and myth spiced with a high dose of perversity. Pathos derives less from a sense of personal release of inner demons than an enjoyment of the tall tale, incredible adventures linking arcane legends, and a mythified present; this is the tone of the curious mixture of genres deployed in *Les Mamelles de Tiresias*, the war-time comic opera inspired by Jarry's *Ubu* cycle, the first "play" or "farce" ever called "Surrealist." Apollinaire launches what could be called a "pathos pseudos" in a mixture of themes tapping unconscious drives like the gender-blending figure of Tiresias, and stylized but delirious scenes. In the collection of stories with the teeming false Messiahs and true impostors, we never forget that all these fictions constitute a *pseudos*; less a direct lie than a creative fiction. True to this program, when answering a questionnaire on "ideal art" in 1914, Apollinaire defined Truth as "authentic lies, veritable ghosts."[29]

By contrast with Apollinaire's deployment of a pseudo-Sadian pathos leading to healthily perverse enjoyment, a sense of humility akin to that of Geulincx appealed more to Jules Romains. Romains had toyed with the idea of documenting anonymous lives as fully as possible in poems, essays, plays or novels. The program launching a collective ethos was realized scrupulously by *Mort de Quelqu'un*, translated as *The Death of a Nobody* (it should be "Death of Someone"). The novel was dated 1910 and published early in 1911. It gives form to the cosmic vision put forward in the poetic sequence *La Vie Unanime* (1908). Romains's aim is to describe the life and death of the most banal person—Jacques Godard. The lonely widower living in Paris catches a cold after a visit to the Pantheon and dies soon after. Godard is dead by page 12, the point being to show how he begins to live after his death.

Godard, a retiree from the French railway system, led an empty life in Paris, rarely returning to the mountains of Auvergne to visit his old parents. After his death, solitude is broken and new groups are being formed. His neighbors learn of the solitary death, and chip in for a crown. The study in sheer banality becomes a sociological analysis of the ways in which the social spirit can be embodied. This becomes explicit when the funeral reaches an avenue in which the police and trade-union strikers are fighting. The battling men are forced to observe a truce: they salute the procession and let it pass. When the mourners enter the church, the dead man assumes the proportions of a vital force: "The dead man was now so great that he needed no one any longer. To think of him was not to do an act of charity but to yield to a force. He gathered himself together and was created anew. He was the master."[30] The presence of this force reassures the priest, who was doubting his vocation! The metamorphoses of a "nobody" makes him turn into a group, a mass, a crowd, and finally express Life. The death of a "nobody" triggers a social rebirth and releases a collective force that culminates in a non-religious apotheosis. Seeing the funeral pass, a young man remembers his own father's funeral, which offers a good exemplification of Hegel's *Sittlichkeit*. Romains's *ethos* connects Jacques Godard, a forerunner of Musil's "man without qualities," with the poetic values evinced by Malte Laurids Brigge. The lack of a true "character" in novelistic terms highlights the collective *ethos:* the group becomes the true hero.

Individuals discover this source of strength in moments of collective ecstasy, feeling then at one with the continuum of life. Any social event can generate one of these epiphanies. Romains had exposed these ideas in *A Manual of Deification* (1910). The task of the artist was to look for spontaneous events betraying unanimist life: they are found at crossroads, in streets, squares, near monuments, wherever an observer captures the collective unconscious. The point is less to seize the instant in a lyrical expression than to push it to the next stage and create a "divine surprise" by forcing a group to become conscious of its own dynamism.

However, Apollinaire did not share these ideas; he even objected to them forcibly. Apollinaire had been a friend of Romains, but in April 1911, just before the Louvre scandal erupted, he launched a ferocious attack on Romains's *The Army in the City*, a play portraying a rebellion in a small city. Romains had presented his play as "classical and national." Apollinaire countered that Romains had sunk to the level of historical melodramas. He quoted a section of the *Manual of Deification* describing how Romains wished to "wake up groups from their somnolence" by "doing violence" to them, unleashing sudden explosions or extravagant actions.[31] Apollinaire derided Romains as a manipulator fascinated by collective violence; he had reduced literature to the level of a speech by "a trade-union leader proclaiming class-war."[32] The clash between these two forms of French modernism was inevitable. Romains's modernism addressed common men in the name of social fraternity. Apollinaire's modernism, like Woolf's modernism, continued Symbolism by other means; its pathos of the new would generate original modes of expression, slowly recreating an ethos. Romains opted for the forceful and deliberate creation of a new ethos on the spot. The rift was ethical as well as political; it would reappear in the divide between various avant-gardes, those that ended up on the left and those that went to the right, and those who insisted on "pure" modernism.

Virginia Woolf admired Jules Romains and would have been shocked by Apollinaire's stories. She owned a copy of *Mort de Quelqu'un*, and in 1913 reviewed Romains's *Les Copains* for the *Times Literary Supplement*.[33] She grasped Romains's "ability to trace the mysterious growth [...] of a kind of consciousness of the group in addition to that of each individual of the group."[34] Woolf was inspired by the idea of doing away with "characters," as she later did in *The Waves*. Unlike *Les Copains*, a ribald riff on friends wreaking havoc in a sleepy provincial town, Romains remained serious with *Mort de Quelqu'un*. It was a novel in which there "were no 'characters,' no humour, no plot, only a few dramatised psychological and metaphysical theories."[35] Romains provided an immediate model for *Jacob's Room*, a unanimist novel dominated by the pathos of the death of the hero, even though we learn about the fact surreptitiously. Jacob himself is barely present, and always mediated by the gaze of others; the true carriers of emotion are things: a lost brooch, an unopened letter from Mrs. Flanders, a chair keeping the imprint of Jacob's body.

Woolf thought that she had found a solution to her growing impatience with traditional "characters" as one finds in the novels of Arnold Bennett, for instance. She imagined a new "character" born in December 1910 who would be endowed both with ethos and pathos. Her aim was to create a new anonymous "character"—that is, an ethos without a subjective or literary "character" as in the stock-trade types defined by tradition. That ethos would double as pathos, but would generate new affects devoid of sentimental emotions, as we will see in detail in the next chapter. When in "Mr Bennett and Mrs Brown" Woolf asserts that "it is to express character—not to preach doctrines, sing songs, or celebrate the glories of the British Empire, that the form of the novel, so clumsy, so verbose, and undramatic, so rich, elastic, and alive, has been evolved,"[36] her examples of "characters" are national, with English, French or Russian filters brought in contact with similar situations but experienced differently. This etymology of "character" harks back to the original sense of "sharpening, engraving, leaving distinctive signs." Character is a form of writing that takes into account human temperaments and historicized ethical evaluations. Our chronotopic mosaic limited to the year 1910 has shown that modernist authors created a modern character for which "courage" and "conceit" were not mutually exclusive. The conjunction was productive for the writers we examined. It gave them the courage to live and create; a courage that they can convey to us, for it is also the courage to create new affects.

5

Affect Effects Affects

Deleuzian Affect vs. Lacanian Pathos

It was inevitable that the "turn to affect" that has marked the last decade in literary studies should generate controversy. One cannot display affects as if these constituted a badge of honor with total impunity. If I endorse Ruth Leys's suspicion that the new field has created fads and allowed rampant subjectivism to return under the cover of neurosciences,[1] I would like to suggest that some bridges linking psychoanalytically inflected studies to affect theory have not been blown up; at least, my ambition would be to build a footbridge. In other words, we may not have to choose between Darwin and Freud, as Leys states.

One of the nagging issues in the current discussions of affects is whether what is often called "emotion" concerns the body or is due to a mental process, or even triggered by the darker psychic parts of subjectivity. The body is given pride of place in the books and articles that have mapped out a turn to affect in literary studies—however, what body is this? Is it the libidinal body of psychoanalysis, or the scanned map of a totalizable system deployed by neuroscience? The editors and authors of *The Affect Theory Reader* devote a good number of their pages to this "between-ness," an interactive, one might even say an "inter-passive," passage from body to text.[2] For Lacan and his school, the question about affects derives mainly from the "Real," the site in which the enigma of a "speaking body" is manifested. As Lacan stated: "The real, I will say, is the mystery of the speaking body, the mystery of the unconscious."[3]

Is "affect" simply a fashionable term used to reintroduce the study of passions and emotions in literature? That would not signal a radical departure, for we have known since Aristotle and Lessing that the recurrent problem of aesthetics hinges around the management of emotions, whether by sublimation or by redirection of bodily functions. When Aristotle introduced terror and pity as the main affects released by tragedy, his aim was to understand how purgation works: is it a quasi-physiological discharge of excremental passions, a collective cleansing of the body politic, or a refinement in perception brought about by higher virtues? Later on, Lessing pointedly asked why a scream of pain or horror like that uttered by Laocoön could not be a fit object for art of the highest order. What attenuation of the spasmodic contractures of the face will be requested to make the pain amenable to a proper expression, thus attaining "the true pathos of suffering"?[4]

Darwin was alerted to this issue, and he quotes Lessing at the beginning of his canonical study on *The Expression of the Emotions in Man and Animals*, a book published the same year as Nietzsche's *Birth of Tragedy from the Spirit of Music*.[5] The cumulative impact of both books was such that they motivated Aby Warburg to begin his investigations of the expression of pathos in the art of the Italian Renaissance. Darwin was attentive to contrasts offered by our tradition of formal beauty with what happens when emotion is expressed by "strongly contracted facial muscles."[6] Lessing focuses his lens on the limits set to expression by historical and cultural codes:

> There are passions and degrees of passion which are expressed by the most hideous contortions of the face and which throw the whole body into such unnatural positions as to lose all the beautiful contours of its natural state. The ancient artists either refrained from depicting such emotions or reduced them to a degree where it is possible to show them with a certain measure of beauty.[7]

Anguish will thus have to be toned down as sadness, wildness turns to sullenness, and the grin of Democritus should be downgraded to a smile. Woe to a materialist philosopher like La Mettrie, who had required to be represented as a laughing Democritus; looking at his portrait, Lessing was filled with "disgust or horror." The painting seems to represent a laughing man at first, but if we gaze at it longer, the philosopher turns into a "fop," his laugh an embarrassing "grin."[8] No disfiguring scream or open mouth will ever be able to create "natural beauty."

Assuming that affects are located in the body, let us first pose the question of whether the "natural" body offers a site that risks disrupting the classical poetics of representation that have dominated from Aristotle to the end of the eighteenth century, when literature was ruled by genres defined by conformity with the topic represented. When extolling the emergence of a new regime of expressivity, Jacques Rancière has followed a historical or genealogical model. If the emergence of a new regime of expression is due to different class structures and modes of social and economic production, the turn to affect has remained closer to a foundational view of the interactions between the human body and the languages of art, such as had been brought to the fore by Mikhail Bakhtin half a century before. To launch the critical vocabulary of affects, no single text was more influential than Deleuze's and Guattari's 1991 "Percept, Affect and Concept," a chapter planned jointly by the two thinkers, but whose final redaction was due to Deleuze alone.[9] This was the text that pushed Brian Massumi and others to work with affects. I will highlight its salient points, and develop some of its implications before comparing it with a Lacanian theory of affects.

The logic of affect

"Percept, Affect and Concept" concludes *What Is Philosophy?*[10] which is probably the most systematic work by the two authors. It opens with a dogmatic statement: the task of philosophy is to invent concepts, and the task of art is to invent affects. Any work of art can be defined as a compound of percepts and affects. These theses entail important distinctions that are too often overlooked:

> Affects are no longer feelings or affections; they go beyond the strength of those who undergo them. Sensations, percepts, and affects are *beings* whose validity lies in themselves and exceeds any lived. They could be said to exist in the absence of man because man, as he is caught in stone, on the canvas, or by words, is himself a compound of percepts and affects. The work of art is a being of sensation and nothing else: it exists in itself.
> (WIP, 164)

Avoiding any subjectivist projection when defining art as the invention of new emotions, Deleuze combines his philosophy of expression with his objectivist anti-humanism. On this view, art produces monuments that are self-sufficient because it creates an autonomous universe that should not be read as the transmutation or sublimation of human passions and affections. Next to examples taken from painting, with Rubens, Pisarro, Monet, Cézanne, two American writers are quoted at first: Emily Dickinson and Edith Wharton. Both understood that a few lines or a few words were sufficient to create this sufficiency, this autonomy, when, say, evoking a being, a landscape or a privileged instant.

Deleuze quotes Wharton's short story "The Verdict," in which Rickham, the narrator, wonders why Gisburn, once a successful painter but a "cheap genius," has abandoned painting after his marriage to a rich woman. Rickham imagines that it is because Gisburn is now rich: he lives in luxury on the French Riviera; his creativity must have been stifled by materialism. However, we discover that Gisburn stopped painting the day he realized that his art lacked any foundation, which dawned upon him when he saw a painting by his former rival, Stroud. It all came because Stroud's widow had asked Gisburn to paint a portrait of her deceased husband. He had accepted out of curiosity and then saw in Stroud's studio the sketch of a donkey done in a few strokes: that was enough to make him gauge the inanity of his own work. The narrator also notices the picture: "What a wonder! Made with a dozen lines—but on everlasting foundations."[11] Shocked by the realization of his lack of talent, Gisburn cannot paint the old man's portrait; he leaves with the sketched donkey. The posthumous victory of the deceased painter is overwhelming: "[A]s he lay there and watched me, the thing they called my 'technique' collapsed like a house of cards. He didn't sneer, you understand, poor Stroud—he just lay there quietly watching, and on his lips, through the gray beard, I seemed to hear the question: 'Are you sure you know where you're coming out?'"

This tale, whose reference is missing in the English translation, offers an interesting example, not only because it is founded on ekphrasis with the imaginary animal, but also because the principle of artistic autonomy is enunciated so forcibly. The living painter left alone with the corpse feels watched by the dead man's eyes, then questions his art and admits that he is a fraud and a failure. Wharton superposes two binaries, truth and lies, and life and death, to assert that because Stroud is dead, he sees the truth. The title of the French translation, *Les Metteurs en scène*, insists on art as artifice, staging, against a Truth emerging from the abyss of death.

Wharton's tale condenses the mixture of formalist modernism and Romantic expressivism that marks Deleuze's theory of art. On the one hand, art does not "resemble" reality: it creates its own universe: "We paint, sculpt, compose and write sensations. As percepts, sensations are not perceptions referring to an object (reference): if they resemble something it is with a resemblance produced with their own methods; and the smile on the canvas is made solely with colors, lines, shadow, and light" (WIP, 166). Such a formalist statement would have pleased Clement Greenberg. On the other hand, Deleuze adds a factor downplayed by Greenberg: the autonomy of art leads to a-subjective affects divorced from any perceiving subject. Far from the neo-Kantian theory of artistic judgments based on the cultivation of personal taste of the mature Greenberg, Deleuze affirms the objective essence of art: "If resemblance haunts the work of art, it is because sensation refers only to its material: it is the percept or affect of the material itself, the smile of oil, the gesture of fired clay, the thrust of metal, the crouch of Romanesque stone, and the ascent of Gothic stone" (WIP, 166). Caught by art, sensible matter creates its own eternity, even if it is to last an instant. Affects are autonomous, unattached to a perceiving subject, eternally out there in their stubborn materiality.

Proust and Pessoa have created sensations as pure and separate beings (WIP, 167). The example of Proust is adduced perversely to argue that memory plays a minimal role in artistic creation. If every work of art is a "monument," it is not a commemorative monument (WIP, 167). Such examples confirm that "affect" does not mean emotion, no more than "percept" would be a perception or a sensation. Thomas Hardy, Herman Melville, Virginia Woolf, William Faulkner, Leo Tolstoy, and Anton Chekhov are all mentioned because their works imply an "absence of man" (WIP, 169). A comparison between Cézanne and Woolf leads the passage in which Woolf presents Mrs. Dalloway gazing at Piccadilly Circus and taking in the spectacle of London:

> She sliced like a knife through everything; at the same time was outside, looking on. She had a perpetual sense, as she watched the taxi cabs, of being out, out, far out to sea and alone; she always had the feeling that it was very, very dangerous to live even one day. [...] She knew nothing; no language, no history; she scarcely read a book now, except memoirs in bed; and yet to her it was absolutely absorbing; all this; the cabs passing; and she would not say of Peter, she would not say of herself, I am this, I am that.[12]

Why include *Mrs Dalloway* and not *Ulysses*? What interests Deleuze in Woolf is her sense of a lacking ego, her recurrent intuition that her self is not there. This makes it possible for her to use the genre of the novel for non-psychological projections of affective states, thus to create an affect. Virginia Woolf "is" not Clarissa Dalloway, a wealthy socialite with a difficult daughter and an absent husband, preparing a party at which Peter Walsh, an old flame, will be present. What matters is not psychology. With Joyce, there is always the suspicion that one should care about the psychology of Bloom, worry with him that his wife is cuckolding him on June 16, 1904. Clarissa's inner life appears on the contrary devoured by the others, spent in exterior stimuli generated by the city. This exteriority allows her to become the mystical double of war-traumatized Septimus, although she barely knows him—a redoubling that could not occur in Joyce's plot construction. As the double of a subject soon to kill himself, Clarissa's intense joy is heightened; her a-subjective vitality projects the affect of a joy to be merely alive—alive in spite of all, the recent war, the dead friends, the returning ghosts of the past, and the future suicide.

The projection of a selfless subject echoes with similar statements in Cézanne's letters: the artist stresses that we have to become the instant, or become the world. Vision is becoming, not possession of the world, but being possessed by the world. Beckett appreciated that aspect of the French painter when he praised his ability to render a "non-organic" world. This dehumanized quality recurred in the paintings of Jack Yeats: "God knows it doesn't take much sensitiveness to feel it in Ireland, a nature almost as inhumanly inorganic as a stage set."[13] In the same way, Ahab is a device allowing Melville to become the whale and the ocean, just as Kleist uses Penthesilea to accelerate passions, his heroine's frantic love indistinguishable from murderous fury. Out of love, Achilles lets Penthesilea defeat him; she has accelerated her affects so violently that she cannot help killing him. She tears his body apart, regrets her actions, and dies. Here, affects are used as stones of weapons, the objects of "sudden petrifications or infinite accelerations" (WIP, 169). Deleuze parallels this instrumentalism with Kleist's essay on the puppet theater, an essay appreciated by Beckett who grafted Kleist's insights on Geulincx's insights. If everything happens because God wills it, we live a permanent miracle, we become divine puppets.[14] The *pathosformeln* of expressive gestures endow subjects with grace, if their gestures can remain untainted by thought.[15] By abolishing the principle of causality, formal grace is produced, a grace combining the elegance of bodies spinning along and the delicate gyrations of automata.

The same grace underpins the affects explored by Deleuze, who, like Kleist, aims at freeing animated bodies from bothersome psychology; apparently autobiographical novels like Henry Miller's *Tropic of Cancer* or Thomas Wolfe's *Look Homeward, Angel* cannot be subsumed under psychology. Psycho-biography has no purchase there, despite some parallels with the authors' lives. Wolfe extracts a "giant" from his father; Henry Miller transforms Paris into a planet, an aerolith (WIP, 171–2): both transcend accidents of their individual lives and render them allegorical, telluric, universal. In spite of differences in tone and plot, both novels end with scenes in which the narrator contemplates the city he is about to leave, feeling life flow through his bodies. In *Tropic of Cancer*, the narrator reaches Auteuil and watches the Seine: "[The Seine] is always there, quiet and unobtrusive, like a great artery running through the human body."[16] A similar interpenetration of landscape and character underpins the monumentality of Wolfe's enterprise.

The novelists and artists gathered by Deleuze display an ability to "write exteriorly" and to "think externally," as Virginia Woolf stated in a diary entry of November 1928. Woolf, meditating on her craft, realized that she wanted to "saturate every atom" of her texts.[17] This "exteriority" acquired more force in *Orlando*, a novel that had brought her fame; in forthcoming books, she planned to "give the moment whole; whatever it includes."[18] Kafka, Woolf, and Wolfe are called "athletes" who confront daily their "inorganic doubles" (WIP, 172). One thinks of Kafka as a "hunger artist," a paradigm from which Peter Sloterdijk has extracted the idea of the acrobat of modern times.[19]

Proust puts us on the right track when he presents affects as bodily manifestations from which material allegories are generated beyond any subjective point of view, which is exemplified by the kitchen maid of Combray who turns into "Giotto's Charity." Allegorical affects rule Proust's epic of Time, from the multiplicity of desired bodies glimpsed together in the collective assemblage of the "Young Women in Bloom" sauntering along the beach, to the contradictory facets of a continuously lying Albertine. What prevents Proust from yielding to his latent Platonism is the awareness that only pain and affect teach a lasting lesson. Proust explains that we become better when the person we love makes us suffer. If we truly suffer, following the *pathos mathos* logic, we perceive that those who hurt us most are thus divinities, true gods or goddesses. Only the pain inflicted will help us progress.[20] Proust's objective is to preserve the unity of the work of art in the face of the multiplicity of teeming and contradictory sensations, which leads from affects linked with singular bodies to a work of art functioning as an autonomous corpus, a glorified Body. The "effect" of totality derives from the affect created by the work. Affects are always effects on the body of hidden passions of which we are unaware: we learn from the effect, after the fact, how much we have been affected.

This theme had been developed by Jean-Paul Sartre in *Sketch of a Theory of Emotions*.[21] This early text stages a confrontation between a not-yet-founded existential phenomenology and psychoanalysis, a program also developed by Ludwig Binswanger. The attempt clashes with the refusal, manifest in later works, of the idea of the Unconscious, for in *Being and Nothingness*, the Unconscious was deemed incompatible with a philosophy of consciousness. Unconscious manifestations were simply effects of "bad faith." However, in this short book from 1938, Sartre treated emotions as bodily affections coming from the outside, and made them compatible with existential affects derived from Heidegger. Quoting Pierre Janet, Wilhelm Stekel, Alfred Adler, and Henri Wallon, Sartre examined cases of paradoxical behavior, like the action of a clumsy thief who wants to be caught in order to be punished, or phobias; as he writes, "anger can signify sadism."[22]

In his reading of affect, Sartre anticipated Deleuze's semiology of exterior signs and Lacan's binary of signifier and signified, and even considers a determination of affects by pure exteriority:

> [I]f we had a consciousness, *even implicit*, of our true desire, we would be in *bad faith*, and the psychoanalyst will not accept this. The consequence is that the signification of our conscious behavior is entirely exterior to this very behavior, or, if one prefers, the *signified* is entirely cut off from the *signifier*. The behavior of the subject is in itself what it is (if we call "in

itself" what it is *for itself*), but it is possible to decipher it by appropriate techniques, as one deciphers a written language.²³

These signs, split between signifier and signified—Lacan was to make much of this conceptual tool—are not available to the consciousness of the subject. Only another person can read them as signs. Soon, however, objections crop up: isn't there a contradiction between this "in itself" and this "for itself" in the subject's *cogito*? If there is a *cogito*, how can it not create all the significations? When Sartre had briefly glimpsed a psychoanalytic truth, he had thematized the binary of signifier and signified, a conceptual couple that Lacan deployed two decades later. Alas, all too soon he closed the door to affects determined by the language of exteriority.

Sartre's harking back to consciousness is at the other end of the spectrum from Deleuze's adherence to a theory of autonomous and impersonal affects. If art produces affects, the artist remains a Romantic "seer" (WIP, 171) who creates a world, often metaphorized as a space. Any dwelling will do, a palace or a house, even a threatened burrow like that of Kafka's paranoid mole. The artist's godlike role is superimposed upon Spinoza's God, an idea enacted playfully by Beckett who gave Murphy a Spinozist motto in a parody of divine self-love: "*Amor intellectualis quo Murphy se ipsum amat.*"²⁴ Murphy replaces God in the famous definition of God's love for himself of *Ethics*, Book V, Proposition 35. Is this love a pure solipsism, a sign of Murphy's isolation after he leaves the social world to enter that of the psychotic Mr. Endon? Deleuze had analyzed the logic of Expression in Spinoza's *Ethics*, distinguishing between suffering, passion, feelings, affection and affect.²⁵ Expression is not just the Romantic privilege granted to the Creator, whether divine or artistic. Expression derives from a concept of infinity, which generates the two main affects in Spinoza's philosophy: joy, when our being is augmented, and sadness, when it is diminished.²⁶

A recent animation film like *Inside Out* (2015), directed by Pete Docter from Pixar Animation Studios, proves to be a Spinozist tale, but with a Lacanian twist. Riley, an eleven-year-old girl suddenly uprooted from Minnesota to San Francisco, is increasingly unable to cope with her growing distress. Her emotions are reduced to five: Joy, Fear, Anger, Disgust, and Sadness. The leading two are Joy and Sadness, at first, it seems, obvious opposites (although Joy's hair shares the blue color that Sadness spreads on any memory she touches, a subtle detail). But the moral of the story is delivered when Joy admits that her power has limits; she yields to Sadness, who achieves the expected reunion of the family members. Then Riley stops her fugue; father, mother, and daughter can cry together. This proves that a limitation in being can be a good thing, provided all the other emotions collaborate and contribute to the final *tableau*.

There are as many lists of affects as there are philosophers; most agree that a combination of Joy and Sadness provides a key to emotional balance. Descartes has only six passions, quite different from the five of *Inside Out*: wonder, love, hatred, desire, and then joy and sadness. Of course, given her tender age, Riley is not supposed to have felt the stirrings of sexuality (Freud would strongly object to this rosy picture), and wonder is left to the viewer. Descartes and *Inside Out* would agree on the allegorical picture of emotions as keys to behavior, all triggered by different types of memories masterminded by little imps at the keyboard of a gigantic technological apparatus of mental switches, controls, and gears. Spinoza's *Ethics* would add to this picture a notion of infinity, ultimately predicated on the unity between Nature and the human soul.

A similar unity dominates in Darwin's book on the expression of emotions in humans and animals, as well as in Nietzsche's pages on pathos and tragedy. Whereas Spinoza links man and God's enjoyment, Darwin parallels human expressions of affects such as anxiety, dejection, despair, anger, disgust, surprise, horror, and shame, with emotional expression among animals. Although expression is a universal feature for Darwin, his belief in the identity of signs denoting affects meets limits. One of these comes to the fore in shame: after some hesitation, Darwin concludes that blushing should appear as a truly human affect. His chapter on blushing, an affective or pathetic manifestation apparent even among blind people or subjects who cannot perceive the others' gaze, is instructive.[27] This suggests that human affects function like colors: the color of the skin reveals a moral and physiological truth in symptoms combining nature and culture, while a Pixar-generated electric blue connects Joy and Sadness.

All this confirms Deleuze's contention that a great artist has to invent an affect: "A great novelist is above all an artist who invents unknown or unrecognized affects and brings them to light as the becoming of his characters" (WIP, 174). If affects are like colors, it means that they can lie while telling the truth. An author invents affects just as a painter invents colors or a musician invents harmonies. Thus Proust "invents" a new concept of jealousy as an original affect:

> When Proust seems to be describing jealousy in such minute detail, he is inventing an affect, because he constantly reverses the order in affections presupposed by opinion, according to which jealousy would be an unhappy consequence of love: for him, on the contrary, jealousy is finality, destination; and if we must love, it is so that we can be jealous, jealousy being the meaning of signs—affect as semiology.
> (WIP, 175)

The presentation of Proustian jealousy as a major invention provides an important addition to Deleuze's 1964 *Proust and Signs*.[28] There is a semiology of affect, which can be approached via color theory.

The colors of affects

Shakespeare, too, invented jealousy as an affect in *Othello:* he grafted this unholy passion onto a new body and pushed it further, thanks to the trope of affects turning into colors.[29] *Othello* foregrounds the black color of its eponymous hero, a Moor whose physical darkness is the counterpart of Iago's moral "blackness." The affect of the play being jealousy, the irascible passion that leads to Desdemona's murder, its effect is the speed with which it spreads. Iago, the villain who slanders Desdemona in order to create suspicion in the mind of a loving husband, lies first by inventing her own lies. Iago's resentment derives from his envy of Othello's sexual and rhetorical power. He tells Roderigo: "Mark me with what violence she first loved the Moor, but for bragging and telling her fantastical lies" (O, II, 2, 218). The object of jealousy has to be a woman, in order to evacuate the same-sex tension between Iago and Othello. Iago postulates a feminine nature in Desdemona, who is presented as a young and immature woman. Her fate is to fall in love with a young man closer to her age and skin color, a role played by Cassio, also "green" because he is as immature as she is. Green reappears in the evocation of Jealousy as an autonomous being or affect. By warning Othello against jealousy, Iago creates it by coloring the vision of the Moor, which makes us understand the self-fulfilling prophecy of affect: "Oh, beware, my lord, of jealousy/It is the green-eyed monster, which doth mock/The meat it feeds on" (O, III, 3). Iago fuels Othello's imagination with visions whose effect is to create doubt, anger, and hatred. Jealousy is created by the effect of the thetic power inherent in language: as soon as anything is mentioned in connection with affectivity, affects begin to take life and thus exist. Cassio is imagined with Desdemona lying naked in bed, which feeds Othello's epistemophilia—he wants to know, then needs to know more. Othello's delirium reiterates "lies" (about who "lies" with her) so that he is trapped in them. The color-coding beginning with white and black expands to include the green of envy. Such a blooming affect becomes an autonomous passion; it acquires power beyond the control of any subject. Once it appears on stage, conjured up by rhetorical tricks, it migrates from Iago's cunning mind to Othello's infected imagination.

Joyce also depicted jealousy as an autonomous affect and achieved this by critiquing both Spinoza and Shakespeare:

As a contribution to the study of jealousy Shakespeare's *Othello* is incomplete. It and Spinoza's analysis are made from the sensationalist standpoint—Spinoza speaks of *pudendis et excrementis alterius jungere imaginem rei amatae*. Bertha has considered the passion in itself—apart from hatred or baffled lust. The scholastic definition of jealousy as a *passio irascibilis* comes nearer—its object being a difficult good. [...] [Richard] is jealous, wills and knows his own dishonor and the dishonor of her, to be united with every phase of whose being is love's end as to achieve that union in the region of the difficult, the void and impossible is its necessary tendency.[30]

Here, Joyce seems to have shed the psychologism that permeated his interior monologues. When he talks about "the difficult, the void and impossible," he thinks of an affect that can only be captured by an oxymoron, the union of non-union, the possibility of impossibility. If jealousy is such a "difficult" or "impossible" affect, how can it be represented? The issue combines the theme of expression with the context of the stage. The realm of the "difficult" in which characters are trapped turns into a technical "difficulty" for the playwright: can one represent pain and suffering on stage? It is on such a difficulty that most performances of *Exiles* have foundered:

It will be difficult to recommend Beatrice to the interest of the audience, every man of which is Robert and would like to be Richard—in any case Bertha's. The note of compassion can be struck when she takes the spectacles in order to read. Critics may say what they like, all these persons—even Bertha—are suffering during the action.[31]

Joyce's aesthetics meets its limits when it tries to envisage the visibility of affects.

In *Exiles*, Richard Rowan, Joyce's alter-ego, carries the brunt of the plot. It revolves around his lack of reaction when he is told that his friend Robert Hand is trying to seduce Bertha, his beautiful common-law wife. Bertha, flattered more than tempted by Robert's attentions, tells Richard of the seduction scheme and begs him to intervene. He refuses, letting her choose freely. When she accepts Robert's invitation, Richard prefers not to know what happens. In the last scene, Richard still does not know whether Bertha has slept with Robert or not, but he renews his vows with Bertha. Their love is not a relationship between complementary partners but a joining of divided and "wounded" subjects, ready to come to terms with the pathos of their irreducible difference. Such belated acceptance of distance creates pain; this pathos thrives on the pain that gave rise to it, but the outcome is to unleash an ethical freedom at the very end.

Lacan's Pathos: The distance of no relation

The play *Exiles* displays an affect that, for Lacan, amounts to Joyce's symptom.[32] Indeed, *Exiles* presents squarely the lack of sexual relation; its technical difficulty stages the impossibility of a complementarity in the male and female sides in a couple. Richard's shocking indifference at the beginning is linked with a strange lability or fragility observable in the Joycean body. In Seminar XXIII, Lacan pointed to this evanescence when he discussed affects in *A Portrait of the Artist as a Young Man*. A vignette condenses it, a memory from Stephen's school days. A group of boys tormented him because of his claim that Byron was the greatest poet. Then overcome by anger but too late, he rushes after them. Suddenly, his anger falls from him: "[E]ven that night as he stumbled homewards along Jones's road he had felt that some power was divesting him of that suddenwoven anger as easily as a fruit is divested of its soft ripe peel."[33] This scene proves that affects can vanish or suddenly fall from the center of one's ego because it has been imperfectly held together by the "envelope" of the body. Other scenes point to a similar dispossession and suggest the agency of what Ernest Jones called *aphanisis*, the sudden disappearance of desire. Joyce's ego constitutes a rim; it is porous, artificial, and it can be dropped. Thus he will re-knot his ego thanks to his writing. His creative artifice will give birth to a Borromean knot linking an extreme jouissance of language with the creation of Beauty.

References to Spinoza would link Joyce, Lacan, and Deleuze. Lacan's doctoral dissertation had an epigraph, the untranslated quote from *Ethics*, from book III, proposition 57: "*Quilibet uniuscuiusque individui affectus ab affectu alterius tantum discrepat, quantum essentia unius ab essentia alterius differt.*"[34] At the end only, Lacan provided a paraphrase:

> Let us say, in order to express the very inspiration of our research, that "any affect of any given individual differs from the affects of another as much as the essence of the one differs from the essence of the other." (*Ethics*, III-57). By this we mean that the *determining conflicts, the intentional symptoms and the instinctual* (pulsionnelles) *reactions* of a psychosis differ from the *relations of comprehension* defining the development, the conceptual structures and the social tensions of the normal personality according to a measure determined by the *history* of the subject's affections.[35]

Lacan's philosophy of drives is Spinozist throughout. In *Ethics*, Spinoza adds the concept of desire to his analysis of affects. If all affects are related to desire, joy, or sadness, desire spells out the specific essence of individuals: "[T]he desire of each individual differs from the desire of another as much as the nature, or essence, of the one differs from the essence of the other."[36] Desire, affect, and differential personal genealogies converge.

There is a need to sketch a theory of "Lacanian affects," as Colette Soler has insisted. She lists among main affects anguish, pain, sadness, joy, guilt, boredom, moodiness, anger, shame, love, enthusiasm.[37] Lacan began to work systematically with affects when he analyzed anxiety in his 1962–1963 Seminar.[38] Anxiety is one of the first symptoms for psychoanalysis for it is an affect with recognizable bodily manifestations. Freud opposed it to fear, which has an immediate object, whereas anxiety would have no clear object, just vague sources of worry like the fear of dying. Lacan reversed this, arguing that anxiety was "the affect that never deceives." As an affect and not an emotion, its object is lack, the paradigm of a-symbolizable objects. In psychoanalysis, the term of affect covers the description of emotions and passions, but relates them to an Other source caught up between language and the drives.

Aristotle taught Freud about the power of terror, pity or anger and their social uses via purgation, since Freud's method was first called a "cathartic method." "Catharsis" was used by Aristotle to describe the therapeutic function of tragedy, which works by the purgation or purification of affects and passions. This term had been discussed by Jakob Bernays, the uncle of Freud's wife, in his *Fundamental Features of Aristotle's Lost Treatise on the Effects of Tragedy* from 1857. In this book, Bernays lays out the Aristotelian theory of affects as "lustration," rejecting the usual translation as purgation. For Bernays, *katharsis* is a "relieving discharge of the affects" (*erleichternde Entladung der Gemüthsaffectionen*).[39] Breuer used the term first, followed by Freud, in their *Studies on Hysteria*. *Studies on Hysteria* argues that language can serve as a tool for the "abreaction" of affects, by which is meant a transformation of energetic reaction to a painful event. Freud systematized the opposition between pleasure and displeasure in order to study negative affects such as anxiety, fear, disgust, boredom, moroseness, along with positive affects such as love, joy, enthusiasm, compassion, and the "oceanic feeling," the sense of a dissolution of the self in the world. The latter reminds us that affects in literature erase the solid boundaries between the self and the world by ushering in a writing of the outside. This Deleuzian notion had been well expressed by Kafka: "[W]e need books that *affect* us like a disaster, that grieve us deeply, like the death of someone we loved more than ourselves, like being banished into forests far from everyone, like a suicide. A book must be the axe for the sea inside us."[40]

Kafka's view of literature as a break with classical psychology unleashed a pathos that viewed Being as such, which can be related to Heidegger's philosophy of "Care" (*Sorge*) facing the ineluctability of our death. For

Heidegger, both man or woman as existence (*Dasein*) are true to their death by accepting that *Dasein* is a "Being toward death." Then we can reach an ethics that had nothing to do with humanism. The anti-ethics of a humanity falling towards death stresses the distance or verticality between Being as capitalized, the pure essence of Being, and lower-case-"b" beings existing in the world. It is no wonder that Lacan's anti-humanism was brought in conversation with Heidegger's philosophy. Their convergence culminated when Lacan translated Heidegger's "Logos" for the first issue of *La Psychanalyse* in 1956. The philosopher Jean Beaufret, who was Lacan's analysand, played the role of mediator. Beaufret became one of the best commentators of Heidegger in French, and he knew Heidegger personally. Heidegger had written the *Letter on Humanism* as a response to Beaufret's questions about the links between his philosophy and French developments via Sartre and Merleau-Ponty. Thus, at Easter 1955, Lacan, accompanied by Beaufret, visited Heidegger in Freiburg, and asked for permission to translate "Logos" for his journal, *La Psychanalyse*. Heidegger accepted, and a few months later spent a weekend in Lacan's country house.[41]

Heidegger's influence on Lacan is perceptible in "Function and Field of Speech and Language in Psychoanalysis,"[42] an essay echoing Lacan's translation of "Logos." Heidegger's "logos" became in Lacan's version "*legs*" (or legacy). The translation was as punning as the original, mostly in imitation of Mallarmé's prose style. When Heidegger played on the proximity in German between the verbs *legen* ("to read" in German) and *legein* (Greek, from "logos"), Lacan exploited a different French homophony of *legs* ("legacy") and *lais* (poetic "lays"). The decision to translate "logos" as "legacy" was the result of a deliberate pun.

Heidegger deplored the inability of Heraclitus, deemed to be the most perceptive of the pre-Socratic philosophers, to understand that *Logos* was not "Reason" but simply the essence of language. For Heidegger, "Logos" should be rendered in German as "*Lege*," or a "Laying that gathers."[43] Heidegger developed the analysis of Heraclitus's philosophical blindness in a metaphor: he compared this process with a flash of lightning that lets, for an instant, Being appear: "But the lightning [*Blitz*] abruptly vanished. [...] We see this lightning only when we station ourselves in the storm of Being [*Gewitter des Seins*]" (EGT, 78). The image was adapted by Lacan to evoke poetically a moment when Truth is glimpsed, or when the Unconscious discloses something for an instant before vanishing or becoming obscure again. For Lacan as for Heidegger, Truth could only be produced when a terrifying storm of Being raged and disclosed its essence as Language.

Lacan's Mallarméan version provided an adequate equivalent of Heidegger's tortuous prose for indeed "*lais*," the "poetic song," echoes the

German *Lege* without any conceptual forcing. If Heidegger is present in "The Function and Field of Speech and Language in Psychoanalysis," another voice looms as importantly; it is that of T. S. Eliot, invoked in combination with poets like Browning, Goethe and Valéry. Lacan quotes Eliot in the original and without attribution:

We are the hollow men
We are the stuffed men
Leaning together
Headpiece filled with straw. Alas![44]

Lacan's manifesto ends with a quote from the Upanishads about the "voice of the thunder," the celebrated gloss on "Da" interpreted successively as *Damyata*, to master oneself, *Datta*, to give, and *Dayadhvam*, to be merciful (E, 265). Early in the 1940s, Lacan had begun to translate Eliot's poem into French; in a talk given in 1960, he connected Eliot's vision of a drab and desolate "Waste Land" following the catastrophe of the First World War with Freud's main insights: "God is dead, nothing is permitted any more. [...] This is what Freud brings us, meeting in the thousand threads of his network a very ancient myth of something wounded, lost, castrated in a mysterious king, that causes the wasting of the entire land."[45]

It made perfect sense to splice Eliot and Heidegger. Eliot's "hollow men" call up the world of empty verbiage, the *Gerede* of inauthentic *Dasein* denounced in *Being and Time*. The fragment from the Upanishads adapted for the magnificent ending of *The Waste Land* demonstrates that the gift of the gods to humanity is not fire, as with Prometheus, but the gift of speech, once the thunder and the fire have died out. In case we had missed the references to Eliot, Lacan then quotes the epigraph from Petronius's Latin novel *Satyricon* chosen for *The Waste Land*.[46] He forgets to explain that, in the original context, the story of the Sibyl at Cumae hanging in a big bottle and requesting death merely testifies to Trimalchio's absurd boasts and spurious claims to fame.[47]

The wish to die uttered by Petronius's Sybil in an epigraph by which *The Waste Land* opens ominously leads in the second section of the poem to a dialogue between a neurotic woman and a man obsessed by death which condenses all diagnoses about modern anxiety:

My nerves are bad to-night. Yes, bad. Stay with me.
Speak to me. Why do you never speak. Speak.
What are you thinking of? What thinking? What?
I never know what you are thinking. Think.

[...] Are you alive, or not? Is there nothing in your head?
[...] What shall I do now? What shall I do?
[...] What shall we ever do?[48]

However, this is not the passage that Lacan highlights when he discusses anxiety in the Seminar devoted to the notion. Twice, Lacan quotes *The Waste Land*, and the concepts that he finds deployed in the poem are those of an excessive female jouissance, followed by the disconnect between desire and enjoyment. Tiresias, called "the patron saint of psychoanalysis" (S.X, 183) had been struck blind by the gods for having revealed that women know a higher degree of *voluptas*[49] than men. How could he know this? He has been changed into a woman, and then back into a man, and knew intimately the power of feminine orgasms than men. Eliot writes in his notes that "what Tiresias *sees*, in fact, is the substance of the poem,"[50] and the substance of the poem has therefore to be understood as sexual jouissance, insofar as it is unevenly distributed: there is an excess on the side of women. The limitation brought to male jouissance is explained by castration—the ultimate cause of anxiety both for Freud and for Lacan, but with a different twist in Lacanian theory. Freud assumes that anxiety is mostly male and derives from a fear that the penis might be cut or maimed; this fear is then repressed but returns without having any specific object in the phenomenon of anxiety. Lacan thinks that anxiety has an object. Anxiety derives from being too close to the object—especially when the object is the phallus or the symbol of castration.

All this would remain abstract without illustrations. Lacan provided one later in his seminar by revisiting *The Waste Land*, focusing on the "young man carbuncular," who has sex with the typist while Tiresias watches. Lacan quotes the lines in English:

> When lovely woman stoops to folly and
> Paces about her room again, alone,
> She smoothes her hair with automatic hand,
> And puts a record on the gramophone.
>
> (CPP, 69)

He adds that the theme of the debasement of sexuality, here reduced to an automatic and unsatisfactory action, leads to a new formulation, anticipating the maxim, "There is no sexual rapport." Lacan states in the Seminar: "Man's jouissance and woman's jouissance will never conjoin organically. [...] It is because the phallus doesn't achieve any matching of the desires, save in its evanescence, that it becomes the common-place of anxiety" (S.X, 265). *The Waste Land* formalizes a basic sexual paradox: on the one hand, women enjoy sex much more than men; on the other hand, their practical resolution to the lack of complementarity in sexuality is to offer their partners an object hidden behind the phallic claim; this object is to be the hard, rigid or non-detumescent object capable of sustaining desire—in other words, it is a purely imaginary phallus. Thus, in the poem, the young woman is glad that the abortive sexual romp is over; music from a record should help her recover from the fiasco. Meanwhile, the young man carbuncular slips away, having kept his illusion of a sexual triumph. The meaning of this scene is left for Tiresias to ponder, that is to the psychoanalyst who meditates on all that one has had to endure or "foresuffer" in the pornographic dramas enacted by the others:

> His vanity requires no response,
> And makes a welcome of indifference.
> (And I Tiresias have foresuffered all
> Enacted on this same divan or bed[...])
>
> (CPP, 69)

I will return to Eliot's private drama, a struggle that turned into a war of the sexes, in Chapter 6. Suffice it to say at this point that when affects are debased in such sordid travesties, when love is merely a cheap poultice thrown on the open wound, we find ourselves in modern times—this is the period of modernism. In his reading of Eliot, Lacan makes it clear that anxiety has a decisive role to play in that cheap modern farce of sexuality, for anxiety opens up the hole of truth and subverts the weak consensus through which partners attempt to breach the gap in sexuality. Thus the pathos of sexual difference as sexual distance will remain a central theme in the later Lacan.

In the last decade of his teachings, Lacan repeated that "there was no sexual relationship"—an apparently paradoxical thesis launched in 1967. In his astute but critical observations on Lacan's controversial statement, Jean-Luc Nancy has pointed out that the logic of this counter-intuitive remark (for we see every day people having sex, or at least pretending to do so) has a Heideggerian ring. Lacan's expression, "There is no sexual relationship," would both be a provocation flying in the face of banal empirical observation, and a derivation from Heidegger's conceit that Being, in some ways, is not. A Heideggerian logic suggests that we should consider the "sexual relationship" as a "being" whose "Being" is not. The Being coupled to the human subjects who are engaged in an active sexual life will not allow itself to be seen, counted, or even defined.

Nancy argues that the provocative force of the Lacanian utterance does more than shock: it tends to prohibit something—perhaps as Eliot meant it. The utterance functions at the level of theory as castration works in Freud's metapsychology. The pragmatic effect of this prohibition can be compared to that of a "*coitus interruptus*," which outlines the horizon of a certain castration, if not of renunciation. Meditating on the theme of "passivity" in philosophy and psychoanalysis, Nancy asserts that the "passive power" implied by couples engaged in sexuality forces one to reach a pathetic mode of thinking: "It is a whole *pathos* (*toute une pathétique*) that cannot be reduced to a pathology. Now psychoanalysis, especially in its Lacanian version, wants to be something different from a medicine of pathology. Let us say that it wants to be the ethics of a pathos (*l'éthique d'une pathétique*)."[51] One might add that this pathos is discovered in poetry, when Lacan reads it in Eliot's *Waste Land*.

Having reached this point, Nancy stops hedging his bets and endorses the Lacanian version of the "non-relation" proper to sexuality when he examines the key term of "relationship," whether sexual or not. It is not the act, sexual or not, even if common usage treats them as synonyms; common usage assumes that the "relationship" is something, whereas in fact it is more an action than a product. Nancy unpacks brilliantly the intertwined meanings that Lacan condenses in his "There is no sexual relationship":

> The claim that there is no sexual relationship might mean that there is no return, no final report, no conformity or pre-established proportion for what is involved when a couple mates. And, indeed, there is not. If the claim is about the relationship *of* or *to the* subject of the sexual act, if it is about saying what this act *relates* or what one can *retain, retell, calculate* or *capitalize* (and hence inscribe or write in this sense) from it, then undoubtedly we have to say that the report, the measure, or even, in general, the appropriation or the determination of it as "some thing" is not possible.[52]

Critical reservations are toned down after we reach that point in Nancy's argumentation. Nancy provides then a profound and subtle philosophical commentary of the *pathos* of Lacan's motto entirely in agreement with its logic.

Lacan's motto, whether one stresses the beginning ("*There is* no sexual relationship") or the ending ("There is no sexual *relationship*"), in other words, whether one stresses the ontology of the relationship or the epistemology concerning the nature of this relationship, nevertheless presupposes a dialectical relationship between two terms: "*no*" and "*sexual*." The question is how to think the negativity and restlessness that the sentence disseminates in relationship with sexual difference itself. Its key resides in the pathos of distance, which is what Eliot's poem had allowed Lacan to understand—he would take another decade to formulate the insight via his logic of mathemes—that the pathos of difference would generate a methodical *mathos* of distance.

6

"Playing Possum"

War, Death, and Distance in Eliot's Poetry

Following Deleuze's and Lacan's intuitions, this chapter will attempt to measure the distance between two types of pathos, each illustrated by one poem. My aim will be to focus on a short segment of the trajectory of T. S. Eliot's poetic development. A first "pathos of distance" will be embodied in a fairly typical poem from 1915, "In the department store," which ends:

> Man's life is powerless and brief and dark
> It is not possible for me to make her happy.[1]

It is clear that this slight and unpublished poem, dated from 1915, could have been written in 1910 or 1911, when Eliot was drafting "The Love Song of J. Alfred Prufrock." What stands out in those early poems is a crippling awareness that the gap between two souls can never be bridged, even by love. There are sexual and social reasons for that: the poet cannot cross the divide separating him from a department store seller whose wares are as spurious as her false teeth ("The lady of the porcelain department / Smiles at the world through a set of false teeth"). Moreover, his shyness prevents him from responding to the sexual invitation implied by her "sharpened eyes"; he will leave her to enjoy the fantasized "heated nights in second story dance halls" with others. As for him, if he goes out at all, it will be to the opera, but his companion will be conceited or boring, at any rate a partner for whom he feels no desire.

What is left of desire organizes the skillful sequence of metonymies that compose the "lady": the porcelain wares she sells call up her false teeth, also a porcelain of some sort, while the pencil stuck in her hair seems sharpened by her very eyes. The penultimate line quotes Bertrand Russell's 1903 *The Free Man's Worship*, a sentence that Eliot liked; he quoted its lilting rhythms in *The Nation* in 1918: "Brief and powerless is Man's life; on him and all his race, the slow, sure doom falls pitiless and dark." Here is a paragraph evoking a post-Nietzschean and turn of the century pathos with gusto:

In the spectacle of Death, in the endurance of intolerable pain, and in the irrevocableness of a vanished past, there is a sacredness, an overpowering awe, a feeling of the vastness, the depth, the inexhaustible mystery of existence, in which, as by some strange marriage of pain, the sufferer is bound to the world by bonds of sorrow. In these moments of insight, we lose all eagerness of temporary desire, all struggling and striving for petty ends, all care for the little trivial things that, to a superficial view, make up the common life of day by day [...] To take into the inmost shrine of the soul the irresistible forces whose puppets we seem to be—Death and change, the irrevocableness of the past, and the powerlessness of Man before the blind hurry of the universe from vanity to vanity—to feel these things and know them is to conquer them.[2]

Then Russell's text concludes his modern *Vanitas* with resounding words:

Brief and powerless is Man's life; on him and all his race the slow, sure doom falls pitiless and dark. Blind to good and evil, reckless of destruction, omnipotent matter rolls on its relentless way; for Man, condemned to-day to lose his dearest, to-morrow himself to pass through the gate of darkness, it remains only to cherish, ere yet the blow falls, the lofty thoughts that ennoble his little day; disdaining the coward terrors of the slave of Fate, to worship at the shrine that his own hands have built; undismayed by the empire of chance, to preserve a mind free from the wanton tyranny that rules his outward life; proudly defiant of the irresistible forces that tolerate, for a moment, his knowledge and his condemnation, to sustain alone, a weary but unyielding Atlas, the world that his own ideals have fashioned despite the trampling march of unconscious power.[3]

In Eliot's poem, the magnificent sweep of Russell's rhetoric has been broken, its spring destroyed by a last line that sounds so wooden and prosaic ("It is not possible for me to make her happy") that its very immaturity, its simplistic despair, its down-to-earth reductiveness all but destroy the lofty eloquence of the philosopher's purple patch. Because of that, Russell's views on tragedy and vanity appear in retrospect as somewhat spurious. The rhyme of "park" and "dark" carried a lethal irony: it is better to have fun in the park than brood in the dark!

A different pathos of distance will be reached three years later in the poem called "Ode," dated "Independence Day, July 4th 1918." This time, the pathos is raw and "hard," not a "soft" pathos as previously. I quote the last lines of the poem, in which, upon awakening, the bridegroom hears:

Children, singing in the orchard
(Io Hymen, Hymenae)
Succuba eviscerate.

Tortuous.

By arrangement with Perseus
The fooled resentment of the dragon
Sailing before the wind at dawn.

(IMH, 383)

The tone has shifted to a dark, disturbing, cryptic, tense, and hyper-coded variation on mythical figures; echoes of Shakespeare's *Coriolanus* and Chapman's *Bussy D'Ambois* lead us to Jules Laforgue's parody of the Perseus legend. Perseus killed Poseidon's dragon and freed the maiden Andromeda, whom he married. Here, the epithalamium of Roman hymen songs does not announce a happy wedding. Marriage has taken place but its aftermath is sinister, loaded with betrayal, violence, and blood-letting. The bride is a sinister "succuba eviscerate," a nightmarish image of predatory and ghoulish sexuality. Classical myths are not ironized as with Laforgue but taken tragically, evoking scenes of murder, incest, and sexual misery with the weight and dignity they deserve. This version of "Tragedy" so well invoked by Russell's 1903 essay is nevertheless coupled with a sense of resentment and indignation.

In the essay, Russell had written rather pompously:

> Of all the arts, Tragedy is the proudest, the most triumphant; for it builds its shining citadel in the very centre of the enemy's country, on the very summit of his highest mountain; from its impregnable watchtowers, his camps and arsenals, his columns and forts, are all revealed; within its walls the free life continues, while the legions of Death and Pain and Despair, and all the servile captains of tyrant Fate, afford the burghers of that dauntless city new spectacles of beauty.[4]

In Eliot's "Ode," a sort of reverse "mythical method" has been applied to a thoroughly dishonored present, to a contemporaneity that is so morally tainted that it cannot be reduced to mere chaos or anarchy.[5]

The date is telling: in July 1918, the war was still raging in France; its turning point, when the Allied offensive led to the German retreat, was still a few weeks away; and the United States were fully invested in the bloody conflict. Eliot believed that he might have to serve in the army. The poem was written at Marlow Cottage, where Bertrand Russell and Vivien, Eliot's wife, were meeting, continuing their intimate trysts during the week, while Eliot would only come back on weekends from his work in London. In other words, the four-year-old Apocalypse was still raging; the dominant mood was the "horror."[6] It has been noted that the poem was published once in the British edition of *Ara Vos Prec* (1920) before being deleted and replaced by "Hysteria"—the prose poem already discussed—in the American edition of *Poems* appearing a few months later in 1920. Subsequently deleted from later collections, "Ode" does not appear in the *Collected Poems and Plays* published by Faber in 1969.

In order to assess the progression from one pathos to another, from a soft and ironical pathos to a hard and tragic pathos, we will have to revisit the war years in London, and understand how Eliot's new experiences were grafted on a post-symbolist aesthetic. Events leading to the sense of a tragedy would have to be filtered by a post-symbolist aesthetics of subjective disappearance, until they made it tremble or even explode.

Eliot and the symbolist "death of the author"

Eliot's modernism found its foundation in late symbolism, which situates him as heir to a French fin-de-siècle tradition. Symbolism had elaborated an original concept of the "death of the author" one century before Roland Barthes. It made this painful subjective "death" a prerequisite for the transmission of a truly living tradition. Eliot referred to the idea in a passage of the Turnbull lectures on Laforgue and Corbière:

> [W]hen I first came across these French poets, some twenty-three years ago, it was a personal enlightenment such as I can hardly communicate. I felt for the first time in contact with a tradition, for the first time, that I had, so to speak, some backing by the dead, and at the same time that I had something to say that might be new and relevant.[7]

The qualification—"so to speak"—would not be necessary for readers of the earlier essays or poems. We hear echoes from two different passages, two different regimes of utterance: the poetic: "I should be glad of another death" as the closure of "Journey of the Magi" (CPP, 104), or the critical mode in "Tradition and the Individual Talent": "Someone said: 'The dead writers are remote from us because we *know* so much more than they did.' Precisely, and they are that which we know."[8]

One needs to assess the importance of the French context to gauge Eliot's sense of a homology between his personal death and the collective death entailed by the idea of tradition. A real collective death would be enacted with a vengeance during the Great War. Living and dying many times through all this, Eliot revisited the ancient trope of a dwarf who sees better because he is sitting on the shoulders of a giant. If giants carrying dwarves need to be living, one cannot avoid a thanatopoeia connecting a "dead poets' society" with modern forms capable of expressing the contemporary world. The symbolist authors mentioned by Eliot in his American lectures include Baudelaire, Corbière, Verlaine, Laforgue, Mallarmé, Rimbaud, and Charles-Louis Philippe. Their ultimate value will be assessed after a comparison of their respective worth among the dead: "No poet, no artist of any art, has his complete meaning alone. His significance, his appreciation is the appreciation of the relation to the dead poets and artists. You cannot value him alone; you must see him, for contrast and comparison, among the dead" (SW, 52).

This key insight led Eliot to adopt a fundamental attitude, encapsulated by Ezra Pound when the latter nicknamed him "Old Possum." The joking allusion to an opossum alludes to Eliot's wish to "pass" for a dead person, which for Pound also meant become a British author. Eliot would pretend to be "dead" so as to identify with the language and tradition of dead authors. If the American nickname hits upon a desire to merge with a collective spirit before inventing a singular mode of expression, the doctrine had roots in French symbolism following Poe's pervasive influence. Baudelaire, a devoted disciple of Poe, was its initiator, while Mallarmé kept a keen sense of his own death as a person to be reborn as pure literature in a process analyzed by Leo Bersani.[9] Mallarmé could write to a friend that he was "perfectly dead,"[10] a conceit that, paradoxical as it sounds, sends us in the direction of the concept of writing proposed by Jacques Derrida. From this literary impersonality, one could reach the idea of a critique of subjectivity, which became Jules Laforgue's main trope. One encounters it everywhere, most poignantly perhaps in "Sundays", a poem admired by Eliot and quoted in the Turnbull lecture.[11] A literal translation gives this:

> Well I was about to blurt out "I love you"
> When I struggled to own
> That first of all I wasn't sure of being my own.
> [...]
> A poor and pale individual,
> Trusting only sparingly my Ego
> I saw my fiancée fade away
> Swept by the ways things go
> As the rose thorn lets fall
> Under guise of approaching night its loveliest petal.[12]

When Eliot discovered Arthur Symonds's book on the symbolist movement, it introduced him not only to Laforgue's works but to "wholly new feelings" that took the shape of a "revelation" (SW, 5). Eliot is usually careful to distinguish "feelings" from "emotions": the foundational essay "Tradition and the Individual Talent" concludes with the notorious idea that "Poetry is not a turning loose of emotion, but an escape from emotion" (SW, 58) whereas the mind of a poet should assemble "feelings, phrases and images" (SW, 53) that will then unite by taking form together. Hence, Eliot is not being sentimental facing Symbolism: what these poets brought to him was a new way of perceiving the world formally, an original articulation between ethics and sensibility as we have seen in Chapter 4. By focusing on another type of affect, an affect associated with one's sense of being subjectively dead, I want to suggest here a pathos that goes beyond the binary of "emotion" and "feeling."

Symonds begins his section on Mallarmé, the acknowledged leader of the movement, by positing an "Absolute" in poetry: "Stéphane Mallarmé was one of those who love literature too much to write it except by fragments [...] he was always divided between an absolute aim at the absolute, that is, the unattainable, and a too logical disdain for the compromise by which, after all, literature is literature."[13] The problematic of the Absolute could not but call up Bradley's late Hegelianism, with which Eliot was struggling in his graduate work and his dissertation. Eliot would struggle with the Absolute both by discussing Bradley and by reading a Mallarmé revisited by Laforgue's irony.

Mallarmé's struggle with the Absolute led him to experience a terrible pathos, condensed for him by an impression that he had died. Several letters testify to this extraordinary existential crisis. In April 1868, he felt that he had "dug down into verse" only to reach a pure nothingness that he called elegantly "the void disseminated in its porosity" (C, 366). Although he would announce several times that he had "perfectly died"[14] (C, 342), at the same time he promised to write two books, one on "Beauty," the other on the "sumptuous allegories of Nothingness." In all this, Mallarmé felt that he was the spiritual son of Baudelaire, whose melancholia needed a new allegory as Walter Benjamin had perceived. Mallarmé could *see* these allegories but felt unable to *write* them: "Really, I am afraid to *begin* (although, it is true Eternity has scintillated in me and devoured any surviving notion of time) where our poor and sacred Baudelaire ended" (C, 367). In the following year, Mallarmé dictated letters to various addressees that his wife had to write, because he was suffering from a hysterical writer's block and could not touch a pen.

Much later, as he was about to die, choking in the grips of a spasmodic crisis, Mallarmé realized that his project of the Book had led him to a dead-end; no-one would take up his quixotic project of writing the pure and absolute Book. The last letter written for his family, as he was gasping between two seizures, mentions a "half-centenarian heap of notes" (C, 642) for the Book that he alone could have deciphered. Mallarmé asked that his notes be burned—they were not. The tension between the absolute *Oeuvre* and the futility of everyday life could only be resolved by a practice of serial deaths, with the hope that they would usher in a rebirth. Eliot added to this dialectical deaths and rebirths another principle—the pathos of distance as verbal irony. Irony was a measure of the impassable distance separating the Absolute from the Everyday. It was exemplified in two late symbolist poets, both disciples of Mallarmé, Corbière, and Laforgue, both extolling irony as a major mode of expression.

Corbière brought to Eliot the sense that a conflation of "hard" form of poetic utterance and high degree of reflexive irony was possible, whereas Laforgue's melancholic self-portraits remained soft even when touched by irony. Eliot saw in Corbière a modern Villon; like Pound, he took *Amours Jaunes* (*Wry-Blue Loves*) as a modernist equivalent of Villon's testament. This familiarity was documented in a Harvard anecdote: when a student, the young Eliot said at the end of a seminar given by Bertrand Russell that the impact of Heraclitus on him was comparable to that of Villon. The remark impressed the British philosopher, left groping for a theme that would unite the Greek philosopher of constant flux and the lyrical poet of Parisian low-life. It is likely that Eliot was thinking of Heraclitus's famous fragment 119, *ethos anthrópoi daímon*, often rendered as "man's character is a fate/demon," a theme that underpins Villon's *Testament*. Russell, who had never read Villon, thought highly of Eliot and sought out the young American when he came to England, with the consequences that we know.[15]

The dominant mode of *Wry-Blue Loves* is parody. Nothing is spared, not even the speaker. One section even looks like a send-up, in advance, of the opening of *Four Quartets*; it comes with several Epitaphs that introduce the sequence, one of which is a prose riff playing on "beginnings" and "endings":

> *Except for lovers beginning or finished who wish to begin with the end there are so many things that end with the beginning that the beginning begins to end by being the end the end of which will be that lovers and others will end by beginning to re-begin with this beginning which will have ended by being only the return of the end which will begin by being equal to eternity which has neither beginning nor end and which ends by being as finally equal to the rotation of the earth whereupon one will have ended by no longer distinguishing where the end begins from where the start finishes which is every end of every beginning equal to every beginning of every end which is the final beginning of the infinite defined by the indefinite . . .*[16]

This strange litany includes "His one regret, not having been his mistress, no less," a regret evoked by the bisexual fantasies of "The Death of Saint Narcissus" already discussed.

One of the most direct re-workings of Corbière in *Inventions of the March Hare* is "Petit Epître," directly written in French and whose literal translation I provide:

> It is not for people to be disgusted
> By the taste of sewer coming from my Ego
> That I make poetry out of everyday incidents
> That smell too strongly of sauerkraut.
> But what did I do, great Lord,
> To have all the jackals follow me?
> I said there were a male smell
> And a female smell
> And these two are not the same.
>
> (IMH, 86)

This poem written in French evokes an anecdote reported by several friends of Baudelaire. Baudelaire was sitting in a Paris brasserie and repeated: "There's smell of destruction." His friends denied this and suggested that the smell came from some "*choucroute*" (sauerkraut) or a "woman somewhat too hot." But Baudelaire insisted: "I tell you there's a smell of destruction."[17] The poem offers a gloss on one of Corbière's memorable lines: "*Pur, à force d'avoir purgé tous les dégoûts.*"[18] ("Pure, by dint of having purged all disgusts!").[19] The effort to found sexual difference on an affect of disgust, itself derived from a hysterical interpretation of human smells, recurs in many poems from the time of *The Waste Land*.

Corbière's recurrent device was to pile abuse on himself, portraying himself as an ugly homeless creep, rejected by all save animals, while highlighting that he embodied an ideal of pure poetry. Always in rut, he wants to have sex with filthy prostitutes, who take his money and rarely care for him. There was a biographical foundation for this outsider status. Corbière was not only sickly and disabled, he also preferred, like Villon, to frequent brothels and stay in the company of prostitutes. Eliot adds to this satirical self-portrayal his recurrent worry about sexual difference, often objectified by body smells. While Corbière felt that he had been reduced to pure abjection and called himself "Eunuch" or "Pederast," Eliot went further in his bawdy verse. His "Ballad pour la grosse Lulu" (IMH, 311-12) piles up American references next to echoes of Corbière's parody of Villon's *Testament*. One of these in *Amours Jaunes* is called the ballad of "Bossu Bitor" and narrates the exploits of an ugly hunchback who goes to a brothel, has sex with a prostitute, and dies—perhaps in a brawl, or because of excessive love-making. Parodies of this kind dominate in "The Triumph of Bullshit," a poem whose refrain is "For Christ's sake stick up your ass" (IMH, 307). Eliot's satirical art consists in obscene deflations while revolving around an important theme, impotence. Here, it is merely the impotence of philosophy searching for an empty Absolute as an "Impotent galamatias." A hyperbolic but stunted maleness inherited from Corbière betrays an uneasiness about sexual potency, an issue that recurs in Laforgue and in Eliot's poems influenced by Laforgue.

After his stay in Paris and further away from Jean Verdenal, a great admirer of Laforgue, the dire limitations of Laforgue's poetic art became apparent to Eliot. In a letter of July 1919, Eliot asserted that Laforgue's technique was inferior to that of Corbière;[20] he conceded the point again later, but added that Laforgue's mind was nevertheless the more interesting one (VMP, 286). Peter Dale comments: "[A]s more biographical details emerge, it may perhaps be seen that another of Eliot's fascinations with Laforgue was not chiefly poetic but with Laforgue's sexual confusions over women—an area in which Eliot has problems of his own and, perhaps, needed some company."[21] This confusion is confirmed if we look at Laforgue's *Pierrot Fumiste*,[22] a farce devoted to the exploration of male impotence: Pierrot gets married, but out of idealism, refuses to deflower the beautiful wife whom he idealizes. She has to remain pure and virginal in spite of herself. After a few months, she starts worrying, asks for advice, consults doctors. Pierrot, reprimanded and put in front of his responsibilities, acts out wildly. One night, he brutally rapes his wife, then leaves, abandoning her forever. This strangely text, nevertheless written with care and fervor, even, was in the books by Laforgue shared by Verdenal and Eliot. In retrospect, Eliot must have perceived parallels between his predicament facing Vivien and Laforgue's partly impotent Pierrot. This defines an unconscious nexus in Eliot's writings, and the issue is linked with the question of the Unconscious.

When Eliot lectured on Laforgue in America, he linked him with the doctrines of Schopenhauer and Hartmann: "Laforgue is the nearest verse equivalent to the philosophy of Schopenhauer and Hartmann, the philosophy of the unconscious and of annihilation [...] in Laforgue there is continuous war between the feelings implied by his ideas, and the ideas implied by the feelings." (VMP, 215). To illustrate this "war," Eliot translated one of the experimental passages in Laforgue's prose, "Grande Complainte de la Ville de Paris." Shouts are heard coming from the crowd:

> Important notice! Redemption Loan has weakened, Panama Canal shares firm. Auction, Experts. Advances against securities quoted or

unquoted, purchase of unencumbered properties or annuities; advances against expectations; time-tables, annuals, new-year's gifts. Circular tours at reduced prices. Madame Ludovic predicts the future, daily, from 2 to 4. Au paradis des Enfants: toys for children and cotillon favours for adults ...Sole agency!...Cylinder machines Marinnoni! Everything guaranteed, everything for nothing! Oh the rapidity of life also sole agency...

(VMP, 215)

Eliot presents this passage as pre-Dadaist; indeed, this text, written in 1884, points to a "state of affairs which we usually date from the Treaty of Versailles" (VMP, 216). It also gestures in the direction of the later Joyce with its composite puns: "Haberdasheries: voluptual standing on ceremony." (Maison de blanc: pompes voluptiales.) [...] And monastic corners, exilent bells of the *dies iraemissibles.*"[23] These prose poems announce the verbal pyrotechnics and associative delirium of Aragon's Surrealist masterpiece, *Paris Peasant.*

Thus the war was not only in the words; it derived from a clash between the sexes, as we see in the question posed to J. Alfred Prufrock by an unnamed woman. Prufrock is ready to say: "I am Lazarus, come from the dead, /Come back to tell you all, I shall tell you all," but she cuts him with: "That is not what I meant at all./ That is not it, at all." (CPP, 16). The woman's repeated rebuttal debunks any apocalyptic revelation. Her studied indifference merely delays an outburst of her latent hysteria, as she urges the speaker to say more while denying he has anything to say. Her infectious hysteria passing from a female to a male speaker can be defused by a dose of humor, as we see in "Short Romance (Conversation Galante)," in which the woman is addressed:

"Giving our vagrant moods the slightest twist!
With your air indifferent and imperious
At a stroke our mad poetics to confute—"
And—"Are we then so serious?"

(IMH, 346)

Exactly as Hegel posited in Antigone an "irony" that destroyed the coherence of the Greek *Sittlichkeit*, Eliot sees in these feminine rebels who remain refractory to his poetics a threat for his art: those arch and seductive women question his lack of relevance. Eliot had alluded to Guido da Montefeltro, punished in Hell for his lack of logics according to the epigraph of the "Love Song of J. Alfred Prufrock." Guido, who is damned for all eternity, assumes that Dante the poet must be dead, damned and forever in Hell if he can talk to him. In *The Waste Land* and after, Hell has come to earth, and the boundaries between life and death are even more porous.

The worry about this type of interrogation impelled Eliot's anguish to new levels after the First World War. We can hear its pathos in a letter that sketched Vivien's plight and his own: "What will happen if I live again? [...] But the dilemma—to kill another person by being dead, or to kill them by being alive? Is it best to make oneself a machine, and kill them by not giving nourishment, or to be alive, and kill them by wanting something that one *cannot* get from that person?"[24] A nightmarish solution was adumbrated in *Fragments of an Agon* when Sweeney mentions a murderer who "didn't know if he was alive / and the girl was dead" or "He didn't know if the girl was alive / and he was dead." (CPP, 125) In between, other traumatic experiences will have been traversed: the Great War on the theatre of Europe; the small war with his wife.

Before the war, Eliot imagined that he might find a solution peacefully, by imitating the Proustian decision to live only for art and become one with a tradition in which material words and spiritual sense are wedded together. Then one could be dead and alive at once, combining in one's mind the teachings of all the dead and all the living. However, in this positive or optimistic fusion, there lurks the danger of a parody of the Passion, a fake ecstasy leading to more dissociation, as we see in a character met in "The Little Passion" (From "An Agony in the Garret") from 1915:

> I recollect one thing he said
> After those hours of streets and streets
> That spun around him like a wheel
> He finally remarked: "I feel
> As if I'd been a long time dead."
>
> (IMH, 57)

We encounter a modern "man of the crowd" who, like Poe's ominous character, might contains the "essence of crime." Nothing can redeem him, because he has nothing to lose—he looks like Judas, his smile unable to hide "a washed-out, unperceived disgrace." An earlier version had: "A thin, unconscious, half-perceived disgrace" (IMH, 58). As Kafka stated at the end of *The Trial*, the pathos of death comes less from one's demise than from the sense of shame or disgrace that adheres to it. A whole mechanism of ethical reevaluation will be needed to avoid this unconscious disgrace.

A disgrace to end all distance

The devastation brought by the First World War to Europe had incalculable consequences that still shape our world, but there were more calculable costs, whether financial or moral. Eliot took on the task of reckoning with these, first as a clerk working on German debts and reparations at Lloyds Bank in London, then as a poet who tried to rethink the foundations of the world order emerging after 1918. A war first imagined as a Napoleonic campaign, with swift defeats and victories, had turned into a general stalemate, a mechanized mass slaughter in a bitter tussle of attrition in which most industrialized nations were forced to participate. Never a "war to end all wars," the First World War heralded worse to come, partly because the map of the world had changed so quickly after the collapse of Russia, the Austro-Hungarian Empire and the Ottoman Empire. Europeans had discovered that, indeed, "civilizations were mortal," as Paul Valéry wrote in his diagnosis of the "crisis of the spirit."[25] The European "spirit," this old Hegelian *Geist* was turning into a ghost; Europe was cut down to size, the mere tip of a "peninsula," a promontory shaken by the reawakening of Russia and Asia. A similar ontological crisis was condensed in the lines from *The Waste Land:*

> Falling towers
> Jerusalem Athens Alexandria
> Vienna London
> Unreal
>
> (CPP, 73)

Like Valéry, Eliot included Smyrna (now in Turkey) and Alexandria (in Egypt) in his map of Europe. Eliot, too, felt that Europe had "exhausted its modernism."[26] *The Waste Land* is a modernist after-war poem because of its themes and its gestation, much as *Ulysses* and *In Search of Lost Time* would be unthinkable without the delays in their publication processes caused by the war. While Joyce and Proust used the extra time they gained to expand and revise their novels, Eliot, collecting and rearranging previous texts, made sense of collective and personal traumas by condensing and refining, with the help of Ezra Pound, as we have seen, a sprawling mass of manuscripts and typescripts so as to reach just 433 lines. Its incantatory and exhortatory affirmation of "Peace," or "Shantih" in Sanskrit, was borrowed from the Upanishads at the end of the poem, but it seems to anticipate a dim European future.

If Joyce's *Ulysses* had memorialized the pre-war society in Dublin, Eliot's poem attempted to look to the future, as Franz Kafka did in his prose. From opposite sides in the conflict, Eliot and Kafka had made similar career choices: both posited a link between the raging military conflict and war in the sentimental and sexual domains. Such a link is exemplified by a short story of which Eliot was fond. In December 1917, *The Egoist*, of which Eliot had become an Assistant-editor, published "War," a story by his friend Mary

Hutchinson.[27] She passed it to Vivien, who "enjoyed it immensely" and promised that her husband would get it published.[28] Given its title, readers might have expected a war story, whereas it treats only modern love. We overhear a conversation between Jane, a rich, married, and fashionable lady of twenty-five and her would-be lover, Giniver, a jaded writer and self-declared cynic. Their banter is interrupted by drums and a brass band from soldiers at drill, marching through London streets. Jane confides to Sabine that she feels drawn to Giniver. Sabine thinks that Jane will be a mere diversion for him. Jane, growing "hysterical,"[29] is convinced that she has fallen in love with Giniver. His night visit should prove decisive. He brings a manuscript but prefers not to read it. Both are nervous, irritable, embarrassed; their conversation trails off. Finally, they keep silent. Choosing a break-up, Jane declares: "I don't suppose we shall meet again for some time."[30] Giniver leaves and Jane remains alone. She falls asleep, to be woken up by a bugle sounding the reveille in the barracks. The reminder of a war going on outside brings relief as the text ends with: "Afterwards she slept as though she knew the earth to be a spherical and comfortable place."[31] This "war" was one to which Eliot was attuned, a blend of the war of sexes, with tangled strategies of seduction, hysteria, and rejection, and distant military campaigns. The war functions as the ultimate Hegelian *Aufhebrung* providing the union of the self with a globalized universe. What had thrilled Vivien was that Mary Hutchinson was slyly referring to the ups and downs of the affair her friend Vivien was having with Bertrand Russell.

Kafka, like Eliot, was not drafted for medical reasons; both had the opportunity to use the wartime years for ongoing discussions about love, the compatibility of married life with literary creation, and the psychic gains to be had from the torture of their partners. Kafka would never marry Felice, his eternal bride-to-be. He tortured her and himself via an abundant and frantic correspondence.[32] Sensing the need to put as much distance between his family and himself as he could, Eliot had taken the war as a pretext for a situation of exception that allowed him to get married with a seductive and brilliant English woman. He would torture her and himself in words, deeds, and inaction, erecting the temple of eternal love on the murky foundations of sexual impotence and gender indecision.

The war forced Eliot to choose a place to settle in. Had there been no war, he might have moved back and forth between Boston and Marburg, Saint Louis and Oxford, New York and Paris. His 1910–11 stay in Paris had given him a taste of cosmopolitan culture and introduced him to a cultivated French milieu. He befriended Alain-Fournier, who died in combat near Verdun in September 1914. Soon Eliot's close friend from Paris, Jean Verdenal, would be a victim of the slaughter. Echoes between Verdun and Verdenal are not coincidental: the name "Verdenal" was linked to a village in the Meurthe and Moselle region on the border with Alsace-Lorraine, a German possession after the 1871 war. The region was the site of many battles in 1914 and 1915; the inhabitants of Verdenal are called "Verdunois."

In Paris, Eliot had shared with Verdenal and Alain-Fournier a love of Wagner and Laforgue, also discovering Dostoevsky thanks to Alain-Fournier. Before 1914, these young intellectuals were more germanophile than anglophile, a common tendency among symbolist poets. While Mallarmé's wife was German, Laforgue had spent five happy years in Berlin as a reader for the German Empress. An American living in England, Eliot bore no grudge to Germany and refused to associate himself with the shrill patriotism that was dominant in France.

Despite signals that an international storm was brewing, Eliot had no inkling that a world war was coming. On July 26, 1914, he wrote to Eleanor Hinkley: "I shan't have anything very exciting to narrate this summer; this is as peaceful a life as one could well find."[33] Two days later, Archduke Ferdinand was murdered in Sarajevo. The assassination triggered the successive declarations of war. I will now survey the timeline of the War's theatres, in parallel with Eliot's experiences.

Parallel wars

In September 1914, while Ezra Pound, enthusiastic about Eliot's poems, wants to print "Prufrock," Eliot mentions that one of his best friends is fighting in the war (LI, 62). Eliot sends a "war poem" to Conrad Aiken; it ends:

What ho! they cry'd, we'll sink your ship!
And so they up and sink'd her.
But the cabin boy was sav'd alive
And bugger'd, in the sphincter.

Eliot comments that the poem was rejected because it paid "too great a tribute to the charms of German youth" (LI, 64). In October, Eliot, still at Merton College, Oxford, entertains hopes of returning to a German university in the spring being a "neutral" (LI, 65).

Even though Eliot finds Oxford "peaceful, always elegiac" (LI, 75), he feels "more alive" in London: "Oxford is very pretty, but I don't like to be dead" (LI, 81). He follows the developments of the war in a new "theater of operations," when in February 1915, the Dardanelles campaign is launched. An Anglo-French army attacks Gallipoli in today's Turkey. "Anzac" soldiers from

Australia and New Zealand, wearing Stetson hats instead of helmets, establish a beachhead, the "Anzac cove." Allied forces combine ground forces and amphibious naval attacks, but they fail; their strategy was compared then with the Roman triumph over Carthage at Mylae, in 260 BC, during the first Punic war: Roman boats equipped with bridges had linked themselves with enemy ships, which allowed legionnaires to fight as if they were on solid ground. Echoes of these historical details are found in *The Waste Land*.

In Oxford, Eliot complains about the war ("the War suffocates me," (LI, 95)), while London appears as the site of artistic innovation because of the agitation around the *Blast* group led by Ezra Pound and Wyndham Lewis. Their friend Gaudier-Brzeska is killed in action on June 5, 1915. In March, Eliot meets Vivien(ne) Haigh-Wood at a party organized by Scofield Thayer in Oxford. On May 2, 1915, Verdenal, Eliot's friend from Paris, a French army medical officer, is killed during the Gallipoli campaign. He had been all night in water up to his waist, helping evacuate wounded soldiers by sea, when he was shot by enemy fire.

On June 26, 1915, after three months of intense courtship, Eliot marries Vivien secretly. Ezra Pound and Bertrand Russell defend Eliot's position facing his family's incomprehension. In July, despite the sinking of the *Lusitania*, Eliot travels to America in order to explain his actions. He returns to England in September 1915. Bertrand Russell, a sort of symbolic father, helps the couple, but soon becomes Vivien's lover when the sexual incompatibility between his two friends is blatant. In July 1915, the second and last issue of *Blast* is published. This "war number" included Eliot's "Preludes" I to IV and "Rhapsody on a Windy Night." In a January 1916 letter, Eliot mentions the death of Verdenal along with news of his marriage (LI, 137). Despite his wife's constant sickness, Eliot's spirits are high: "I am having a wonderful time nevertheless. I have *lived* through material for a score of long poems, in the last six months" (LI, 138).

Eliot explains to Aiken that his wife suffers from "nerves" (LI, 157). He justifies his decision to stay in England to his father because he has "succeeded" in what he has undertaken, but confesses that when Vivien is worried, "she bleeds internally" (LI, 177). He begins working at Lloyds Bank as a clerk in the foreign department, preferring this to teaching schoolchildren. He specializes in international accounts, which forces him to brush up his French and Italian, and to study Danish, Swedish, Norwegian, and Spanish.

After the United States declares war on Germany in April 1917, Vivien worries that her husband will be drafted. Eliot becomes the contributing editor to *The Egoist*, a pacifist review. Eliot explains that he cannot understand "war *enthusiasm*" because the war is "something very sordid and disagreeable which must be put through" (LI, 203). His first book, *Prufrock and Other Observations*, is published, dedicated to Jean Verdenal "mort aux Dardanelles."

Eliot is tempted by pacifism in June 23, 1917, when he publishes a letter by his brother-in-law, Maurice Haigh-Wood, that describes vividly the horrors of trench warfare, "swollen and blackened corpses of hundreds of young men," "the appalling stench of rotting carrion," and "mud like porridge, trenches like shallow and sloping cracks in the porridge—porridge that stinks in the sun" (LI, 205). A frightening evocation follows: "Wounded men lying in the shell holes among the decaying corpses: helpless under the scorching sun and bitter nights, under repeated shelling. Men with bowels dropping out, lungs shot away, with blinded, smashed faces, or limbs blown into space. Men screaming and gibbering." Maurice sneers at those who can forget everything like army officers "who have never stopped to think in their lives" (LI, 205). Eliot does not for all that endorse Bertrand Russell's militant pacifism. Russell is helped in his courageous activism by Vivien.

In November 1917, the Bolsheviks overthrow the Tsarist government in Russia. Eliot is not surprised: he had foreseen the possibility as early as July 1917, expecting things to "go to pieces in Russia" (LI, 211). In April 1918, he rejects the expression "fight for civilization," for the term has lost its meaning (LI, 262). From August to October 1918, Eliot attempts to be enlisted in the US Navy as an Intelligence officer or as a non-combatant interpreter; the plan fails, and he returns to the bank. In July 1918, Bertrand Russell is sentenced to six months in prison as a pacifist. Eliot writes the "Ode" quoted above.

In December 1918, Eliot feels exhausted by his dealings with the army and by influenza. He requests complete mental rest after his father has died on January 7, 1919. Eliot experiences a "collapse" in February 1919. Meanwhile *Poems* is published by the Hogarth Press in May 1919, just when Vivien makes a firm decision to stop seeing Bertrand Russell. In February 1919, the Polish–Soviet War begins, lasting until March 1921. Soviet Russia and Soviet Ukraine fight against the Polish Republic and the Ukrainian People's Republic, in an attempt by the Soviet regime to spread the revolution westward. The first draft of *The Waste Land* mentions "hooded hordes swarming / Over Polish plains," which is then crossed out and changed to "endless plains."[34] In August 1919, Eliot takes a walking tour in the South of France with Pound. He feels in better health. He publishes in the last issue of *The Egoist* (December 1919) the second and last installment of "Tradition and the Individual Talent."

On December 18, 1919, Eliot criticizes American delays to a global peace, pointing out the starvation of the Viennese population: "I suppose Americans realize now what a fiasco the reorganization of nationalities has been: the 'Balkanisation' of Europe" (LI, 425). He has to sort out pre-war debts between the bank and Germany, which gives an opportunity to study the effects of the Peace Treaty, with the knotty issue of war reparations to be paid by the

German state. Following the Treaty of Versailles, the Danzig corridor is created to give Poland access to the Baltic Sea. "Gerontion" mentions "cunning corridors," alluding to the new map of Europe reshaped by the complex and often devious schemes of the Allies—ultimately a Pyrrhic victory, since the tensions unleashed led to a second world war.

Demobilization or demoralization

The war years offer a good "theatre" to present the series of mental collapses and psycho-somatic depressions that Eliot experienced in 1921, which led to his stay at Margate and the cure in Lausanne with Doctor Vittoz. In the same way as Eliot had been told that the demobilization process had been a failure in the United States, which accounted for the American public opinion's swing against Wilson's misguided international politics, his poem dramatizes the difficulty of returning to a "normal" life after the sacrifices made in the name of "civilization." We hear this in "A Game of Chess" when Lil is reproached for not knowing how to keep her looks—her recently "demobbed" husband wants to enjoy himself and can be excused for having a roving eye:

> [A]nd think of poor Albert,
> He's been in the army four years, he wants a good time,
> And if you don't give it him, there's others will, I said.
>
> (CPP, 66)

We soon learn via Tiresias that the post-war sexual freedom leads to mechanical and meaningless love-making. We saw how the typist is only glad that sexual congress is quickly over, while the young man does not even notice her indifference. Given this landscape of barrenness (Lil's problems come from her having aborted with dubious pills) and sexual apathy, it may come as a surprise that, as we have seen, Tiresias's lesson to the gods is to teach them that feminine orgasms are stronger than men's. It is as if the demobilization has triggered a general demoralization, which would be marked by a loss of sensual appetite and a vanishing desire.

Such moral and sexual detumescence cannot be blamed on the fact that Eliot felt guilty for not having seen combat, even if Gerontion confesses his absence from the battle-field:

> I was neither at the hot gates
> Nor fought in the warm rain

> Nor knee-deep in the salt marsh, heaving a cutlass,
> Bitten by flies, fought.
>
> (CPP, 37)

This passage is often read as an echo of Jean Verdenal's death near Gallipoli. Even if the friendship with Verdenal may have remained asexual, it had conveyed a sense of shared delight and the enjoyment of life's little pleasures—pleasures that have vanished after the war. Or the remaining thrills appear as perverse or sterile, as we see in "Gerontion." The "chilled delirium" evoked by "Gerontion" is related to a "wilderness of *mirrors*," a startling image that conceals an allusion to the *Galerie des Glaces* at Versailles, the huge Hall where the International Treaty was signed on June 28, 1919. Hence a loss of enjoyment, an *aphanisis*, to use the term coined by Ernest Jones in 1927 to denote a sudden loss of sexual interest, the disappearance of desire. *Aphanisis* defines the new sexual morality, the modern ethos in which sex has lost its pathetic intensity, in a drift brought about by post-war demobilization, a demobilization hiding a deeper demoralization.

This sexual tussle was confirmed by a letter to Eleanor Hinkley from 1917 in which Eliot rehearses his absence from combat while stressing that he waged his "other war," a discrete allusion to his sexual tug of war with Vivien caught between him and Bertrand Russell. Eleanor evokes an America in which life went on as usual, which was not the case for Eliot:

> Life moves so rapidly over here that one never hears twice of the same person as being in the same place or doing quite the same thing. It is either killed or wounded, or going to gaol, or being let out of gaol, or being tried, or summoned before a tribunal of some kind. I have been living in one of Dostoevsky's novels, you see, not in one of Jane Austen's. If I have not seen the battlefield, I have seen other strange things, and I have signed a cheque for £200,000 while bombs fell about me. I have dined with a princess and with a man who expected two years of hard labour; and it all seems like a dream. The most real thing was a little dance we went to a few days ago, something like yours used to be, in a studio with a gramophone.
>
> (LI, 210)

If this reveals a curious loss of reality experienced during the war, there were nevertheless small pleasures like listening to rag music on the gramophone and dancing to its tunes so as to ward off sexual and psychic upheavals. Eliot alludes here to Russell, who was almost jailed in 1917—and then was in 1918. The Great War generated a double unreality: the unreality of the unspeakably traumatic scenes of trench warfare described by Maurice Haigh-Wood, and the unreality of everyday life in London.

At the same time, Eliot experienced life more deeply and felt more alive than before. He could gauge life in all its "horror" because he finally experienced pain, excess, and ecstasy fully. He was granted what he was asking for before the war, as expressed in July 1914, when he complained of "lacking inspiration" and "suffering from constipation." The only cure would be a good *pathos mathos*, or the crazy intensity displayed by Dostoevsky's characters:

> Some people say that pain is necessary ("they learn in suffering" etc) [. . .] what is necessary is a *certain kind* (could one but catch it!) of *tranquility*, and sometimes pain does bring it. A kind of tranquility which Dostoievsky must (on second thoughts I delete the line) have known when he was writing his masterpieces at top-speed to keep from starving.
>
> (LI, 45)

Six days later, in guise of illustration, Eliot sends several poems, including "The Love Song of St Sebastian" in which he dwells on sado-masochistic fantasies. The speaker flogs himself till he bleeds then strangles a woman (LI, 51). The trope of *pathos mathos*, suffering bringing knowledge, applies to a pre-war poet who dimly sensed that he could not experience life—he felt like a virgin in sexual matters and in his apprehension of reality.

In the 1917 letter, Eliot refers to novels, not to poetry or tragedy, in order to get a grip on the unthinkable reality of the war. The Great War imposes a paradigm shift in the choice of literary examples: before the war, life was a Jane Austen novel; during the war it turns into a Dostoevsky novel. Eliot alludes to the fact that he had acted in "An Afternoon with Mr. Woodhouse," a sketch based on Jane Austen that Eleanor had organized at Cambridge, Massachusetts, in 1913. The reference to Jane Austen is apt: it captures the pre-war world of young men and women aiming at making a good marriage. Dostoevsky's novels bring in a different mode of excesses, a heady hysteria coupled with metaphysical anguish well summarized by Bertrand Russell, who knew that Vivien Eliot loved reading the Russian novelist. Russell confides to Ottoline Morrell that Vivien happens to be cruel facing her husband: "It is a Dostoevsky type of cruelty. . . . She is a person who lives on a knife edge, & will end as a criminal or a saint—I don't know which yet."[35] Russell evokes the cliché of Russian characters, people going to extremes easily, hinting that Vivien was a bipolar seducer capable of murdering her husband or her lover on a whim. Her "Russian" psychology would be exemplified by Dostoevsky's characters. It presents a combination of hysteria and sado-masochism, as we see with "Fresca" in the first draft of *The Waste Land*:

The Scandinavians bemused her wits,
The Russians thrilled her to hysteric fits.[36]

Before writing a psycho-biography of Dostoevsky in 1928, Freud had mentioned "Russian character-types" in "The Economic Problem of Masochism" (1924) in order to describe people prone to commiting sinful acts just in order to trigger endless reproaches from their sadistic moral conscience.[37] Eliot gives a similar diagnosis in the "London Letter" for *The Dial* of September 1922. He discusses Dostoevsky, who "had the gift, a sign of genius in itself, for utilizing his weaknesses; so that epilepsy and hysteria cease to be the defects of an individual and become—as a fundamental weakness can, given the ability to face it and study it—the entrance to a genuine and personal universe."[38] These terms echo Hermann Hesse's apocalyptic essay on "*The Brothers Karamazov* or the Downfall of Europe" that Eliot had read while in Lausanne. The last words of Hesse's essay are quoted in German in the notes to *The Waste Land*.

In his impassioned meditation written in 1919, Hesse was linking Nietzsche and Dostoevsky—he, too, stated that they had used their neuroses creatively. The convulsions of the Karamazov family, leading to the murder of a demented father, allegorize the downfall of Europe. The fate of Dmitri, the immoralist with an artist's sensitivity, who follows the promptings of his inner voice, points to a possible renewal. This is only possible if one leaves behind the old Christian morality and looks for wisdom in Asia.[39] According to Hesse, Dostoevsky was calling for an "Asian ideal" of mystical sainthood that would avoid the dichotomies of "good" and "evil."[40] For Hesse, Asia was the spiritual mother of Europe, and the only way of avoiding another catastrophe was by combining Eastern and Western mysticism, a theme alluded to by Eliot's endnotes as well.

Hesse's essay has too often been reduced to a condemnation of the Soviet revolution. Indeed, it ends with: "Soon half of Europe, at least half Eastern Europe, is on the road to chaos, reeling into the abyss in a state of drunken delirium, singing drunken hymns as Dmitri Karamazov did. These songs are heard with wounded laughter by the bourgeois, and with tears by the saint and the seer."[41] In fact, Hesse was not so much rejecting the Soviet revolution as condemning the bourgeois complacency exhibited by Western Europe. If both Dostoevsky and the Russian revolutionaries suffer from "hysteria," as he argues, such neurosis can be productive provided it be sublimated by an artist whose mystical visions bring about a rejuvenation. Meanwhile, innocent non-conformists like Dmitri Karamazov, condemned for a murder that he has not committed, are still unjustly punished. Dostoevsky accused the prejudiced and bigoted bourgeois who have taken Dmitri's drunken singing for an actual confession. It has no ground in reality, as we know if we have read book twelve of the *Brothers Karamazov*.

Hesse's interpretation of Dostoevsky paves the way for Eliot's understanding of the artist as a renovator of values. Hesse places Dostoevsky in close proximity with Nietzsche, for whom any upheaval of ancient values would lead to a positive outcome. Moreover, Hesse and Eliot aim at avoiding being trapped in binary logics opposing reason and emotions, the normal and the pathological, divisions that have plagued European rationalism since the Enlightenment. Their parallel attempt to think beyond these dualities has far-ranging political consequences. Hesse's thinking follows the reasoning of a Catholic thinker of politics like Carl Schmitt, who was just then rethinking the foundations of politics.

Schmitt had attempted to make sense of the situation of "exception" caused by the war. Indeed, *The Waste Land* was published in the same year as Schmitt's *Political Theology*, whose first volume began with the famous definition: "Sovereign is he who decides on the exception."[42] Like Valéry's "La Crise de l'Esprit" already quoted, Schmitt thinks beyond the dichotomy of order and chaos. Schmitt writes: "What characterizes an exception is principally unlimited authority, which means the suspension of the entire existing order. In such a situation it is clear that the state remains whereas law recedes. Because the exception is different from anarchy and chaos, order in the juristic sense still prevails even if it is not of the ordinary kind."[43] Valéry compares the European man of 1919 to a Hamlet overwhelmed by his discovery of too many Yorick's skulls, and thus unable to philosophize about them: "Our European Hamlet looks at millions of specters.... He thinks of the tedium of rehearsing the past, and of the madness of always innovating. He staggers between two abysses, for two dangers constantly threaten the world: order and disorder."[44] This useful admonition should remind us not to reduce Eliot's thought to a simple opposition between order and chaos.

A last binary that Eliot was trying to overcome was that of defeat and victory; his depression came to him not during the war, but after. By a relatively common paradox, the victory of the Allies heralded a new debacle. The war had provided an "exception," but without the exception, one would fall back on an impossible choice: either order or chaos. It was such a Kierkegaardian choice that led to Eliot's mental and moral collapse.

Eliot had found this moral debacle treated by his first role-model, Laforgue, and he confessed to it publicly, albeit obliquely, in "The Metaphysical Poets" (1921). At the end of the essay, Eliot quotes one of Laforgue's last poems in order to show that the French poet is at times difficult, allusive, indirect; Laforgue's impact has been "to force, to dislocate if necessary, language into his meaning."⁴⁵ The example provided is taken from the first stanza of Poem X in *Last Poems*. It begins "*O geraniums diaphanes...*" and reiterates the startling expression of "*débâcles nuptiales*" (nuptial fiascos). Laforgue evokes mysterious geraniums that were at war ("*guerroyeurs*"); then people were waiting in vain for the "big party" ("*grands soirs*") of total Revolution, but are now stuck in the familiar litany of "transfusions, reprisals, churchings, compresses and the eternal potion" (lines 7–8). This dismal view of the consequences of reproduction frames the speaker's horror at the thought of "nuptial fiascos," a phrase repeated twice (line 10) The sexual fiasco brought about by a bad marriage is intolerable in times of peace; however a return to peace is called up at the end of the poem, but in lines not quoted by Eliot. Indeed, Laforgue has added his own exception to the rule of disastrous sexual encounters when he sings of the sexual bliss felt in his recent marriage. Laforgue was not to enjoy this bliss long: he died one year after his marriage. Eliot did not die, whereas his marriage did.

The victory of the Allies allowed Eliot to probe deeper further *debacles*. The term was commonly used for the French defeat of 1870–71. Emile Zola's *La Débâcle*, a historical novel about the Franco-Prussian war of 1870–71, somehow explained the Great War, just as 1919 would explain 1939. The serious task would be to understand the conditions needed for redemption, as Franz Rosenzweig argued in *Star of Redemption*, a book that he drafted from the trenches. The war's aftermath had left too many loaded nationalisms or tricky Danzig corridors ready to explode, all the while contributing baffling instances of Hegel's "cunning of reason," as "Gerontion" puts it:

> After such knowledge, what forgiveness? Think now
> History has many cunning passages, contrived corridors
> And issues, deceives with whispering ambitions,
> Guides us by vanities ....
> These tears are shaken from the wrath-bearing tree.
>
> (CPP, 38)

These urgent admonitions sound less a "*rappel à l'ordre*" (as Cocteau and Gide implied when launching a modernist classicism to which we will return) than a "reveille," not with a military bugle, but with words. The emphasis is on the possibility of an awakening, as Walter Benjamin argued in his *Arcades Project*. One should no longer sleep but wake up from the four-year trance of "sleepwalkers"⁴⁶ going unscathed through mined terrain. Then, even if we have learned that the earth is a small sphere, and that it has become a comfortable place to inhabit, we should try to "redeem the times," that is to look at it from the point of view of redemption (Benjamin's or Rosenzweig's *Erlösung*). The concept of redemption, the "buying back" of innate sin is above all a "solution" to a problem (*Lösung*) and not a "dissolution." What matters is to preserve fragments of everyday history and arrange them for their final judgment.

We find this preoccupation in an often-quoted line from *The Waste Land*: "These fragments I have shored against my ruins" (CPP, 75). Eliot had initially written: "These fragments I have spelt into my ruins." He added above the line: "shored against."[47] The two versions convey different meanings. The first version can be construed as: "My poem made up of fragments will spell my name, write my words on my ruins." The revision adds the meaning of "propping up, supporting." This time, the poetic fragments are called upon to ward off an impending ruin. In the first concept, the poet's task is to mobilize the "withered stumps of time" (line 104) and transmute them into the poet's signature. The poem offers itself as a ruined monument, able to survive among the ruins of an ancient culture left by the war. In the second concept, the poem provides a rampart of words, a tentative construction whose prosthetic props help the wounded poet survive after he has witnessed the destruction, material and moral, brought about by European madness. Whether the ruins are construed as negative or positive, what stands out is first that there remains a conceptual tension between the "monuments" arranged in an "ideal order"[48] of culture and the "ruins," and then that the syntax balances the deictic "these," which testifies to the objective existence of the poem and the possessive "my." Even if there are ruins, they are *my* ruins.

Ruins offer the only "true refuge," as Beckett wrote in later prose texts.[49] Ruins offer material reminders of a pathetic past along with a memory of petrified horrors. In a ruin, a half-dead monument, one can die and be reborn. In a ruin, past tragedies can be exhibited along with old joys frozen in stone. A ruin is always between two deaths: the death of the ancient cultural context, and the impending death of the contemporary viewer, feeling empathy for the actual decay of something that was grandiose. Lacan showed in his seminar on *The Ethics of Psychoanalysis*[50] that *Antigone* presented the paradigm of tragedy because ethics and esthetics were knotted together by the theme of a "second death", a theme allegorized by the heroine's condemnation to be buried alive. In *Oedipus at Colonnus*, the chorus states that it would be better "not to be" (*me phynai*, line 1224) or "never to have been born" than to continue living on. Death or non-being would be preferable to endless suffering. Freud quoted a *Witz* about this, quoting the sentence with a twist: "Never to be born would be the best thing for mortal men. But adds the philosophical comment in *Fliegende Blätter*, this happens to scarcely one person in a hundred thousand."[51] Eliot, much more optimistic despite his recurrent despair, asserted that he was longing for rebirth after serial deaths. A good gloss on this death is given by a draft of section V of *The Waste Land*. Just after lines that evoke the calamities of the Great War, Eliot recycled a passage that we have encountered in "The Little Passion" (IMH, 57):

> A man lay flat on his back, and cried
> "It seems that I have been a long time dead:
> Do not report me to the established world."[52]

This was changed to: "The world has seen strange revolutions since I died."[53] Eliot then crossed out "The world," writing: "It," and added "catalepsies" under "revolutions." The line became: "It has seen strange revolutions: let me bide," with "I abide" inserted above. The uncanny and even shocking superposition of "revolutions" and "catalepsies" confirms the aptness of Eliot's nickname of "old Possum." Eliot would "bide," which means "endure," and also "bide his time," always drawing some advantage from his games with real and symbolic death.

If Eliot could pretend to be dead like his totemic animal the opossum, he also knew that the American idiom of "playing possum" yielded other hints— on the one hand, it comes close to the Latin phrase of *"Non Possumus"* ("We cannot"), the recurrent tag by which several Popes, from Pius IX to Pius XII, justified their refusals to engage with the Italian regimes surrounding them; on the other hand, the abbreviation of "opossum" into "possum" grants more freedom: Eliot can utter sub voce, even while pretending to be dead, "Possum!" which means: "I can, I am able, I am not impotent." In Eliot's "Possum" would be the source of his indomitable urgency to write, the root of his unbreakable, resilient, hard-won, and durable creativity.

7

Let the Lips of the Wound Speak

Cocteau's *Pathosformel*

Jean Cocteau could never "play possum": he was as flamboyant in his gay sexuality as he was intense in his artistic endeavors. I will now focus on a different medium, one in which he illustrated himself, film, with the idea of testing the relevance of Nietzsche's "pathos of distance." Film will allow me to put in contact the Nietzschean expression both with Aby Warburg's "*Pathosformel*" and with Benjamin's theory of allegorical expression. In these three critical analyses, the idea of certain pathos emerges, a pathos needing distance to find expression. Here again, distance is not simply a lack, a defect, or a limitation, but a space into which the artist or thinker can project herself or himself, first because of the opacity or irreducible resistance to immediate apprehension that marks the formal process of allegory. I will take as my main "text" Cocteau's *Blood of a Poet*, a first film for a poet who later produced many others and reached celebrity with them. This film offers a good example of modernist allegory, especially in the specific meaning given to allegory by Benjamin.[1] Benjamin insisted on the artificiality of the allegory, and presented it as a non-organic ruin hesitating between neo-classicism, the gothic, and surrealism.

In one of his preliminary sketches for the *Arcades Project*, Benjamin evoked the neo-classicism of Cocteau; he placed it in a temporal series, aligning it with the return to classicism advocated by Stravinsky, Picasso, and de Chirico: "[T]he traditional space of awakening in which we now are living is, wherever possible, traversed by the gods. This traversal of space by gods is to be understood as lightning-like" (AP, 843). Benjamin links the intermittent appearances and disappearances of the gods with the motif of homosexuality, which works well with Proust and Cocteau. However, one may query his reduction of *Blood of a Poet* to a historical genre or fashion called "neo-classicism." Exactly contemporary with Buñuel's *L'Age d'Or*, produced in the same conditions and the same budget, *Blood of a Poet* cannot be subsumed under any generic category. It is no more surrealist than it is an expressionist extravaganza; it is no more a gothic horror film than it is a film about opium addiction—and yet it plays with all these themes, ties them up together in a curious knot that we can call a modernist allegory. Cocteau's caption calls the film that follows a "group of allegories," implying that his allegories can and should be decoded: "Every poem is a coat of arms: it must be deciphered." (*"Tout poème est un blason. Il faut le déchiffrer"*).² Here is our task. I assume that Benjamin' allegory is a good tool to decode the film's numerous riddles and enigmas. As Cocteau noted, he had let himself be "trapped by his own film," which suggests that his meanings were not so transparent.

Blood of a Poet has fascinated audiences since it was released in 1932. It has retained an aura that none of Cocteau's subsequent films managed to acquire. Besides, the scandal that it caused was worse than the fracas occasioned by the release of Buñuel's *Chien Andalou*, a film with which it is often compared. With this first foray in the art of filmmaking, Cocteau managed to alienate both the Right and the Left: the Surrealists violently rejected it and attacked it, unfairly, as a pale copy of their experiments, and a sign of the author's "pederasty," while the rich and privileged patrons who had financed it tried to make it disappear for good. The story has often been told, both by Cocteau and by his biographers. Spending New Year's Eve with the Viscount de Noailles, whose wife was an old flame of the young Cocteau, the well-off Maecenas offered Cocteau and Buñuel each one million francs to produce films that they would own after completion. Cocteau had first imagined that he would produce an animated film, with the help of his friend the composer Georges Auric, but soon realized that the task was too specialized, finicky, and difficult. Meanwhile Buñuel was able to shoot *L'Age d'Or* with the same offer from the de Noailles. Cocteau's film was shot from April to September 1930.

Intractable difficulties surrounded the shooting, including mattresses full of bedbugs, absurdly long hours, the exhausted director's sciatica, and Cocteau's blissful ignorance of the most basic requirements of film-making (he did not know how to make a tracking shot). As he was to note later, it was precisely this sense of improvisation, of bold risk-taking, of solutions found at the last minute for technical problems that gave *Blood of a Poet* its unique allure and rare vitality. However, when Cocteau screened it in Paris at the de Noailles in November 1930, the de Noailles were so afraid for their reputation that they confiscated the film. It was released two years later, on January 5, 1932, after actors had replaced the de Noailles, who were seen clapping at the death of the Poet in the fourth part. The fact that it was titled "The Profanation of the Host" did not make things easier. In order to understand the reasons for such resistance, one needs to survey the plot, although it is rather hard to follow. Cocteau provided his notes from memory, and they are often slightly wrong. The storyline is divided into four "episodes" linked two by two, making it a sort of diptych of the Life of a Poet (this was the original title of the film).

My notes are intended to guide viewers who have watched the film available for free on the internet.

"To write means to kill death"[3]

The first episode is introduced by the Author, Cocteau himself, who is masked, with a plaster hand. Soon, a huge industrial chimney collapses in slow-motion, and the frame freezes. The action begins when the section entitled "The Wounded Hand, or the Scars of the Poet" takes us back to 1745: the events take place during the battle of Fontenoy, when Louis XV's army was attacking the town of Tournai. The Poet, a rather athletic young man, naked to the waist but wearing a wig, draws a face on a canvas. The mouth he has drawn comes alive, moves its lips, shows strong teeth. He tries to erase it with his hand, the mouth remains there. A friend bangs on the door, enters and retreats with a horrified stare. The Poet washes his hands—the mouth is now inside his hand. Swinging his arms, he attempts to get rid of it. The mouth screams, "*De l'air!*" ("Give me air!"). The Author appears as a statue; then the Poet applies the mouth to his own body. With the mouth still gaping and gasping in the middle of his hand, he caresses his torso, moves it down slowly on a nipple, lets the hand go down in a rather torrid evocation of masturbation; soon we see the Poet swoon in ecstasy. The next day, the Poet's room displays a woman's statue. The Poet moves behind it and presses the mouth against the statue's face. It remains there, which brings the statue to life. The Poet smiles, apparently relieved: he has got rid of a mouth that felt like a vampire.

The second episode, "Have the Walls Ears?" follows from the first. The statue asks the Poet whether one can get rid of the "mouth of a wound" so easily. In fact, the Poet appears locked up in his room. The statue explains that he can only get out by entering the mirror, and repeats: "Try." Stepping on a chair suddenly materializing, the Poet moves along a high vertical mirror, jumps into the surface as the mirror turns to water, which allows him to swim away in the dark. He reaches the corridor of a hotel named Hôtel des Folies-Dramatiques. A Vietnamese man walks along the corridor to the camera, listening to voices speaking in Chinese from a room. The Poet walks slowly along the surface of the sordid corridor, each time peeping into a succession of keyholes. Each room discloses a curious dumb show. In room 17, a Mexican man, hero, revolutionary or bandit, it is not clear, is shot twice in slow motion by four rifles. Each time, he revives and a statuette of the Virgin reconstitutes itself. The Author's voice comments cryptically: "Early at dawn, Mexico, the ditches of Vincennes, Boulevard Arago and a hotel room are just like each other," which is the most "Surrealist" moment in the film.

Room 19 presents "*ombres Chinoises*," a shadow play of hands that prepare an opium pipe, and a smoker begins to smoke. Room 21 has a sign saying "Flying Lessons." Inside, a little girl is whipped by a middle-aged woman played by Pauline Carton, the only professional actress. The girl is made to move on the chimney and crawl up the wall. She reaches the ceiling, from which she pulls her tongue at her tormentor. Room 23 presents a mixture of drawings, paintings, and bodies under the heading of "Hermaphrodites." A reclining man-woman has limbs emerging from holes in a wall, while a spiral whirls around on a disc like Marcel Duchamp's "roto-reliefs." When the creature lifts a cloth covering the lower belly, a sign appears stating: "Danger of death." Masculine and feminine voices are heard. Finally the Poet reaches the end of the corridor, where the hand of a sales-woman from a department store appears, gives him a gun, and explains how to shoot. The Poet shoots himself in the head. Blood gushes but soon turns into a cloth, and then into a laurel wreath. The Author comments: "Always the glory!" as if to suggest that death is relative or merely symbolic. However, seemingly flustered or annoyed, the Poet mutters "shit" three times, adding: "I'm fed up." He rushes back along the same corridor, returning to the night from which he emerged, to be "expelled" by the mirror. The Author adds an often-quoted sentence: "Mirror ought to reflect better before sending back images." The Poet confronts the woman's statue and violently hammers at its head. He destroys it, which covers him in plaster and he soon metamorphoses into a statue himself.

This segues neatly into the third episode, "The Snowball Battle," in which the Poet is now a statue in an enclosed yard where schoolboys are playing roughly with snowballs after school. As Cocteau notes, the setting was the Cité Monthiers in the ninth arrondissement, a sort of wild playground where the rough boys used to settle their accounts after leaving the Lycée Condorcet (SP, 54). The tone, the style, and even the lighting change completely. We witness fierce battles between groups of boys, teenagers' jousts that Cocteau's novel's *Les Enfants Terribles* depicts so well. The name of Dargelos reappears and comes directly from these childhood memories. The boys are pitted against each other in ferocious snowball fights, during which they destroy the statue bit by bit. A pale boy is hit twice by a snowball, the last one hurled viciously by the bully Dargelos, who stands out as the alpha male of the group. The younger boy falls to the ground, spits a spurt of dark blood in a quasi-orgasmic passing, and then apparently dies.

For the fourth and last episode, "The Profanation of the Host," we remain in the same setting, but the snowy playground has turned into a theatrical space. In the back wall, two boxes are filled with spectators in evening dress, among whom Barbette, a well-known cross-dresser at the time, is recognizable.

Expecting a theatrical play or an opera, but it is simply a game of cards opposing the Muse (Lee Miller who was the statue before) and the Poet. The body of the wounded or dead boy is visible at the foot of the table. A friend called the Indifferent is watching, first in a mask, then without it. The Muse tells the Poet that he is lost without the ace of hearts. He quickly takes it from the inner pocket of the boy directly under him. Then a guardian angel appears: he is black, beautiful, half-naked, his back decorated with strange bee-like wings. He comes down the stairs limping, lays his body over the boy's body, and seems to absorb it in the process. Turning all white by a trick of the film shot as a negative, he swallows the boy, whose body leaves a faint trace in the snow. Before walking up the stairs, the angel steals the ace of hearts from the Poet's hand. Dumbstruck, the Poet folds his cards, his Indifferent friend starts while the Muse looks at him contemptuously. His heart beats so loudly that it makes the lapel of his jacket rebound. The Poet takes a gun from his inner pocket and shoots himself in the head. Again, blood flows from the wound, which turns into a star. The two groups in the boxes clap and one hears the confused medley of their voices. The Muse wears black gloves up to her arms; her black eyes are painted on her eyelids. A curious metal ball crosses the screen slowly from right to the left and later from left to right. Majestically, the Muse walks down inner stairs before calling for a carriage. Instead, a bull appears. The bull carries fragments of the map of Europe as tatters glued on its back. The bull vanishes and its horns turn into a lyre. The Muse is now a chalked profile, after which she is seen lying next to the lyre and a globe. The Author utters: "Mortal tedium of immortality." A second chimney is seen collapsing as the sign "The End" appears.

Given some obvious sexual "symbols," it was hard to resist the temptation to interpret the plot along Freudian lines. In a conversation with André Fraigneau, Cocteau made fun of Freudian exegetes who insisted that the collapsing chimney was a phallic symbol.[4] At the same time, he claimed that Sigmund Freud had written an essay on *Blood of a Poet*—which sounds like wishful thinking. This invention suggests that the very question of an interpretation, whether Freudian or not, facing the dreamlike sequence of opaque images summed up previously, is built into the film itself. Cocteau is both claiming his prerogative as an Author who appears as the absolute master of his creation, while killing the Author as a divine owner of meaning. "Blood of a Poet," the prime *auteur* film, narrates the suicide of an Author who searches for his own image among narcissistic doubles. What he obtains is an allegory revolving around his own blood, a *sang* calling up the "lessness" of "*sans*." Blood rites inscribe the poet's "*Sans/Sang*"[5] in an allegory of hieratically and ritually spilled blood.

A private mythology: The death of the gods

All the signs highlight this film as a *"film d'auteur."* Cocteau appears at the start, proclaims his control over images in which his own death is recurrently described. Cocteau hides in full sight; he appears masked, maimed, or dead, in order to confess more. Beyond the plaster mask that he wears and the many sketches of his head (it even appears as a revolving wire sculpture), one of his masks includes the character of the Poet; he is also, quite obviously, the dead schoolboy whose body is lovingly absorbed by a black angel. The presence of the Author takes on an impersonal turn—the Poet is an Oedipus who confronts the gods and asks about his fate.

Blood of a Poet poses a question that recurs in Cocteau's entire oeuvre—whether one can still make the ancient gods appear. Are the gods of the Greek pantheon more than mutilated statues, and if so, what are the conditions needed to grant them a voice? Cocteau's preoccupations were close to those of his friend Ezra Pound, who had been impressed by the French poet's ready wit, unrivalled eloquence, and proficiency with all artistic media. In his *Cantos* and elsewhere, Pound evokes Cocteau nervously playing the drums in a jazz band. Cocteau added to Pound's recurrent preoccupations with the gods his specific sense of provocation, of sexual transgression, his games with profanation and queer subversion, which were foreign to the American poet. Moreover, Cocteau's innovative *bricolage* with the medium of film itself announced original practices of late modernist writers and artists like Samuel Beckett, who co-directed *Film* in the 1960s and was thus forced to rethink the very medium for his own ends.

The Author's main prerogative allows him to deploy his private mythology. This is evident in the first historical reference given by the film. If the action takes place during the battle of Fontenoy, the apparently absurd precision (given the fact that most the film looks like a dream covering several historical periods) hides an oblique homage: Cocteau pays back the generous offer by Marie-Laure and Charles de Noailles by alluding to the glorious past of their ancestors. In 1745, the French armies, defeating Austrian and British armies as the climax of a campaign in what is now Belgium, were led by Marshal Adrien Maurice de Noailles. For French schoolboys, who have to memorize the date, the battle of Fontenoy inevitably evokes an example of absurd politeness between officers: the *mot* handed down by tradition is that the count d'Anterroches shouted to his British approaching enemies: *"Messieurs les Anglais, tirez les premiers!"* This self-defeating call reverberates in a film in which we see several characters shot to death or shooting themselves with a gun before being revived.

We realize that most events in the plot occur twice. An industrial chimney falls twice. The Poet commits suicide twice. A Mexican man is shot twice by guns. A schoolboy is hit twice by a snowball. The statue is destroyed twice, first the woman's head exploded by the Poet, then the Poet's figure dismantled by children looking for snowballs. Blood flows, but it never looks real, except for the close-up of the schoolboy's groaning face when he spits blood. With these dramatic shots, Cocteau was trying to relive what he had not been able to witness: he was imaginatively processing the first trauma of his life. His father had shot himself to death when he was only nine years old; this hushed event remained a family secret for a long time. The rich and idle father's main activity had been drawing and painting, which explains why the film's Poet is never seen writing but only drawing. In his confessional *White Book*, Cocteau guesses that his father committed suicide for sexual reasons. His father would have been caught up in desires resembling those of his son, desires that he tried to repress: "At that time, one would kill oneself for less."[6]

The *White Book* gives more details about Dargelos, the evil and sexually mature schoolboy, than does the *Enfants Terribles*. The film presents him as "*le coq de la classe*,"[7] while the *White Book* develops the portrait. Dargelos was not only beautiful but "endowed with a virility beyond his age."[8] Dargelos masturbated openly in class, exhibiting himself to the others and to the teachers. In a classroom stinking of sweat and sperm, the young Cocteau could not avoid falling in love with him. He evokes his misguided efforts to attract Dargelos's attention. In the fiction of *Les Enfants Terribles*, Dargelos does not kill the waiflike Paul, but knocks him out with a snowball loaded with a stone; then he gets expelled from the school for his arrogance. One might be tempted to connect this phallicized young "*coq*" with the name of "Cocteau," whose etymology goes back to "Coquet," meaning a "young cock," with innuendoes both of excessive amorous propensities and silly affectation or coquetry. It is not by chance that Cocteau's first book, published in 1918, was *Le Coq et l'Arlequin*. Later Cocteau meditated on the reasons why the ancient Chinese used the sharp beak of cocks to take out their own eyes: they were forced to blind themselves if they saw the emperor, since this was forbidden.[9] Thus Orpheus, Oedipus, and Cocteau blend together in visionary blindness.

The second death of the Poet seems caused by contradictory desires, more precisely by his inability to love the Muse. He first smashes her head, and then loses a game of cards with her. When the seductive black angel steals the ace of hearts that the Poet himself had stolen from the dead child (a child representing the child that the Poet was), the confusion about stolen love objects is made clear. The dead boy lying in the snow can be superimposed on the little girl who had to learn to *voler*, meaning to fly but also to steal. The constant confusion generates a sort of sexual panic.

The beating heart preceding the second suicide makes it more dramatic than the first suicide, since it was accomplished for glory and not for love. Lee

Miller's beauty and her pout of contempt evoke Cocteau's domineering, possessive and vain mother. Nothing short of suicide could release her maternal grip. All this calls up a double genealogy, one turned toward Cocteau's particular history, the other to recent history. There was of course the suicide of his own father when he was a little boy, and unresolved mourning for his lover, the gifted Raymond Radiguet, who died in 1923 of typhoid fever at age twenty, and also remorse for the suicide of Jeanne Bourgoint, the model for the incestuous sister of *Les Enfants Terribles* in 1929. There was on the other hand a world history marked by catastrophes like the Wall Street crash of 1929 and the slow but painful termination of the glittering 1920s.

Cocteau and Ucello: *Pathosformeln*

The main cause of the social scandal that affected the de Noailles, which was so severe that they were excluded from the Jockey Club and almost excommunicated by the Catholic Church, had to do with the title chosen by Cocteau for the last episode of the film: "The Profanation of the Host." The scenes depicted look indeed irreverent and blasphemous. De Noailles objected to the original plan, in which he and his friends appeared clapping in a theatrical balcony just as the wounded boy dies and the Poet commits suicide. They were replaced by actors. Cocteau's title quotes a famous sequence of six paintings by Paolo Ucello and his school. This is foregrounded when the film begins with a series of dogmatic statements inscribed in cartons, and one of them is a dedication of this group or reel (the term is *bande*, a signifier with sexual connotations of erection) of allegories, in "memory of Pisanello, Paolo Ucello, Piero della Francesca, Andrea del Castagno, painters of coats of arms and enigmas" (SP, 15).

Cocteau had seen Paolo Ucello's panels from the series of "The Profanation of the Host" in an Italian art exhibition in London (SP, 65, note). The main filmic reference is to the second panel of the 1467–1469 Predella at Urbino. It is a dramatic scene, divided in two spaces marked by a sharp left-leaning perspective: on the left-hand side, the four members of the Jewish family look dumbfounded as they realize that from the profaned host, placed on a pan under a fire in the chimney, a steady rivulet of blood is flowing. The Jewish pawnbroker had bought a sacred host from a Christian woman in the first panel, because he wanted to cook it. To his dismay, blood is trickling along the geometrical black-and-white squares of the floor and seeps through the wall. His little daughter is distraught and clutches her mother's dress, while the older son turns away, a hand on his eyes, also panic-stricken.

Outside, on the right, a group of soldiers and night-watchmen is already banging at the entrance door, battering it with an axe. They have seen the "miracle" of the blood flowing through a wall and have come to stop the profanation.

The blood flowing freely in that panel gave Cocteau his main image—the image of the little boy wounded by a snowball containing a stone, who spits blood and dies. As his notes state, the close-up had to be accompanied by a moan of pain: "He moans. He half-opens his eyes. This image has to be painful" (SP, 65). In a 1932 talk, Cocteau explained that in his school memories the boy just bled from his nose. In *Les Enfants Terribles*, he is badly wounded but survives. In the film, he dies indeed (SP, 66, note). This point is crucial for the hidden allegorical plot of the film. Cocteau saw the sequence of the six paintings, and was attracted by the last panel depicting the body of the Christian woman who had almost been hanged in a precious scene for having pawned the sacred host. An angel had come to save her at the last minute. There was no such pity for the family of the money-lender: the father, the mother, and the two children are burned at the stake in a vicious *auto-da-fé*. In the last panel, the supine body of the young woman is watched over by supernatural figures: to her left, near her head, are two angels, but to the right, next to the feet, two devils—all four seem about to fight over the soul of the dead woman. There is a blue-black devil and a yellow-brown devil; both have enormous wings, and served as models for the half-naked and very handsome black angel who saunters down the steps in the film.

Ucello's allegorical sequence was one of the most disturbing examples of the rabid anti-Semitism that cropped up repeatedly in medieval Europe; it is the scene analyzed by Stephen Greenblatt as the "wound in the wall,"[10] a theme that chimes in with Cocteau's recurrent device of animating objects, creating a mouth in the Poet's hand, and having statues that speak. Nobody can be saved in the Jewish family; they are all burned alive for the "profanation" of the sacred Host. As Greenblatt and others remind us, Christians had to believe that the Host contained the "real presence" of Christ's body, at least his blood and flesh. The real but divine presence in a host was something that Cocteau had experimented during his "conversion" to Catholicism in 1926. He had gone to communion, seduced by the captious Christian rhetoric of the philosopher Jacques Maritain. This season of contrition and purification did not last, but nostalgia for the moment when he had felt "atoned" with God had left a mark. Hereafter, only desecration could allow him to return to a holy bliss glimpsed then. However, in 1932, Cocteau wrote more dismissively about the meaning of Ucello's title: "The meaning of the title of *Profanation of the Host*? Blood profanes the snow. That is all."[11] Was it then only a perfect form that had caught his eye?

Cocteau had been entranced by the formal beauty of Ucello's geometrical composition and by the fact that the plot underlying the sequence has kept its mystery. The same mystery had attracted the attention of Aby Warburg, who included the entire sequence of the six Ucello paintings in section 28–29 of *Atlas-Mnemosyne*.[12] This panel came first in the series devoted to the Renaissance (they went from 28 to 64). Warburg's *Tafel 28* contains other reproductions from the works of Paolo Ucello: the famous painting of Saint George killing the dragon from the London National Gallery, and the battle of Saint Romano. All the paintings and *cassoni* reproduced by Warburg come from the middle of the fifteenth century. The "*Pathosformeln*" that they exemplify hesitate between celebration and combat, joyful wedding scenes and intolerant social exclusion and punishment. A subtext in the arrangement is a clash between Jewish and Christian values: the most sacred object, the Host, is profaned by the most despised group, the Jewish moneylender and his family. The mode of representation of the clash entails a symptomatic image, that of the "wound in the wall" that betrays the desecration. Warburg had planned to systematize his views on the mistreatment of Jews in later sections of his Atlas, but never completed the project. One sees the lineaments of such a political denunciation in the last panels, 77, 78, and 79, in which Mussolini and the Pope appear.

This may not have been Cocteau's intention when, just two years after Warburg's death, he combined these allegories borrowed from Paolo Ucello; however, like Warburg, he worked systematically in a materialist and formalist manner at once. The fact that a wall speaks by spouting blood was enough of a prompter for his sequence of animated objects. The pathos of a boy's mouth spitting blood provided the emotive impetus for a series of sexual and religious metamorphoses. His innovative practice with film calls up the analyses of Jacques Rancière when he points out that changes in the "distribution of the sensible" always derive from new poetics of expressivity. Rancière sees the change happening in the middle of the nineteenth century, when Victor Hugo's *Notre-Dame de Paris* collapsed prose and poetry in 1831.[13] Rancière shows that Hugo's novel becomes a prose poem when, by a process of contamination, prose style "petrifies" in order to give life to the stones of the cathedral. Hugo's material language of expressivity thus overthrows the stable hierarchies defining the order of earlier poetics. What Rancière has called the "distribution of the sensible" proper to the poetics of expressivity began much earlier for Warburg, who identified the main change in the poetics of expressivity around 1450. It consisted in unleashing new pathos forms in the Renaissance, especially in the Florence of the fifteenth century.

Like Warburg, Cocteau wanted to blend the physical attributes of the devils and the moral function of the angels; creating a new pathos through a new form of expression, he invented a composite supernatural being, half guardian angel as far as the boy is concerned, half trickster who steals the winning ace from the Poet's hand. The angel's action is enigmatic: while he presses his body against the boy's, one hears the deafening roar of an airplane engine. His action—is he "saving" the boy's soul, or having sex with the little corpse?—is just called "work" ("*travail*").[14] The metamorphosis of the angel is rendered allegorical by a trick only film can permit: suddenly, we see the negative of the black man's body; he turns white while he somehow absorbs or devours the boy's body, which then disappears. This metamorphosis could not be read as a Christian scene of redemption or a Salvationist miracle. It is much closer to sexual or biological devouring, which is enhanced by the detail that the angel's wings are held by a model of the "bee's nervous system" (SP, 72). Cocteau insisted that the aristocrats in the boxes clap not for the death of a young boy, but applaud the suicide of the Poet. No matter what causes their collective applause, one cannot help finding their attitude callous, if not downright perverse. The Catholic hierarchy may have sensed something suspect when attempting to excommunicate the de Noailles for having been instrumental in bringing about the birth of *Blood of a Poet*.

Cocteau did not think in Christian terms; neither did he want to suggest a black mass or Satanic possession. He liked the form of medieval mysteries—the content, full of dark riddles as it was, was left for others to unlock. His personal myth revolved around the aura of an angel that was as "terrible," "frightening," and "beautiful" as the angels called upon by Rilke at the beginning of the *Duino Elegies*. However, unlike Rilke's angels regrouped in their "orders," Cocteau's angel is always alone. He appears under the guise of "Angel Heurtebise" in a series of poems from 1925 that display common features with the characters of *Blood of a Poet*. Here are the first two stanzas of this elliptic sequence:

(I)
Angel Heurtebise, on the tiers of the theatre,
Shot-silk winged
Beats me to refresh my memory,
The rascal, alone, motionless
With me on the agate
Broken, you ass, by your supernatural
Pack-saddle.

(II)
Angel Heurtebise, with unbelievable
Brutality, jumps on me. Please

Don't jump so hard
Beastly boy, flower of huge
Stature.
You've laid me up. And that's
Bad manners. I have the ace; check.
You got it?[15]

These poems confirm the sexual aspect of the encounter with the Angel. As in the film, the narrator has an ace that he shares with Heurtebise. The Angel is shot by God's soldiers, as in one of the rooms, he is limping because he has been wounded, his mouth is full of blood. The pathos mixing tortured powerlessness and enjoyable surrender dominates in the film; and it was expressed not by virtuosity but by technical poverty. Whereas Cocteau was a dazzling poet and a virtuosic master of language, he found with film a medium in which his very lack of expertise would turn into a paradoxical asset.

Re-inventing the medium

Cocteau described the success of his film as due to two main factors: its hermeneutic indecision, and his own ability to overcome technical obstacles at the last minute: "[T]he lasting success of the film is largely due to my mistakes, and to the possibility I give to the spectators to enter into it and play a part in it."[16] Let us take a look at what he calls his mistakes. Cocteau was the first French writer who took the risk of directing a film himself, working on it hands-on, tirelessly even, and learning from the very process. He had succeeded in so many different media, from music to painting, drawing and ballet, that he had not foreseen the specific difficulties of film as a collective medium. The initial idea for *Blood of a Poet* had been to make an animated cartoon, as we have seen. What remains of the animation effect is the recurrent use of Cocteau's drawings; they are used to sketch a face or draw his signature star with five points on the poet's back (which allowed him to hide an old scar), or when the star returns after the poet has committed suicide. Faces turn into drawings as with Lee Miller's face at the end, chalked as an outline; even the indifferent friend's mask is transformed into its drawn outline after the Poet's second suicide.

These metamorphoses offer a key for the comprehension of the film's narrative logic. Its construction is underpinned by a series of visual metaphors, after which they developed a network of interconnected metonymies. These two systems create a dense web of tropes working together to achieve the passage from the animate to the inanimate, from the visual to the spoken, and conversely. A first dialectical image is that of the "lips," a catachresis that functions as well in English as in French: in both languages, one speaks of the "lips of a wound" to mean its edges; the catachresis is literalized when the statue says that it is impossible to close "the lips of a wound" (SP, 31). If a wound has lips, these lips have to speak, and one cannot silence them. Where is the "wound" coming from? Why speak of a "wound" at all? The Poet is first seen drawing with white gloves on; he takes off the glove from his right hand, the better to erase the mouth after it has spoken. If the image owes something to the famous hand from which ants keep crawling out in the *Chien Andalou*, the sense is different. A sign states: "Emerging from a painting where the naked hand had caught it like leprosy, the drowned hand seemed to extinguish itself in a little zone of white light" (SP, 23). The Author's hand seen in plaster substitutes itself to the Poet's hand, the mouth is open, water flows from it, and it keeps a white halo around it. This conveys the idea that the wound is productive. It is not just a shock-image as in Dalí's recurrent nightmare of ants and rotting donkeys. The wound is pre-given; it conditions the Poet's vocation before any physical or moral trauma. The wound is animated, it screams for "more air"—therefore it taps a dynamic life force, looking very much like the wound in W. H. Auden's "Letter to a Wound" from *The Orators* (1931). It is a confession that strength and humanity derive from sexual misalignment, personal losses, and other disasters of life, not an image of castration as with Buñuel and Dalí's terrifying images.

Cocteau boasted of ignoring the most basic cinematographic techniques. Charlie Chaplin thought that the sudden movement forward of the Asian man walking along the corridor sudden brought to a close-up was a great innovation. In fact, as Cocteau explains, this was only a "bad cut," another creative mistake.[17] In the "Profanation of the Host" section, it is clear that Cocteau knew nothing of the shot and counter-shot technique; he presents his "audience" watching the scene of the card-game and the suicide of the poet, frontally, which makes these "spectators" a simple background and reinforces the allegorical quality of their participation.

Similarly, the sound effects are a little off; the constant discrepancy creates an interesting tension—this was due to regular mishandling of the soundtrack. When the Poet shoots himself the second time, the dull report is heard only after his head falls, thus enhancing it. The film is one of the first "talkies" and Cocteau uses to his advantage the fact that voices can be heard or not in the soundtrack, as we overhear the murmur of voices in the theater boxes, or when we hear Chinese voices blabbering. He also deliberately avoids anything like a descriptive or accompanying use of music. He explains that he reshuffled the score composed for each sequence: "I shifted and reversed the order of the music in every single sequence. Not only did the contrast heighten the relief of the images, but I even found at times that that 'displaced' music adhered too closely to the gestures, and seemed to have been written on purpose."[18] Such an accidental synchronism endows the film with an uncanny atmosphere that evokes the fuzzy logic of a dream. The startling presence of the dead child near the gaming table, the apparition of the black angel, all look like images from a rebus or an oneiric collage while following the hidden laws of an auto-poesis. The displaced sounds, like the droning engine of a plane heard whereas strange metal balls rebound in parabolas in total silence, create a sensation of disorientating slowness. Even the fact that Lee Miller had to be dubbed, or that when the bourgeois chat together, the murmur was produced by mixing sentences spoken by Cocteau, contribute to the defamiliarization in which one recognizes the Freudian Uncanny.

A remarkable feature of the film is its speed. The rhythm is dominated by an excessive slowness. The dumb show sequences in the hotel rooms are shot slowly, with painstaking hallucinatory precision. This should not be blamed on the lack of technical ability. Cocteau had raised this drowsy slackness to the dignity of an ontological principle before, as we can see from a letter he wrote to Jacques Maritain in 1926:

> Slow films made me understand that everything revolves around speed. Watch a rugby game. Thirty brutes turn into cigar smoke.
> Nothing interests me more than this angel whom a slowing agent forces to emerge from all things like a chestnut from its spiky skin. Why? In comparison with God, our centuries fly in the wink of an eye, we are being shot in slow motion.[19]

As an Author, Cocteau always tries to write from God's point of view, which is from the point of view of unlimited patience, even if, as the "wounded" Poet he knows that the ancient gods' demise was due to boredom—being immortal, they were bored to death. Hence the meaning of the last sentence in *Blood of a Poet*: "Mortal tedium of immortality." The sentence echoes Nietzsche, who stated that the Greek gods had died from being immortal: "dead from immortality."[20] He added: "One pays dearly for immortality: one has to die several times while still alive."[21] Death is thus freely dispensed in the film's plot, which leads to a weirdly repetitive logic, whose desultory rhythm creates a quasi-hypnotic fascination.

One consequence of this alliance between repetition and fascination is another paradox: the excessive slowness of the plot gives the impression of a heightened speed. Cocteau was aware of the phenomenon; he comments on it when the Poet takes the ace of hearts from the dead schoolboy's jacket:

"Interminable documentary, this is how the cheater imagines his gesture, more rapid than lightning" (SP, 70). In fact, the gesture is shot in slow motion, and its speed is hard to assess. Here, the word choice seems strange, but we may remember that the whole film had been described as a "documentary" at first, as a sign has this: "Free to choose faces, forms, gestures, pitches, actions, places that please him, he composes with them a realistic documentary of unreal events" (SP, 15). A documentary is of course an official trace of an event, but it is as well an echo of the old "*docere*" of the Latin precepts. A documentary teaches you about facts, history, and the freedom of narration.

When Cocteau says "*Documentaire interminable*" in his Parisian accent, making the words sound like "*Docu-menteur*," we are ready to find a lying document, as it were to suggest, as he often said, that art is a lie that tells the truth. Art is a creative *pseudos* that keeps the imagination at work. Cocteau, like Beckett experimenting with *Film*, never abandoned his control over the most oneiric material as an Author, but decided to create not a web of universal symbols, but an imaginative narrative (a narrative that we can re-imagine for ourselves), which progresses via strings of opaque modernist allegories. Finally, in the same way as Beckett produced a filmic masterpiece, *Film*, by working from the misguided assumption that one can distinguish between angles of 45 degrees and angles that would be less or more when the camera faces an actor, soon realizing that this was impossible,[22] Cocteau created a modernist masterpiece because of the conjunction between his technological virginity and the virtuosity of his poetic skills.

"No symbols where none intended"[23]

In a presentation given in 1950 to a young audience, Cocteau declared: "This film presents no symbol. It proceeds only by allegories and it might be that these allegories remain as obscure to you as the meaning of coats of arms in heraldry and even the names of your families. It is nevertheless true that these coats of arms remain loaded with a meaning that grants them prestige."[24] The idea is expressed from the start in the mute captions of the film: "Every poem is a coat of arms. One has to decipher it" (SP, 14). The "reel of allegories" thus includes poetry and painting, since this is followed by the reference to Pisanello, Ucello, della Francesca, and del Castagno. It is no coincidence that Pisanello should be named first—he was known to have launched the fashion for portrait medals, and was praised for his hieratic profiles in the *Tempio Malatestiano* of Rimini by Aby Warburg, Ezra Pound, and Adrian Stokes.

Stokes wrote that Pisanello exemplified the rage for emblems that marks the Quattrocento. Such efforts, typical of the early Renaissance, were a sign that the externalization of hidden fantasies, accompanied by their inscription in hard materials like stone or metal, would give the courage to live. Stokes's words could serve as a good commentary of Cocteau's film: "Marble statues of the gods are the gods themselves. For they are objects as if alive which enjoy complete outwardness."[25] For Cocteau, plaster statues work as well as marble ones, and they externalize our deepest fantasies—besides, they are much easier to smash.

Cocteau's film offers a good example of modernist allegory if we take the term of allegory in the sense given to it by Walter Benjamin, a meaning that came to him via Baudelaire. Benjamin insists on a certain artificiality of the allegory that presents itself as a non-organic ruin from the start. It is an unstable category, since it hesitates between neo-classicism, the gothic, and surrealism. I have already quoted Benjamin's sketch for *The Arcades Project* in which he links a modernist neo-classicism with the myth of Orpheus: "With the neoclacissism of Cocteau, Stravinsky, Picasso, Chirico, and others, it has this in common: the traditional space of awakening in which we now are living is, wherever possible, traversed by gods. This traversal of space by gods is to be understood as lightning-like."[26]

Benjamin met Cocteau in June 1926 at the premiere of *Orphée*, a play that he admired, and praised the novel *Les Enfants Terribles* to Adorno.[27] He perceived that *Blood of a Poet* offered the most self-conscious staging of a modernist allegory. Benjamin had begun exploring allegories with the German baroque theater, but then found them in the poetry of Baudelaire as a more modern series of exemplifications. Remaining in line with the position taken by Adorno and Horkheimer, Benjamin presented the modern allegory as the dismantling of myth and symbol: "It was owing to the genius of allegory that Baudelaire did not succumb to the abyss of myth that gaped beneath his feet at every step" (AP, 268). Baudelaire's allegorical genius relies on tactics of shock and surprise; his allegories are not just static, for they embody a "flight of images" and a "petrified unrest" (AP, 325). In this version, allegory is destructive, whereas myth holds to a fake sense of the constructive: "Allegory holds fast to the ruins" (AP, 329).

As we have seen, a destructive impulse is as prevalent in Baudelaire as in Cocteau. Both poets systematically destroy the Romantic illusion that one should strive to recreate a healthy and living organic whole: "[A]llegory has to do, precisely in its destructive furor, with dispelling the illusion that proceeds from all 'given order,' whether of art or of life: the illusion of totality or of organic wholeness which transfigures that order and makes it seem endurable" (AP, 331). To illustrate this, Benjamin quotes Baudelaire's sonnet "Destruction" in *Flowers of Evil*. Its last stanzas describe the negative action of the Devil who never leaves the Poet in peace by activating unholy desires even when they are limited to women and art: "He [the Devil] thrusts before my eyes full of bewilderment, /Dirty filthy garments and open, gaping wounds, /And all the bloody instruments of Destruction!"[28] Benjamin comments:

> Of all of Baudelaire's poems, "La Destruction" comprises the most relentless elaboration of the allegorical intention. The "bloody retinue," which the poet is forced by the demon to contemplate, is the court of allegory—the scattered apparatus by dint of which allegory has so disfigured and so unsettled the world of things that only the fragments of that world are left to it now, as objects of its brooding.
>
> (AP, 349)

Similarly, one can say that the site of Cocteau's work is the "court of allegory," which explains the dark brooding in *Blood of a Poet*, a film in which the dialectical transformation of the "wound" into "glory" is never assured of reaching a final apotheosis. The "court of allegory" is walled in by "sentences" inserted by the Author, most of which keep a ring of sententiousness: these abstract mottos, witty one-liners or enigmatic maxims can be mulled over because they carry more than one meaning. In Baudelaire's sonnet as in *Blood of a Poet*, a similar sense of fragmentariness dominates. What happens after the death of the Poet when the Muse turns into a statue again? The map of Europe in tatters glued together by cow dung betrays a sense of dispersal or dissolution of values. Such a dispersal would be another proof of the crisis of the "aura." Another exemplification of the metamorphosis of the aura in the modern age would be the transformation of the black guardian angel into a white auratic being, however rapidly fading, in a scene shot in negative, with the intense noise of an engine signifying the triumph of the machine. Cocteau's commentary compares the angel's gaze as he accomplishes his "work" of transubstantiation to that of "a dying animal" (SP, 73). One could hardly call this "work" a triumph of artistic transfiguration!

Allegories as rethought by Benjamin testify to the survival of the ancient gods, which is what happened with the submerged classicism of the Renaissance, its pagan gods resurfacing in spite of Christianity, as Aby Warburg knew. Thus when critic Friedrich von Bezold mentioned "the survival of the ancient gods in medieval humanism" a propos of Baudelaire, Benjamin added: "Allegory is the vehicle for this survival" (AP, 367). Altogether allegories reflect a frozen history testifying to a crisis of the aura: "[T]he image of petrified unrest called up by allegory is a historical image. It shows the forces of antiquity and of Christianity suddenly arrested in their contest, turned to stone amid unalloyed hostilities" (AP, 366). Here is another meaning of the Profanation suggested by the fourth panel of Cocteau's filmic sequence. The "Profanation" would open less a door to satanic rituals than an aperture for the rays released by profane illuminations. These illuminations are not produced by a seamless adequation of form and content as in a Romantic "symbol," but generated by constructive dehiscence and formal excess—Beauty is not the object of the quest, on the contrary—a disturbing slowness allows viewers to fantasize on a pageant of petrified images. "Allegory, as the sign that is pointedly set off against its meaning, has its place in art as the antithesis to the beautiful appearance in which signifier and signified flow into each other" (AP, 374). This dehiscence of sign and meaning would account for the last allegorical cluster of the film, when a bull replaces the car called for the departing Muse. The Muse is clearly presented as Europa raped by Zeus. Was this a prophetic image?

In his 1950 presentation of his film, Cocteau singled out the striking image of a bull carrying a map of Europe in tatters, a map torn up, recomposed, and glued together on the skin with cow dung, identifying it with a prophetic vision: "[P]arts of the film became strange because they were prophetic. Thus when the Muse calls her car—it ends up being a bull—(the rape of Europa) but on this bull Europa becomes Europe and the spots of the animal present the terrible spectacle of Europe dismembered, torn apart and maculated with mud."[29] The Muse becomes "inhuman" again after her task has been accomplished. Perhaps the dead poet full of glory will be reborn from his ashes. It seems that we have returned to ancient myth, were it not, according to Benjamin's formula, for the destructiveness of the allegory, a destruction which prevents myth from delivering a stable or unique message. This is confirmed by the detail of the *bouse de vache* (cow dung), a precision given by Cocteau since it would be difficult to smell it on the reel (SP, 82), a "glue" whose lowness does not simply betray decadence but brings along Bataille's tribute to the constructivism of "low" or "base" materialism.[30]

Cocteau's caption called his film a "reel of allegories," which implies that if they do yield "enigmas," they avoid religious "mysteries," to go back to Benjamin's opposition (AP, 365). Everything must be decoded, for the film unfolds like a poem: "Every poem is a coat of arms: it must be deciphered" (SP, 14). Allegories accompanied by their retinue of destruction generate both traces and auras. Benjamin's coupling of opposites, trace and aura, helps here: "Trace and aura. The trace is appearance of a nearness, however far removed the thing that left it. The aura is appearance of a distance, however close the thing that calls it forth. In the trace, we gain possession of the thing; in the aura, it takes possession of us" (AP, 487). Benjamin's theory of allegory allows us to decode the film's enigmas as a dynamic tension between the status of trace and that of aura. Traces at times replace auras—we barely discern the traces left in the snow by the body of the dead schoolboy, or the last drops of blood oozing from the Poet's temple, whereas the Muse exits without leaving any footsteps in the snow: "Her task fulfilled, the woman turned back into a statue, that is to say an inhuman thing, with black gloves denounced by the snow on which ... her steps would then leave no trace" (SP, 78–9). Are we taking possession of the film, or is it taking possession of us? Cocteau felt trapped by his own film: "The sleeper seen in close up, or the surprises of photography ... or how I was trapped by my own film" (SP, 28). Have we, too, been trapped by the profanation enacted in its images? Not really, at least not if the wound speaks, for in all its profane pathos, Cocteau's loquacious wound tells the truth.

8

The Pathos of History

Trauma in Siri Hustvedt's *The Sorrows of an American*

My sorrow is my knight's castle, which lies like an eagle's eyrie high up the mountain peaks among the clouds. No one can take it by storm. From it I fly down into reality and seize my prey; but I do not remain down there, I bring my prey home; and this prey is a picture I weave into the tapestries in my palace. Then I live as one dead.[1]

Cocteau's speaking wound sends us back to the etymology of trauma (a wound), which poses the question whether a trauma can "speak," that is be treated by literature, or whether the only thing to do—which is easier with earlier films—is to remain silent. Eliot's poetry also takes us to a point of distance in pathos as unspoken ecstasy, as we see in *The Waste Land* when an unnamed man speaks to a woman called "the hyacinth girl":

> —Yet when we came back, late, from the hyacinth garden,
> Your arms full, and your hair wet, I could not
> Speak [...]
> [...] and I knew nothing,
> Looking into the heart of light, the silence.
>
> (CPP, 62)

Mainstream literature has always attempted to deal with traumatic experiences, whether poetic and lyrical as this one, or ineffably horrible as in most cases. This insight underpinned Eliot's essay on "Hamlet and his Problems," in which the mainspring of the play's plot is called a forceful "emotion" that keeps so many traces of the "excess" that produced it in the author that it has become unmanageable. Eliot agrees with most commentators that "the essential emotion of the play is the feeling of a son towards a guilty mother" (SW, 99), an emotion that Freud would sum up in one word: "Incest." In Eliot's careful reading, we cannot jump to conclusions so quickly. Hamlet the character is "dominated by an emotion which is inexpressible, because it is in excess of the facts as they appear" (SW, 101). Eliot concludes that because Shakespeare was unable to tame or channel his character's emotional excess, the play *Hamlet* is a failure on the artistic plan. The play is not only too long and contradictory but it is too "pathological": we can leave Hamlet's case to "pathologists" (SW, 102).

For Eliot, this type of emotive "excess" is not uncommon; many people have had the opportunity to register it: "The intense feeling, ecstatic or terrible, without an object or exceeding its object, is something which every person of sensibility has known; it is doubtless a study to pathologists" (SW, 102). However, as we have seen, Eliot postulates that what makes a good artist is his or her ability to control his or her material by presenting "feelings" that blend with sensations, and not an overload of raw emotion. He blames Shakespeare for having lacked artistic control: "We must simply admit that here Shakespeare tackled a problem which proved too much for him. Why he attempted it at all is an insoluble puzzle; under compulsion of what experience he attempted to express the inexpressibly horrible, we cannot ever know" (SW, 102). This was Freud's position facing *Hamlet*, but for Freud, this excess was presented in a positive light: it testifies to the truth of the symptoms described. Eliot argues that art has to sublimate the ineffable horror upon which these symptoms are founded. Joseph Conrad had managed this feat in *Heart of Darkness* when he put the urbane skepticism of a narrator like Marlowe between Kurtz's awareness of the African "horror" and his more genteel British audience. We have a double problem therefore: how to tame one's "passions" and make them amenable to literature, and how to find a narratological model capable of universalizing them.

In this chapter, I will start from a personal illustration about trauma and post-traumatic stress disorder for it throws some a light on the vexed issue of the links between pathos and history. The vignette is provided by Siri Hustvedt, a writer always ready to share and analyze her own symptoms, as she did brilliantly in *The Shaking Woman*, with its ironical subtitle deftly evoking Freud's Schreber case, "*Or a History of My Nerves.*" This time, Hustvedt described the emotional impact of an automobile accident in which she was involved ten years before. The crash that destroyed the car in which she was sitting next to her husband and daughter took place in 2002. Ten years later, attempting to document the double process of traumatic repetition and attendant dissociation and forgetting, she published "Reliving the Crash" in *The New York Times* of February 18, 2012. Here is a passage from this thoughtful piece:

> My husband is speaking to me from the driver's seat, but I cannot answer him. All I know is that I do not want to move. I feel at once serene and distant. I have this thought: *If I'm going to die, this is not such a bad way to go.* [...]

After the accident, I was clearly in a dissociated state—weirdly detached from myself – and although I left the hospital without an injury that could be seen on a CT scan, both my memory and my sense of self had been altered by the shock. My amnesia for the accident and the flashbacks that followed, belong to my psychological state, but they are also, of course, part of my physiological state that involved changes in my brain. This is obvious, and yet this truth has led to a lot of confusion, not only about PTSD, but all mental illnesses. [...]

My late father, who fought in New Guinea and the Philippines during the Second World War, had repeated flashbacks at night after he returned to civilian life, and once while he was awake—the intrusive memory seemed to have been triggered by a hymn he was listening to in chapel. As the horrible images unfolded before him, he began to shake uncontrollably, and he found himself back in the Philippines witnessing what he believed was the unwarranted killing of a Japanese officer.

[...] In 2006 I developed a mysterious seizure disorder that manifests itself in violent shaking, which I now control with medicine. The shaking symptoms first appeared when I gave a speech in memory of my father, but I also once had a seizure while climbing a mountain, which was probably caused by hyperventilation.

It is tempting to link my shaking and my flashbacks to my father's. The question is how? If there is a genetic susceptibility to PTSD, it remains unknown, but both strong emotion—a psychological state—and a lack of oxygen—a physiological one—are known to cause seizures.[2]

I have quoted this article because of the double reference to the 2008 novel *The Sorrow of an American*. The sections that I have italicized condense problematics deployed by Hustvedt in her fiction and essays. What has caused her father's trauma? If it was clear that there was a link between the father's symptoms and her own symptoms, why was there a transgenerational reiteration? Can one understand the root of such traumatic events by writing a fiction or a memoir? Hustvedt's novel attempts to provide an answer to these questions, and uses the device of a narrator or hero, a male psychiatrist, and psychoanalyst eager to make sense of his father's war trauma. Erik develops a series of meditations on trauma that can be inscribed in the context of current debates about the concept.

Trauma: The debate

Erik is a psychoanalyst who knows that the term of trauma has its roots in Freudian concepts. One of the most outspoken advocates of trauma studies,

Cathy Caruth, systematically goes back to Freud as one can see in *Unclaimed Experience: Trauma, Narrative, and History*.³ Caruth's point of departure is Freud's notion of a "traumatic neurosis" insofar as it is applied to history, especially to the history of Jewish religion. Freud introduced a loaded analogy between patients who have suffered a shock from a wound or after an accident, and what happened to the Jewish people as it accepted an originally Egyptian monotheism. In most cases for victims of a trauma, it is only later, after a period of "latency" or "incubation," that they develop symptoms that repeat the initial traumatic situation.⁴ Most of the time, moreover, victims of the trauma are not fully conscious of the events that happened. Although at first they have the impression that their emotions are under control, it is only later that symptoms appear. Trauma thus refers to a psychic "wound" that cannot heal, and hence triggers endless repetitions. The notion of trauma implies a break in the integrity of the psychic apparatus, to the point that it cannot absorb, register or process the shocking or excessive event. If such excess is not controllable or even fully perceptible, it generates intolerable anxiety or endlessly repetitive symptoms.

Deferred action implies the idea of the re-inscription of previously repressed excitations, often sexual in nature. Its temporality is thus not linear but recursive, which complicates the work on memory that psychoanalysis presupposes. It is also the specific temporality of literature. The structure of deferred action is taken as a fundamental hermeneutic paradigm by Caruth. According to her, there is something like an "unclaimed experience" and historical narratives do not follow the experiential model defined by the sequence of events witnessed by observers and later consigned in chronicles. There is no immediate understanding when trauma is concerned. This insight finds obvious applications in the field of Holocaust studies.

Following Caruth's lead, Giorgio Agamben took Primo Levi's memoirs of Auschwitz as the starting point for his far-ranging meditation on the unspeakable in history.⁵ As Levi argued, the true witnesses were not the survivors, they were those who had abandoned all hope in the camps, those who were called the *Müselmänner*. All died because they had gone too deep into the horror. However, some critics objected to the fetishization of the unspeakable. Ruth Leys attacked Cathy Caruth for what she sees as a misreading of Freud on the concept of trauma, and aims at showing that there are at least two models of trauma for Freud, one in which he believes in the reality of the event, the other in which it may just be a simulation.⁶ Thomas Trezise published a virulent debunking of Agamben's account of Auschwitz in *Witnessing Witnessing: On the Reception of Holocaust Survivor Testimony*. Trezise rejects the theme of an unspeakable event, so excessive that it cannot not be inscribed in subjective consciousness or collective memory. Suspicious of the rhetoric of pathos deployed by Agamben, he highlights a dangerous consequence of this position: if one can merely repeat the trauma, this will prevent victims from giving any testimony about their experiences, whereas most victims insist upon their ability (or wish) to provide a true account of their condition.

This is the heated discussion out of which trauma studies have grown; they include memoirs of abuse, rape, murder, and stories about extreme situations. These events being by definition "excessive," they cannot be inscribed either in the memory or consciousness. They have to be repeated compulsively, literally and mutely. Caruth takes examples from Marguerite Duras (*Hiroshima My Love*), Lacan, and Kleist, that all insist on missed experiences and on the inability to inscribe the trauma in a linear and coherent narrative.

Ruth Leys questioned the conclusions reached by physician Bessel van der Kolk and Caruth, who both argue that the symptoms of traumas are literal and veridical repetitions of events that have happened. If those events happened but implied some kind of excess, which explains why they were not fully registered, then the Freudian concepts of repression cannot apply here.[7] The "wound" of the trauma would have been so deep that it affected the organs of perception and memory. Leys compares this thesis with the abundant medical and legal literature produced about Post-Traumatic Stress Disorder since the 1980s. The term "PTSD" became official in the *Diagnostic and Statistical Manual of Mental Disorders* (*DSM*) *III* in 1980. The more recent versions of the *DSM* were more cautious in attributing a literal and truthful nature to traumatic phenomena. The growing number of persons suffering from recurrent memories, flashbacks, hallucinations, and nightmares generated by traumatic injuries or experiences has given rise to an enormous archive that is hard to interpret. Freud, who was aware of the phenomenon, ended up thinking that it testified to the existence of a death-drive that he posited beyond the pleasure principle. However, if the traumatic suffering is undeniable and real, how can we be sure that the cause is a real event? This question takes us back to the interrogations of Freud as he was changing his views about the reality of the seduction of hysterical daughters in the hands of perverse fathers in 1897.

For Caruth, victims of trauma can only repeat the events because they have no possibility of narrating them to themselves. Traumatic events are literally happening over and over again. "The truth of the trauma [is] the failure of representation,"[8] she summarizes. Caruth interprets Claude Lanzmann's film *Shoah* not as a representation destined to make people understand the transportation toward death camps but as a way of transmitting the trauma as such in its incomprehensible horror. The "pathos of the literal" is then Leys's critical response to a combination of scientism about overwhelmed neurotransmitters and a performative literary theory of the contagion of the unspeakable.

More damaging has been Thomas Trezise's refutation of Agamben's application of the paradigm of trauma to discuss the quandary in which Holocaust survivors found themselves. Agamben exploits some of Primo Levi's hesitations about his own role. Levi felt that he was inadequate as a witness, and left that role to those who could not fulfill it by definition since they were the glassy-eyed vanquished, the haggard mute shadows, those who had abandoned any hope. Trezise's question is whether the way survivors have witnessed historical events can lead to disclose a truth, whether the silenced speech of survivors brings about a reconstruction of the crime. If the only true witnesses of the Shoah were the catatonic "Müselmänner" who believe that they will never return to the world of the living, their passivity does not leave a chance to those intent upon narrating their experiences.

Trezise multiplies examples of witnesses who insisted on their witnessing abilities. For them, it was crucial to convey to the outside world the extent of the horror they had experienced. Important books like Charlotte Delbo's *Auschwitz and After* and Robert Antelme's *The Human Species* are memoirs presenting the survivors of the camps engaged in a frenzy of talk. There was an outpouring of stories about their experiences as soon they were able to do so. Narrating the horror was a way to begin understanding it, which contradicts the paradox of an unspeakable account of the unspeakable. One should be attentive to whether witnesses are capable or not of narrating the trauma.[9] Are such witnesses the carriers of a message of which they are unaware, or should there be an ethical decision to be a witness of something that bordered the unspeakable but that can begin to be ordered and sorted out before turning into a narrative? Moreover, there is a transmission of trauma, as has often been observed with children of Holocaust survivors, and such a transgenerational genealogy has also impacted Siri Hustvedt's relationship with her father's war trauma.

Either/Or

True to the title of Kierkegaard's book on which Inga, Erik Davidsen's sister, has written her dissertation, Hustvedt's novel is caught up in an *Either/Or*. It cannot avoid taking a position about the reality and unspeakability of trauma. On the one hand, indeed, *The Sorrows of an American* seems to side with Caruth. Erik Davidsen, the hero of the novel, a middle-aged and divorced male psychiatrist who works at the Payne Whitney Psychiatric Clinic in New York, meditates on trauma and history:

> History is made by amnesia. In the American Civil War, they called it soldier's heart, and over time it changed its name to shell shock, then war neurosis. Now it's PTSD, post-traumatic stress disorder, the most antiseptic of the terms for what can happen to people who witness the unspeakable. During World War I, in the barracks of field hospitals French and British doctors saw them coming in droves—men blind, deaf, shaking, paralyzed, aphasic, catatonic, hallucinating, plagued by recurring nightmares and insomnia, seeing and re-seeing what no one should see, or feeling nothing at all. [...] Trauma isn't part of a story; it is outside the story. It is what we refuse to make part of the story.[10]

This opinion would fall in line with Caruth's thesis; it underpins the main narrative drift in the novel, the parallel between Erik's theories and his progressive deciphering, helped by Inga, of the notes and diaries written by their father during the Second World War. As we saw, the main source of the trauma experienced by Lars Davidsen was the killing of a Japanese officer who was trying to surrender in the Philippines. The Japanese officer was shot unfairly by an American officer even though he posed no threat. This image of the killed supplicant haunts Lars Davidsen's memory. It functions as a ghostly remorse and he superimposes it onto older memories of ancient family dramas. His son Erik must tease out the root of his father's symptoms in order to understand his own predicament. This is now Erik who is speaking:

> I knew that my research was confirming what I had always felt was true in my patients: their memories of war, rape, near-fatal accidents, and collapsing buildings aren't like other memories. They are kept separate in the mind. I remembered the images from PET scans of PTSD patients and the colored highlights showing increased blood flow to the right side of the brain and to the limbic and paralimbic areas, the old brain in evolutionary terms, and decreased flow to the left cortical areas, the language sites. Trauma does not appear in words, but in a roar of terror, sometimes with images. Words create the anatomy of a story, but within that story there are openings that cannot be closed.
>
> (SA, 85)

Another passage is devoted to the father's return to civil life after the war, when he went back to college thanks to the G.I. Bill. The father explains in his diary that one day that he heard the Lutheran hymn "O Day Full of Grace," he was seized by unstoppable shaking: "*To Don's alarm, I began to tremble. I lied and said it was a touch of malaria. This was my only daytime flashback, but I lived in fear that more might come.* I read these sentences to myself many times, trying to penetrate their meaning. [...] Traumatic memory arrives like a blast in the brain" (SA, 136-7). The son then compares this experience with that of traumatized survivors of 9/11: "They came to us later with their wounds of indelible memory, the images that were burned into them and then released again and again in a hormonal surge, the brain flood that accompanies a return to unbearable reality" (SA, 137). American history has a rich store of similar experiences.

On the other hand, these theories of trauma are inserted in a dense narrative web that promises to expose a few "secrets," that is to let them speak, which obeys to the logic of what Barthes has called the hermeneutic code.[11] On the first page, Erik declares: "I think we all have ghosts inside us, and it's better when they speak than when they don't" (SA, 1). There are three main "secrets" in the novel: a secret concerning the past sexual life of Inga's deceased husband, a famous novelist with a complicated past life (solved when compromising letters are bought at the end by a rich friend); a secret concerning Lars's youth, implicating a woman called Lisa who had mentioned a dead person very early on (solved when Erik and Inga meet the very old woman at the end); and a secret concerning Miranda, the beautiful Jamaican mother of Eggy, both of whom become lodgers in Erik's house, who is stalked by a photographer (solved when we discover that the photographer is the father of the child and that he desperately tries to have access to her, and to the mother). The three secrets are skillfully intertwined in a complex web of stories marked by suspense and a progressive resolution. Soon, the narrative of the novel picks up speed and gains a Freudian dynamism of its own. As the Kierkegaardian philosopher Inga admits at some point: "We were looking for one story and ran into another" (SA, 200). This is a good exemplification of how ramified networks of verbal knots, Freud's famous theory of the "*Knotenpunkte*" in *The Interpretation of Dreams*, generate narratives.

In the novel, we witness other traumatic events from the past, like the 1924 fire that destroyed the family farm, but it does not matter whether this caused the original trauma. The second family secret finds a solution at the end, when we learn that Erik's father had helped Lisa Odland give birth to a stillborn baby in the woods one night. The stillborn child was not his. Lars, who was fifteen then, buried the little corpse and avoided mentioning the disturbing incident again. It was henceforth buried in his unconscious. The secret is not only a locked crypt, a hidden ghost in the closet; it is also presented as the most precious possession. Inga, Erik's sister who is a philosopher, quotes Kierkegaard: "Maybe you've kept a secret in your heart that you felt in all its joy or pain was too precious to share with someone else" (SA, 252). Knowing that "[s]ecrets define people" (SA, 201), Inga sums up the opening pages of Kierkegaard's *Either/Or*. From a statement about the secrets we all have, and philosophical considerations on the voice as the sense of our interiority and hearing as the sense of the other's exteriority, Kierkegaard conflates the "secret" and the "secretary" or "escritoire," the chest of drawers in which the editor pretends to have discovered manuscripts by various authors that constitute the entire book. The secret has to do with writing more than with speaking, which is why Hustvedt follows Kierkegaard's device of using proliferating masks, gender-bending projections, multifaceted personas in a calculated use of fictional alter egos.

The "secret" concerning Miranda is easier to decipher, and defines a different type of "event." The characterization of the crazy and narcissistic artist Jeffrey Lane, Miranda's estranged father, is that of a radical skeptic, who refuses to attribute any reality to trauma or affects. When he has become aware of Erik's attraction to Miranda, he stalks them and takes numerous photographs that he displays in and around the house. Lane is a typical "post-modernist" who believes that everything is a simulacrum or replica like Andy Warhol. His art of repetition and intrusion also appears as a parody of the philosophy of Jean Baudrillard or Paul Virilio. This subplot focuses on a series of photographs taken by Lane and showing Erik in an unflattering light: he was so angry that he looks furious, deranged, a true madman, in a sly dig at his profession. When Lane exhibits the photographs in a Chelsea gallery, to great acclaim, one has a caption saying: "Head Doctor Goes Insane." The show is called "Jeff's Lives: Multiple Fictions, or an Excursion into DID" (SA, 260). The outcome is a legal suit won by Erik, but the public humiliation remains. It has one positive consequence: an old patient dreams of the hammer he is wielding in the photograph and is lifted from her acedia (SA, 266–7). When Lane chooses this title, he calls up his real or staged "Dissociative Identity Disorder" (SA, 157), but creates art with it. Here is a case of art imitating not life but psychic disability. Jeffrey Lane is a male version of Sophie Calle, the artist who has most exploited the blurred limits between art and life; she too has exhibited photographs of lovers and even of break-up letters.

This part of the novel can be linked with Hustvedt's forceful rejection of a dated and grating post-modernism. We see this best when she discusses a show organized by Paul Virilio in Paris, in which images of 9/11 were used to argue that reality has ceased to exist in a technological age. I too saw this show at the Foundation Cartier, and in spite of the brilliance of Virilio's impassioned rhetoric, I have to agree with Hustvedt: the overall result felt indeed sickening. Hustvedt is unusually snide: "The alarm in Virilio's writings is palpable; his voice is pitched high. (I venture to say that had he been a woman his fate as a thinker would have been far more uncertain.)"[12] The novel offers a neat parable about the impossibility of post-modernism insofar as it tries to negate reality. Lane is brutally brought back to the real world when Eggy, his beloved six-year-old daughter, falls from a window when she was in his care.

We soon realize that it is impossible for Erik and Miranda to have an affair. Erik has helped Miranda overcome a different trauma, the murder of her uncle Richard in Jamaica but, in fact, he will be instrumental in bringing her and Lane back together as a more or less "normal" family: they will be reunited if the miracle of the child's survival after her coma happens. Stories have their own logic, and one "trauma" can be cured by a narrative generated by another trauma. The little girl played tying up Erik, who then muses: "Telling always binds one thing to another" (SA, 276).

The last section of the novel should bring about a resolution to the vexed issue of trauma when Miranda and Lane, united in their grief, wait for young Eggy to wake up from her coma. Even if the news is good, the girl will have to live with the aftermath of her fall: "I knew that it wasn't over, that even if she recovered fully, Eggy would live with the story of the fall inside her. She would be changed by it" (SA, 300–1). The ending concludes on an uncertain note: it not sure whether Erik will let his relationship with Laura become dominant, or whether he will remain single as before. At least he has understood the role Miranda has played as a figure of pure longing and impossible desire. Even if the solutions are partial and imperfect, the drift of the novel follows a Freudian paradigm, because it affirms that talking, like writing, can lift the weight of traumas. Writing transforms the unspeakable wound into a metaphorical scar, making it a true "scar-letter."

The difficulty of writing a psychoanalytic history when concealment and forgetting have impacted records can be solved by an old and imaginative recourse to the dialectics of fiction. The logic of the Greek *pseudos* (the lie, and any creative mask or departure from truth) provides a bridge between unspeakable facts and the need to bring a testimony. A similar solution is given by Hustvedt's novel, and it also recurs in her essays and memoirs. A first theoretical key can be found in Hustvedt's essay on "The Real Story," in which she juxtaposes fiction with memoirs. Hustvedt rejects the idea that writers are "professional liars" (LTL, 95). A good novel does not lie, even if some "facts" taken as a point of departure can be altered, transposed or distorted. Jean-Jacques Rousseau's *Confessions* took some liberties with a few data in his biography, yet what stands out is that he was able to provide "emotional truth." Hustvedt rightly praises Rousseau: "His appeal is to the truth of sentiments, to *emotional truth*" (LTL, 103). She quotes William James's *The Principles of Psychology*: "There is no such thing as mental retention, the persistence of an idea from month to month or year to year in some mental pigeon-hole from which it can be drawn when wanted. What persists is a tendency to connection" (LTL, 104), which resembles the principle laid out by E. M. Forster of the need to "Only connect." Such emotional connections contribute to forge a global history, a poetic history, as the universal history envisaged by Giambattista Vico, for whom memory was the same as imagination (LTL, 106).

Hustvedt explains that her imagination was stirred once she hit upon the idea of her main character, Erik Davidsen. Erik, she felt, could help her by becoming an "imaginary brother" (LTL, 163). This brother would have to be a psychoanalyst, which led her to invent a fictional therapist obsessed with his father's war trauma—the fictive alter-ego allowed her to overcome the grief that she had felt at her own father's death. Writing as one's imaginary twin who happens to be male and in a position of authority facing medical knowledge was not a manner of deferring to a male-centered ideology of the scientific domination of the psyche. It is rather a bold exploration of otherness and mourning. The logic of mourning colors the affect of "sorrow." For Freud, the work of mourning (*Trauerarbeit*) implies that, after a certain period of time, the subject can process a loss, is ready to move on and invest new objects of desire. Because such a process entails "killing the dead person," it can be blocked or inhibited, which would generate the melancholic position in which the lost object of love cannot be abandoned. In this case, the mourning process entails a certain play with fiction, with fictive others caught up in a bigger history. Thus we find topical allusions to 9/11 (SA, 4) and to the beginning of the Iraq war. Indeed, Hustvedt's title has been carefully chosen, for "sorrow" derives from *sorg*, as in the German *Sorge*, and generates both "sorry" and "sore." The "sore spot" points to where the trauma has impacted either flesh or the mind, whereas the main character feels the need to apologize, being "sorry" for being an American.

For beyond obvious allusions to Goethe's famous *Sorrows of Young Werther* (*Die Leiden des jungen Werthers*, 1774) and to Shakespeare's *Tempest* and George Eliot's *Middlemarch* (Miranda is improbably named Casaubon, which alludes to the stymied and disappointed male mythographer of the novel), we can think of Marie Corelli, whose novel *The Sorrows of Satan* from 1897 happened to be both the first British best-seller and the worst novel ever written. What are then those "sorrows" and whose sorrows are they? We have shifted from a discussion of trauma as unspeakable hole left in the fabric of history to a discussion of narratives embedded in a web of "secrets" that have to be explained one after the other. One of the main features of Lars's war trauma is that it has not been caused by a personal wound; Lars, who could have been killed many times in battle, does not seem to have suffered from an accident or a near-death experience. On the contrary, the "trauma" with the Japanese officer reveals the depth of his empathy and guilt facing the shooting of an unarmed enemy, a clear metonym for a much greater mass murder with atomic bombs. The compassion for an unjustly murdered enemy puts a face on the anonymous reality of warfare. The unfairly killed Japanese officer haunts Lars's dreams more because his murder appeals to his sense of ethics, which includes his participation in a mass slaughter of immense proportions, a juggernaut machine in which he was only a tiny cog. The "sorrows of an American" call up a post-9/11 world in which many have discovered that in some parts of the world, to be an "American" can mean to have the face of "Satan."

Thus the author's recurrent symptom as the "shaking woman" sends us back to a longer legacy, a Lacanian or Heideggerian *legs*, whose roots are found in a traumatized Father. What has been transmitted was not just any wound but the danger of disseminating the traumas, of spreading the wound to others. We have all been wounded by the trauma of birth, of separation, of sexuality—traumas buried in dark forests, the forests of all myths, like the stillborn baby whose memory haunted Lars all his life. Writing the novel thus took the function of a therapy, but as Hustvedt notes, one cannot "psychoanalyze" oneself: "Obviously, writing fictional versions of psychoanalytical sessions is not the same as being in analysis. There is no *real other* in a novel, only imagined others. But writing novels is nevertheless a form of open listening to those imagined others, one that draws on memories, transmuted by both fantasies and fears" (LTL, 165).

Hustvedt's fiction rejects the hypothesis of an unspeakable trauma that remains inaccessible to words, but she also rejects the opposite view, the postmodern thesis that because there are only virtual copies, and because traces are bound to cover and destroy the aura of any original event, no trauma will ever take place outside of a simulation. Not so for her—on her view, there are real events at the root of any trauma and they can be couched in words although never fully presented. Hustvedt confirms a basic Lacanian insight: truth can only be brought to us through language; hence it is always "half-said" (*mi-dite*) in a steady structure of fiction.[13] Therefore the part that has to be left unsaid, the other half of the half "well-said," cannot be simply equated with the traumatic. The pathos of trauma is superfluous, for the "holes" that any narrative contains are due to structural conditions of language.

Language possesses its own logic: Hustvedt explains that she always listens to the music of words when she writes, all the while running after "wild thoughts," thoughts that, as Bion claimed, had no thinker; thoughts determined by the recursive temporal logics of *Nachträglichkeit*: "There are always things that are left unsaid—significant holes. I was aware that I was writing about memory. Freud's notion of *Nachträglichkeit* haunted the book. We remember, and we tell ourselves a story, but the meanings of what we remember are reconfigured over time. Memory and imagination cannot be separated" (LTL, 40). Thus *Nachträglichkeit* implies a retrospective arrangement of the past and organizes a temporality that is not linear but recursive. It is the temporality of literature, insofar as it tries to express the truth, a truth that is not just a subjective projection, a glib fiction or a shared hallucination.

This was the first question posed by J. M. Coetzee about the unstable mixture of truth and fiction in psychoanalysis when he began a series of conversations with a psychoanalyst, Arabella Kurtz. Is psychoanalysis a process by which one slowly pieces together a deeply hidden, unpalatable, and unconscious truth, or a convenient narrative by which one fabricates an empowering fiction that will help one live better? Pressed on the question of a truth that "works," Arabella Kurtz replied sensibly, echoing Hustvedt:

> There is a need for the psychotherapist to help the patient dig deeper and come to a way of understanding why they are so unhappy that has not been possible before, usually because something painful or difficult cannot be faced. When this happens, however imperfect or incomplete, it feels like truth. Not historical or scientific or philosophical truth, but emotional truth.[14]

Is this emotional truth founded on the pathos of proximity or distance, on empathy, sympathy or the distant hospitality for an absolute Other? We will have to turn to Coetzee's recent fiction to answer these questions.

9

Pathos of the Future

Nihilism and Hospitality in *The Childhood of Jesus*

To take up the question posed by Hustvedt's treatment of trauma, one can say that the first novels of J. M. Coetzee tried to let the wounds of colonial and post-colonial times South Africa speak, often by having them bleed openly. This was be the case of the notorious ending of *Disgrace*, in which the last image of euthanized dogs serves as an ambiguous and haunting reminder that nothing has been settled politically or ethically in post-apartheid South Africa. The novels and texts that followed have opened other fields, either by launching a sort of "auto-fiction" in which one cannot distinguish between "real" memories and invented stories, or by creating new novelistic spaces to explore. I will focus on the latest of these, *The Childhood of Jesus*.[1]

Virgin soil

The first thing that strikes one is that, when we follow the engrossing adventures of Simón and David as they try to adapt to a new world in which they are refugees from another continent, one hesitates when assessing Novilla, a city that seems designed for immigrants rescued from their former lives. Some aspects of life there are admirable, others revolting. It may be too soon to judge, for "Novilla" in Spanish refers to a young heifer, a cow that has not borne a calf, a "virgin" cow in which we see the foreshadowing of the choice of Inés, the Virgin of the plot. It also sketches the futurity contained in the novel's allegory. Is Novilla the site for a utopia or a dystopia? In many ways, *The Childhood of Jesus* inverses the Russian novel of *The Master of Petersburg*, both being linked by the theme of a father coming to terms with paternity by facing a "son" who is not really his son. *The Master of Petersburg* begins after the death of Pavel, and what stands out is the struggle between two types of "Russian" pathos and two utopias. The novel of Novilla/Australia would offer a development of the moment when Dostoevsky and Anna make love for the last time in the novel, and she blurts out: "So was that meant to bring about the birth of the saviour?"[2] Meanwhile, the clash between a self-tortured Dostoevsky, who understands his failings as a substitute father for Pavel, and the nihilist Nechaev, who exploits the novelist's guilt for his revolutionary aims, is the narrative backbone of a novel full of sexual crises, epileptic swooning, existential despair, metaphysical anguish, and deep pathos. It looks as if the world of "Russian characters" exalted by T. S. Eliot during the First World War had come back to life, with echoes of *The Devils* (*The Possessed*) or *Brothers Karamazov*.

There could be no stronger contrast with the programmed destruction of affect in the world of Novilla. If it is a utopia, it is mostly because peace and good will are offered to all newcomers; there is work to be found, however badly paid and exhausting, and enough to eat in times of scarcity. The side of dystopia comes to the fore once we understand that this world is deprived of pathos, emotion, and sexual desire. All strong affects, mostly those connected with love and sex, have vanished, perhaps because they are perceived as responsible for the unnamed disaster in the old world. The drift of the novel is to suggest obliquely the need for a Savior, someone capable of breaking with a weak consensus against pathos. A Savior will bring back the missing salt of life. Such a program implies reawakening not only pathos as the unleashing of unholy passions, but also the Nietzschean "pathos of distance," whose drawback is that it entails a rejection of egalitarian equanimity. As Nietzsche repeated, the death of God led to a worse nihilism, the "flattening" of affect, since all strong values have vanished.[3]

The question of messianism facing an all-too-bland or flat nihilism is less a religious question in *The Childhood of Jesus* than a linguistic question, as suggested by a remark made by Coetzee to Paul Auster. Coetzee refers to Jacques Derrida's *Monolingualism of the Other* in an exchange of letters from May 2009,[4] and he quotes the beginning of this book in which Derrida imagined that someone, looking very much like him, was to proclaim in French: "I only have one language; it is not mine."[5] Coetzee compares his relation with the English language with Derrida's assertion that he does not "have" the French language and writes:

> What interested me is Derrida's claim that, though he is/was monolingual in French (monolingual by his own standards—his English was excellent, as I am sure, was his German, to say nothing of his Greek), French is/was not his mother tongue. When I read this it struck me that he could have been writing about me and my relation to English; and a day later, it struck me further that neither he nor I is exceptional, that many writers and

intellectuals have a removed or interrogative relation to the language they speak and write, in fact that referring to the language one uses as one's mother tongue (*langue maternelle*) has become distinctly old-fashioned.

(HN, 65–6)

Coetzee develops the implications of Derrida's remark by adducing his own sense of non-ownership facing English. For him, English was one among other subjects that he had to learn at school. Even though he spoke English fluently, Coetzee imagined the "English" language to mean, literally, the property of the English. The English alone could own English. English would be the language of one human group, a group owning an empire in which large parts of Africa happened to be. English was the language of those who defeated the Boers and ruled South Africa. As Joyce said about Stephen Dedalus who was aware that he was using the language of the conqueror of his nation, the same words do not have the same value for the oppressed and for the oppressor: "The language in which we are speaking is his before it is mine. How different are the words *home, Christ, ale, master*, on his lips and on mine! I cannot speak or write these words without unrest of spirit."[6]

What Joyce experienced as a young man in colonial Dublin was not different from Coetzee's youth in South Africa, a former British dominion plagued by the rise of Apartheid. If Coetzee's family was bilingual, switching easily from English to Afrikaans, this was not the case for Joyce's family: they spoke English and not Gaelic; only Nora Barnacle did. Later, Joyce and Nora used the Triestine dialect to converse in the family. In Derrida's family, no other language but French was spoken. However, at the age of ten, Jackie Derrida was turned away from his French high-school. In 1942, Vichy's racial laws set a quota for Jewish children—an anti-Semitic zeal of the French administration that could not be blamed on the Nazi regime: the rules were imposed by the French colonial administration to please the German authorities. The trauma had lasting effects for Derrida and explains his complex position facing the French language—the language in which he spoke, wrote, and thought was never fully his "mother-tongue." When British and American troops landed in Algeria, Morocco, and Tunisia, Derrida, who had been sent to a Jewish school and felt that he did not belong there either, went back to his old school after French nationality had been restored to the Jewish community. At the other tip of the same continent, in Cape Town, Coetzee was just two years old.

These biographical details apprehend a larger history that is envisioned, at times obliquely, by Coetzee's novels. In the context of colonial history, we understand how the author was caught in conflicting allegiances when he went to England at the age of twenty-one. He could speak English better than most of the "natives," but as soon as he opened his mouth, he betrayed that he was a foreigner. When they were speaking their mother tongue, he borrowed it as a guest (HN, 67). The predicament seems universal: how can anyone conceive of language as his or her own? Paul Auster's response from New York stresses the dispossession always implied by linguistic inheritance. Auster was well placed to grasp the contingent character of one's relation to language: "Just three generations ago, my great-grandparents spoke Russian, Polish, and Yiddish. That I was raised in an English-speaking country strikes me as a wholly contingent fact, a fluke of history" (HN, 70).

Auster's letter mentions an involuntary joke, the ridiculously serious assertion made by a Southern fundamentalist he heard on the radio. This person said that the United States should stop wasting money teaching foreign languages and added: "If English was good enough for Jesus, it's good enough for me" (HN, 69). Here would be another version, hilarious or sinister, as you want, of the "monolingualism of the other"! Auster generously decides that this remark does not just betray provincial stupidity and American backwardness but confirms his intuition that "your world is your language." Indeed, it is difficult to see anything beyond your language, especially if you live in the Bible belt. He writes: "It is inconceivable to you that the son of God could have spoken a language other than your own, for he is the world, and the world exists in one language only, the one that happens to be yours" (HN, 70). Could Auster's funny vignette have triggered an associative process and planted the seeds of a story about the childhood of Jesus? If this had been the case, it would leave us wondering what language Jesus really "had." What do we know about the language of Jesus, let alone the language of God? The riddle was often solved in this manner: God would have written the first tables of the law, before Moses destroyed them, and spoken to Moses, in Hebrew; Jesus, or Christ, or Rabbi Jeshua, spoke and wrote in Aramaic, the lingua franca of Palestine in the first century AD, a language that gave birth to Arabic.

Language lessons

This linguistic divergence suggests that we should examine the name of one of the main protagonists of *The Childhood of Jesus*, Simón. It alludes to a foundational pun for the Gospels, no less crucial for the subsequent institutional history of Christianity. John 1:42 presents Jesus's address to his most faithful disciple as: "You are Simón son of John, you shall be called Cephas", which means "Peter." Cephas, a nickname given by Jesus to the apostle usually known as Simón, turns him into "Simón Peter." The Greek of John 1:42 is transliterated as Κηφᾶς (Kēphâs). There was no etymological link between the apostle's given name (Simón) and the Aramaic nickname, kêpâ, meaning "rock" or "stone." In Greek, a sigma had to be added to kêpâ so as to make the name sound masculine. We now accept the Greek translation of Πέτρος (*Petros*) as Peter. We can think of other famous translations: the name of Joyce deriving from a French name, Joyeux; Freud's name translated into German to mean "joy"; a French Huguenot family giving to Beckett the liquid echoes of Bequet; not to mention another immigrant, most likely also French, Dirk Couché, born in 1655—possibly a Huguenot too—whose name was transliterated as Coetsé after he had settled in The Cape. He settled on a farm in Stellenbosch that would be called Coetzenburg.[7] All this should make us look closely at diacritics like accents.

If the main protagonist's name is Simón with an accent on the "o," this name is not even his real name, since he mentions Belstar, their port of arrival: "This is where they gave us our names, our Spanish names." (CJ, 2) In fact, Simón, the focalizer of the narrative, is always called "he." We are reminded of his name when he is addressed by other characters or has to decline his identity. Similarly, David is not the child's name: Elena notes that Simón keeps referring to him as "the boy." Simón explains his use of the generic: "David is a name they gave him at the camp. He doesn't like it, he says it is not his true name. I try not to use it unless I have to" (CJ, 56). Such a denial of one's name takes us to the domain of what Freud called a "family romance," in which one is likely to imagine one's parents as noble personages if not supernatural beings.

Foundations entail new baptisms, often a wholesale renaming process. Joyce quipped that the Catholic Church was founded upon a pun—Peter's name. An early mode of Christian punning corresponded to a linguistic baptism working via translations from Hebrew to Aramaic to Greek and to Latin. From the Hebrew Shim'on, meaning "hearing, or he who hears," we have Cephas, Petros, Petrus, and Peter. Such an accretive punning process played a huge role in the constitution of the Gospels themselves. In order to follow these investigations, we should not limit ourselves to the "authentic" or "canonical" gospels but take into account a larger tradition that includes deviant, apocryphal, or even subversive gospels. One of these is called the Gospel of Thomas. I want to quote a passage that has always intrigued me and seems relevant in the context.

The gospels alluded to by the title of the novel should include the gospels of pseudo-Thomas or pseudo-Matthew if only because they describe the childhood of Jesus. Those important years of formation are skipped or dealt with cursorily by the canonical gospels: their attention focuses on the circumstances of the birth before meeting Jesus as an adolescent and an adult. In the apocryphal gospels, we discover a wild and often terrifying younger Jesus. He kills with one gaze at the least provocation. In the Gospel of Thomas, Jesus has killed two boys who annoyed him and has blinded all those around for refusing to recognize his divine status.[8] Hearing of the deaths, curses, and unsocial behavior, Zacchaeus, a schoolteacher, decides to teach Jesus to read, which, he assumes, will subdue his fierce spirit, even though Joseph denies that it is possible, for only God can teach Jesus anything (IGJT, 113). Jesus agrees: nothing can be taught to him because he was alive before the teacher was born; he can bring wisdom to the teacher and tell him the date of his death. The others stare in awe: the child is barely five years old and he speaks like a prophet. The teacher insists: "Bring him to the classroom and I'll teach him the alphabet" (IGJT, 115). Here is the scene:

> The teacher wrote the alphabet for him and began the instruction by repeating the letter alpha many times. But the child clammed up and did not answer him for a long time. No wonder, then, that the teacher got angry and struck him on the head. The child took the blow calmly and replied to him, "I'm teaching you rather than being taught by you: I already know the letters you're teaching me, and your condemnation is great. To you these letters are like a bronze pitcher or a clashing cymbal, which can't produce glory or wisdom because it's all just noise. Not does anyone understand the extent of my wisdom." When he got over being angry he recited the letters from alpha to omega very quickly. Then he looked at the teacher and told him: "Since you don't know the real nature of the letter alpha, how are you going to teach the letter beta? You imposter, if you know, teach me first the letter alpha and then I'll trust you with the letter beta."
>
> (IGJT, 117)

Jesus asks the teacher to describe alpha. Zacchaeus remains silent. Then, with the audience listening raptly, Jesus explains the letters. He makes the teacher notice "the arrangement of the first letter"— "How it has two straight lines or strokes proceeding to a point in the middle, gathered together, elevated, dancing, three-cornered, two-cornered, not antagonistic, of the same family (*omogeneis*), providing the alpha has lines of equal measure" (IGJT, 119). Jesus minutely describes Alpha, the first letter of the Greek alphabet, with its loop crossing in the middle, not Aleph, the first letter in Hebrew and Aramaic. Zacchaeus hears the child present intricate allegories (*allegorias*) regarding letters, and feels that he is a fraud. He cannot justify his profession and complains that he is "utterly bewildered" (IGJT, 119). In a highly rhetorical passage, Zacchaeus laments his disgrace: a mere child has shamed him by proving his ignorance: "I just don't know, friends," (*agnoô, ô philoi*). He did not know either the *arche* or the *telos* of the alphabet (IGJT, 122). Once he confesses that he has been an "ignorant schoolmaster," as Jacques Rancière has it, Jesus pardons him. His pardon includes the others, and now the blind can see. Those he had blinded open their eyes and see. After the recantation of the pedagogue, Jesus appears less vicious and unpredictable. The letters have had a sanative effect: another series of miracles resurrect the dead children and heal other people's wounds.

However, the farce is not over yet. Despite the clash with the teacher, Joseph changes his mind and now wants Jesus to learn the alphabet. He enlists a second teacher, who having heard of what happened to Zacchaeus is cautious but also impatient. Soon exasperated, the teacher hits Jesus on the head. Jesus curses him; the teacher falls to the ground, apparently dead. Joseph draws the lesson: "Those who annoy him end up dead" (IGJT, 133). Surprisingly, a third teacher is summoned. This time, Jesus does not waste time discussing letters. He grabs a book at random and interprets it: "Jesus strode boldly into the schoolroom and found a book lying on the desk. He took the book but did not read the letters in it. Rather, he opened his mouth and spoke by the power of the holy spirit and taught the law (*nomos*) to those standing there" (IGJT, 135). Apparently satisfied with his own performance, he revives the second teacher.

These narratives present Jesus as a gifted but willful and contrarian child quite aware of his divine powers. Jesus states in fact, "I am Alpha and Omega," as Revelation 1:8 has it. Being the first and the last letter of the Greek alphabet, he exists from before and after time, hence he is everything. Pedagogues cannot understand the mystical links connecting the first and the second letter of the alphabet, or the first and the last: this would mean understanding Jesus himself.

We find an equivalent of this scene in *The Childhood of Jesus* when David says: "*Yo soy la verdad*" ("I am the truth," CJ, 225). David was asked to write "*Conviene que yo diga la verdad*" ("I must tell the truth") but distorts the sentence willfully. The Jesus of the canonical gospels would say in Spanish: "*Yo soy el camino, la verdad y la vida.*" At this point, however, the teacher explodes and complains about the child's insubordination, stating that there can be only one authority in a classroom (CJ, 225). Authority will have to be subverted, if not discarded in the name of the freedom of the Imagination opening to the otherness of the future.

We have an echo of the Alpha-Omega trope in *The Childhood of Jesus* when David claims that 888 is bigger than 889—for his visual logic of which Jarry would approve, three juxtaposed 8's have a larger volume than 8+8+9. Trying to assert authority and to teach the child the basic rules of arithmetic, Simón thinks:

Why is it that this child, so clever, so ready to make his way into the world, refuses to understand?
"You have visited all the numbers, you tell me," he says. "So tell me the last number, the very last number of all. Only don't say it is Omega. Omega doesn't count."
"What is Omega?"
"Never mind. Just don't say Omega. Tell me the last number, the very last one."

(CJ, 150)

The boy remains silent. Simón reflects that he may have overestimated David's I.Q. He shakes the boy, awaking him from a trance. The boy screams: "You are making me forget! Why do you make me forget? I hate you!" (CJ, 151).

This tense scene echoes Plato's idea that any uneducated child, like the slave of his friend Meno, can "remember" numbers and geometrical shapes because they were already in his soul. Meno's young slave "already had the knowledge in his soul," as Socrates asserts. Unwittingly, we have shifted from a discussion of letters to a discussion of numbers—for both entail a specific pathology for David. This is why he distorts in an amusing fashion Mickey's dog Pluto into Plato. Simón manages to have David leave Daga's apartment where he was watching television (a tricky situation any parent has had to face at some point):

"You can look at Mickey next time," says Daga. "I promise. We will keep him here just for you."
"And Plato?"
"And Plato. We can keep Plato too, can't we, sweetie?"

(CJ, 183–4)

Linked with the Platonician question is the question of autonomy or independence. Plato always tries to bring back written language to a situation of spoken dialogue: there, speakers can be called the "fathers" of their words. What is dangerous, as Derrida has demonstrated about *Phaedrus*, is when writing functions like a wayward son, a son who is not accountable to the authority of the father. Thus, in the scene with the television and Plato, David blurts out: "I haven't got a mother and I haven't got a father. I just am" (CJ, 184). This echo of "I am who I am," can be compared with "I am the Alpha and the Omega." We understand the implications of this specific grammatology: they are both pedagogical (where does the authority of the teacher, of the father, of the mother come from? Is there a "nature" to invoke if we are in a new society where children can be raised by the state, as Rousseau meant it?)

and ethical (can one let a child be seduced by an adult who takes advantage of his naivety?). The quandary has political consequences as well.

David is not a child of television yet, but he wants to learn words visually, that is in a synthetic manner, not letter by letter; this fear is repeated when he counts, for he is afraid of not being able to jump from one number to the next. David succeeds in a synthetic or "global" method as a beginning reader; he has to struggle against similar odds when he tries to master numbers. Letters are tied up to each other, and one is never sure whether counting begins with one or with zero; Simón explains David's innate verticalism to a friend:

> One and one and one make three, you say, and I am bound to agree. Three men in a car: simple. But David won't follow us. He won't take the step we take when we count: *one* step *two* steps *three*. It is as if the numbers were islands floating in a great black sea of nothingness, and he were each time asked to close his eyes and launch himself across the void. *What if I fall?*—that is what he asks himself. *What if I fall and then keep falling for ever?* Lying in bed in the middle of the night, I could sometimes swear that I too was falling—falling under the same spell that grips the boy. *If getting from one to two is so hard*, I asked myself, *how shall I ever get from zero to one?* From nowhere to somewhere: it seemed to demand a miracle each time.
>
> (CJ, 249)

Indeed, there is a need for a daily miracle. Eschatological issues frame the sense of mystery conveyed by each page of the novel. In *The Childhood of Jesus*, the protagonists face a problem posed by what could be called "divine dyslexia," which offers parallels with the "writing lesson" in Claude Lévi-Strauss's *Sad Tropics*.

Thus one nagging question kept returning when I read the novel for the first time: What language did David and Simón speak before they learned Spanish together in Belstar, where they were given daily Spanish lessons for six weeks? I have mentioned the passage in which Simón says that their new names were given in Belstar. Simón and David often complain about having to speak in Spanish. Simón says to Elena: "What do you think I am doing in this country where I know no one, where I cannot express my heart's feelings because all human relations have to be conducted in beginner's Spanish?" (CJ, 106). Is this beginner's Spanish the language the novel is written in and that we read as if it had been translated from the Spanish? We are obviously reading an English text, but the dialogues that we are reading in English are spoken in Spanish by the characters. Once in a while, we are given the actual signifier, as on the first page: "*Centro de Reubicacion Novilla*, says the sign. *Reubicacion*: what does that mean? Not a word he has learned" (CJ, 1). A reader familiar with Coetzee's work will remember the word in Afrikaans or in English from the section of *Life and Time of Michael K.* when Michael endures the Jakkalsdrif Relocation Camp, a resettlement camp.[9] In many ways, *The Childhood of Jesus* rewrites the desperate plight of Michael in a utopian manner.

At first, Simón and David did not share any language. The little that we know is murky: both were on the same boat, the boy's parents were not with him, he might have been sent there to be reunited with his mother. During the trip, David lost a precious pouch containing the name of his mother. Simón met him during the search for the missing letter. They have come to a country in which Spanish is the official language. Immigration is encouraged provided people become fluent in that language. Most of them also come from abroad. There is an uneven progression in language acquisition, for at the beginning, David does not know what *padrino* means (CJ, 28) whereas Simón does (CJ, 33). Simón knows the meaning of *residencia* but later wonders: "*Anodina*: is that a Spanish word?" (CJ, 64). Does Simón only know words with Greek roots? However, when he decides that it is time for David to begin reading, he finds a tattered copy of *Don Quixote* adapted for children. David is so engrossed in it that he never abandons the book and teaches himself to read with it. When they need toilet paper at the end and have only this book, he refuses to tear off a page to clean himself. *Don Quixote* plays a crucial role in the novel, first of all because it is not a book for children, even in a simplified version with illustrations, and we need to turn to this classic.

Don Quixote's dagger

Coetzee ended his Jerusalem Prize Acceptance Speech by alluding to Cervantes: "[H]ow do we get from our world of violent phantasms to a true living world? This is a puzzle that Cervantes' Don Quixote solves quite easily for himself. He leaves behind hot, dusty, tedious La Mancha and enters the realm of faery by what amounts to a willed act of the imagination."[10] At one level, this is what David stands for: he refuses to let himself be gagged by official knowledge and takes up the knight's quest for a more promising future. In which case, Simón plays the part of a reluctant Sancho, who nevertheless accompanies the knight on his quest.

David's enthusiastic reaction to the story of the cave of Montesinos, in which Don Quixote claims that he spent three days and three nights, whereas he was there one hour only, provides a point of entry. Cervantes describes the cave into which the valorous knight slips to converse with the old Montesinos, famous for having cut out the heart of Durandarte, his cousin, after the latter's death. He then brought the heart to Belerma, Durandarte's wife. After this, Merlin had put them under a spell, which imprisoned them in the cave; he had also prophesied that Don Quixote would lift their enchantment.

Why is this episode so often discussed? It is because in the following chapter we find a hand-written note by Cid Hamet Ben Engeli, who asserts that he cannot believe the Montesinos cave story because "it exceeds all reasonable bounds."[11] Notwithstanding this witty inner dialogism, the pseudo-translation (hence the whole story) continues. In the Montesinos cave episode, Don Quixote asks the old Montesinos whether it is true that he has cut out the heart of his friend Durandarte with a dagger. Montesinos confirms the truth of the story, but with one exception: "He replied, all was true, excepting as to the dagger (*daga*): for it was neither a dagger, nor little, but a bright poniard (*puñal buido*) sharper than an awl." (DQ, 615).[12] It is from this passage that Daga derives his name; and his weapon is the knife with which he wounds the gentle Alvaro (CJ, 46).

Daga bypasses the local laws; he seduces both David and Inés, but his name confirms that he is a deceiver, akin to Simon Magus who wanted to buy Jesus's powers and whose name gave the medieval concept of "simony." The fact that Simón shares this very name should alert to such dangerous proximity. However, David trusts Daga because he embodies the very idea of magic. David believes in the efficacy of the spurious cloak of invisibility that he is given at the end, exactly in the same way as he believes in the presence of the treasures glimpsed by Don Quixote in the cave (CJ, 165).

To prove that he can write, David copies one sentence from *Don Quixote*: *Deos sabe si hay Dulcinea o no en el mundo.* ("God knows whether there is a Dulcinea in this world or not." (CJ, 218)). Apart from a misspelling (David writes *Deos* instead of *Dios*), the sentence is correct. Of course, this leads him to ask: "Who is God?" Simón avoids a direct answer, and the child asks again. Simón then says: "God is not no one, but he lives too far away from us to converse with him or have dealings with him. As for whether he notices us, *Dios sabe*" (CJ, 218). The sentence comes from an exchange between the knight and the duke and the duchess, whose aim was to assert the possibility of fiction; Don Quixote himself says: "God knows whether there be a Dulcinea or not in the world, and whether she be imaginary: this is one of those things, the proof whereof is not to be too nicely inquired into" (DQ, 680). This triggers a moment of doubt for Alonso Quixano, the real name of the knight in Cervantes's novel.

Soon, however, "Don Quixote" will die, first in a metaphorical way, because he never existed. The knight can only survive as long as someone (if only the narrator) believes in him. This is followed by Quixano's physical death; a death not caused by illness or old age, but triggered by a melancholic depression. Melancholia engulfs him after he rejects his romantic adventures as delusions. He dies from being "disenchanted" in the modern sense, above all losing his belief in Dulcinea. When Sancho realizes that Quixano is about to die, he pretends to believe in his chivalric delusions, but too late. Sancho even urges him to start a new adventure: "... and who knows, but behind some bush or other we may find the lady Dulcinea disenchanted as fine as heart can wish?" (DQ, 941). Cervantes's novel ends with a paradoxical appeal to romantic fiction once it had been made impossible. When Quixano is restored to sanity, he cannot survive in a rationalistic world. Cervantes suggests that we cannot live without some belief in magic, even if the belief is based on romantic delusions.

The choice of *Don Quixote* as the equivalent of a non-religious Bible of literature is accounted for in the brief but sharp analysis of the novel that Coetzee gave in 1980, in connection with René Girard's theory of triangular desire.[13] "Triangular desire makes its first appearance and becomes a target of analysis in *Don Quixote*, which marks the beginning of the Romanesque tradition of critical fictions. It is thus a specifically modern phenomenon. It arises as a consequence of post-religious humanism and multiplies as social differences are leveled."[14] All of this cannot but call up a canonical essay of the postmodern moment, Jorge Luis Borges's "Pierre Ménard, Author of Don Quixote." That *"fiction"* had been suggested to Borges by the fact that he had first read Cervantes's novel in English as a child. He was disappointed when he later discovered that it came from a Spanish original. In the wonderful exercise of meta-translation that he provides, the narrator takes one sentence from *Don Quixote*, "Truth, whose mother is history, rival of time, depository of deeds, witness of the past, exemplar and adviser to the present, and the future counselor ..." only to disparage the original, "mere rhetorical praise of history,"[15] and heap praise on Pierre Ménard's identical passage, deemed to be groundbreaking, staggering, opening new vistas: a contemporary of William James asserts that history is the foundation of reality: "Historical truth, for Ménard, is not 'what happened'; it is what we *believe* happened."[16] The ironical insertion of belief in what would otherwise be a mere succession of facts also resonates in Coetzee's novel.

Coetzee's novel looks back to the gospels and also to the Bible of modern literature, *Don Quixote*. The main common point between the gospels of Jesus and *Don Quixote* is that both texts deal with the complex links between the old and the new. In *Don Quixote*, the knight labors under the delusion that the ancient code of chivalry still obtains when we know that it is obsolete. The comedy derives from his attempts at reestablishing a code that is at odds with reality. In the gospels, we assume that Jesus is the Redeemer capable of buying our sins back and hence of undoing original sin. Not anyone will accept the validity of the gospels, of course, since it is not a sacred text for the Jews, in the same way as not everyone will accept the canonicity of the apocryphal gospels.

In his Preface, Cervantes flaunts the originality of his conception. He explains that *Don Quixote* will not provide catalogues of other authors as in other books of the times. As he argues tongue in cheek, it is all too easy to take these books, copy the authors' names from A to Z, and "transcribe that very alphabet into your work" (DQ, 19). Of course, we know that Cervantes parodies previous romances and "overthrow[s] that ill-compiled machine of books of chivalry" (DQ, 20). When David asks who was the author of *Don Quixote*, Simón replies that it was "a man named Benengeli" and adds that Benengeli is easy to recognize: "He wears a long robe and has a turban on his head" (CJ, 154). Is Simón making fun of the idea of authorship? He seems to have read *Don Quixote* in his previous life and describes the main character competently for David, explaining that the hero is "a knight in armour, from the old days" (CJ, 151). Readers of *Don Quixote* will remember that the story, as we have seen, is supposed to have been written in Arabic by "Cid Hamet Ben Engeli" (DQ, 104). It would only have been translated into Spanish by Cervantes; indeed, Ben Engeli means in Arabic the "son of the stag." Since stag is "*cervo*," this translates Cervantes's name, splitting it between a totemic animal and the temporal adverb "*antes*," meaning "before," hence suggesting anteriority. Here is another link with the Bible: in both cases, authorship is uncertain, and most interpretive debates derive from thorny issues of translation.

From language games to hospitality: Welcoming the Other

Such meta-fictional games with authorship partly explain why the characters of *The Childhood of Jesus* speak Spanish while looking often frustrated with the language. David expresses his unease close to the end of the novel: "Why do I have to speak Spanish all the time?," he asks, and David answers: "We have to speak some language, my boy, unless we want to bark and howl like animals. And if we are going to speak some language, it is best we all speak the same one. Isn't that reasonable?" (CJ, 186). The dialogue on language continues:

> "But why Spanish? I hate Spanish."
> "You don't hate Spanish. You speak very good Spanish. Your Spanish is better than mine. You are just being contrary. What language do you want to speak?"

"I want to speak my own language."
"There is no such thing as one's language."
"There is! *La la fa fa yam ying tu tu.*"

(CJ, 186)

A demonstration of the otherness of language is provided by a baffling passage, when David, to show that he can sing, intones a song that he says is in English:

Wer reitet so spät durch Dampf und Wind?
Er ist der Vater mit seinem Kind;
Er halt den Knaben in dem Arm,
Er füttert ihn Zucker, er küsst ihm warm.

(CJ, 67)

Readers who know German recognize the most famous poem in the language, Goethe's "Erlkönig." But the text is not accurate. The original goes like this:

Wer reitet so spät durch Nacht und Wind?
Es ist der Vater mit seinem Kind;
Er hat den Knaben wohl in dem Arm,
Er faßt ihn sicher, er hält ihn warm.[17]

(Who rides so late through the night and wind?
It's the father with his child;
He has the boy safe in his arm,
He holds him secure, he holds him warm.)

"Dampf" (mist) has replaced "night," the third line is grammatically incorrect ("halt" should have an umlaut), and the last line distorts the original grotesquely, meaning: "He feeds him sugar, he kisses him warm." Why, above all, is the language English, according to David? Simón doesn't seem to know either, merely adding: "I don't speak English" (CJ, 67). He does not seem to know that David is wrong when he asserts that he loves this English and prefers it to Spanish. I want to stress this moment of dispossession as it emblematizes a certain textual Uncanny. However this moment of singing in German/English is the prelude to the momentous encounter with Inés at *La Residencia*. Here is an extraordinary Annunciation: Simón offers the child to her, asking her to become David's mother. Uncanny ambivalence dominates here. Has Simón sensed a desire for a child in Inés, or has he imagined that she would make a good mother?

Is David a bright child endowed with prophetic powers, or a difficult, opinionated, almost autistic child, who happens to be indulged too much by adoptive parents? The title gives away that David might be a new Christ in disguise, a radical novelty in a world in which Christian lore and the gospels have been forgotten. At the end of the novel, we recognize the mythical pattern of an older father, living in an asexual relationship with a younger woman who may be a virgin, and running away from repressive laws threatening their preternaturally gifted child. They leave Novilla and go north into the unknown in order to start "a new life." Here all is the same, but totally different. The traditional paradigm has been transformed by the Uncanny. As Yoshiki Tajiri argues in "Beyond the Literary Theme Park: J. M. Coetzee's Late Style in *The Childhood of Jesus*,"[18] one finds all the themes of the previous novels in this recent one, which is true but one has to add that they are all impacted by a Freudian Uncanny. The root of this Uncanny seems to be both linguistic and political.

Derrida's analysis of monolingualism ends up proving that language is always an Other's language, a notion we find in Proust as well: the most beautiful books of the world are all written in some kind of foreign language, he famously stated. In Coetzee's work, this generates a different Uncanny from that of Beckett or Kafka. The theme of linguistic alienation combines political denunciation with a curious estrangement predicated upon the Freudian "uncanny." This meditation can be paralleled with what Derrida has to say about hospitality and the "democracy to come." The theme of Hospitality has been treated by Mike Marais in *Secretary of the Invisible: The Idea of Hospitality in the Fiction of J. M. Coetzee*,[19] a book published in 2009, which leaves out *The Childhood of Jesus*. I am providing its missing chapter. Coetzee's novels are political in the sense that they often take up the issue of Hospitality. However, unlike most previous novels that started by describing or evoking a situation of oppression and alienation deriving from the horrors of the Apartheid, here, since we are in a sort of utopia, at first, everything looks positive, bathed in the rosy light of futuristic experiments with the good life. Indeed, life in Novilla is defined by a willingness to accept all immigrants, to provide for them by offering cheap housing, free food, and allowing adults the right to work even when they are unskilled or older like Simón.

However, we soon realize that hospitality has strict limits in Novilla. The first night David and Simón spend there, because of a mishap with a key, they have to sleep in a provisional shelter built from scratch in Ana's garden. They are only given bread and water. Simón, exasperated, miserable with the night's cold, knocks at her door in the middle of the night; she simply throws them a blanket. Simón shouts angrily: "Why do you treat us like this? Like dirt?"

(CJ, 8). They are woken up roughly, given just bread and water. Ana refuses to lend money despite Simón's pleading.

Later on, Ana appears less hostile; she even invites them for a picnic but wants to prevent any sexual innuendo. We guess that, given her enviable status as a nude model for the arts center, this was her concern before. We understand, given the different role played by Elena, that hospitality can entail providing sexual services. This leads to Derrida's powerful meditation on Hospitality, a point of departure for Mike Marais and Derek Attridge. Derrida contrasts an absolute law of Hospitality that he calls "unconditional" with a limited version of hospitality. There is in Derrida a Quixotic quest for an absolute that he knows is impossible, and yet he keeps trying to use as a yardstick to measure diminished reality with it. Hyperbole becomes a dominant trope, which is why Derrida speaks of a hyperbolic hospitality. However, at times Derrida looks like a solid Sancho Panza who keeps his feet on the ground and does not forget the network of performative constraints and rituals imposed by society. For Derrida, thus, "pure" or "unconditional" hospitality implies extreme consequences, since it consists "in leaving one's house open to the unforeseeable arrival of the guest, who can be intrusive, even dangerous, eventually susceptible to cause harm."[20] Pushing the request for unconditionality to a limit, one risks losing one's safety—this would be one of the lessons of *Disgrace*. In contradistinction to this absolute law, there is the array of relative norms that regulate access for the others. They are old customs, written or unwritten rules specifying when and how one can accept a guest, and distinguish between others who are close enough to be considered as brothers and cousins, and other others who are excluded and can be considered as non-human or even animals.

The power of Derrida's analysis comes from his ability to combine those two forms of hospitality. As Samir Haddad states in *Derrida and the Inheritance of Democracy*, "the unconditional law, on its own, is not enough to achieve hospitality, for following this law as such is impossible."[21] However, the conditional laws provide imperfect instantiations of the unconditional law, without which hospitality would be impotent. Haddad sums up this aporia thus: "One could say that the unconditional law depends on the conditional laws *in order to be a law*, whereas the conditional laws depend on the unconditional law *in order to be hospitable*" (DID, 15). In this asymmetrical relationship, there should be a radical openness of the home to the other, but there should be at the same time multiple regulations limiting access to the home. In order to keep its efficiency as a law, unconditional hospitality calls for its own transgression, but in order to be hospitable, the conditional laws of hospitality similarly call for their own transgression.

This paradoxical mechanism is at work in *The Childhood of Jesus*, and it is exemplified by Daga. Unlike Simón who is immediately accepted as one of the stevedores and does not question their regulations, at least not immediately, Daga rejects the status quo on his first day; he refuses the rule prohibiting smoking, takes extra breaks, and demands more than his share of the salary. He quantifies the number of sacks he carries with the productivity limit that he sets: fifty sacks per day, no more. When he is paid for his days of work, he throws the coins at the face of the paymaster and screams contemptuously: "Rat's wage" (CJ, 45). He slashes Alvaro's hand with a switchblade knife, takes the money, and leaves the scene of communal work for good after having stolen the bicycle of the paymaster. David, terrified by the sudden outburst of violence, is not reassured when Simón pretends that nothing has happened.

The whole struggle, brutal and jarring as it is, has the eerie feeling of a dream. If the point is to mount a critique of violence, Simón's apparent acquiescence to Daga's exactions is curious. Daga embodies the human desire to get more than one's share. Why is Simón not critical or active facing a dangerous guest who can turn into an enemy or a rival? He is as conflicted as Conrad's Lord Jim facing the exactions of his evil double, gentleman Brown, in Patusan. Simón gives a little speech about "feeling special" in one's deeper self even though all work the same, which is lost on David, who already betrays an interest in Daga for being different and fun. David then wonders why the workers don't imitate Daga, that is revolt and take all the money. Finally, David, as much a literalist as a budding anarchist, asserts that there will always be money in the moneybox because it is called the moneybox (CJ, 50).

Simón turns away in the scene of the fight; he does not intervene to help his friend Alvaro because the sudden rupture produced by Daga's violent and illegal actions has woken up Simón's nostalgia for the old days. The clash with a rowdy guest shatters the consensus established by the group about happiness. Daga sounds the note of dangerous desire, the asocial need to dominate, the insatiable craving to possess more. He is ready to get everything quickly and by all means. He rejects the measured, simple, and easy enjoyment of a prudently limited present. This issue recurs in the discussion with Elena, who insists that in their new world, no-one should regret the loss of passion for absent delicacies, or miss the old hankering for always missing objects of desire: "This endless dissatisfaction, this yearning for the something-more that is missing, is a way of thinking we are well rid of, in my opinion" (CJ, 63).

Indeed, collective life in Novilla is underpinned by an all-too-rational decision to abolish longing and the endless frustrations of desire, an anhedonic code which corresponds exactly to Nietzsche's definition of nihilism. Not only have they "killed God" but they also erase the differences underpinning desire. The people of Novilla accept the present as it is not only because they live in a state of bare survival, but because the rule is that desire is evil. Once the basic needs are satisfied, there should be no excess of value, neither surplus-value nor lust-value; one has to get rid of surplus enjoyment, as Lacan would say, which might be a good way of leaving capitalism behind, were it not almost impossible. The philosophical discussions with the other stevedores revolve around whether one should live in a timeless present or in a historically conscious society. Simón invokes history when he pleads for more machinery, asserting that a crane would be more efficient to lift and carry the heavy bags from the ships than their backs. He sees history as defined by technological progress, which meets the resistance of the others: they claim that they do not feel history in their bones, a neat echo of Eliot's "historical sense" which should make one feel the history of Europe in one's very bones (CJ, 116). After Simón has convinced them of the progress brought by machinery, he is the first to suffer the consequences when the badly operated crane almost kills him.

The point made by Coetzee's political allegory is clear: no society can abolish its link with history even with the best intentions. What he attacks here is democratic totalitarianism, a collective agreement to limit desires by leading a simple life of labor and occupying evenings with classes on philosophy and the arts. Novilla's Platonician Republic smacks of totalitarianism, even if it is the soft totalitarianism of a meliorist culture. It displays a tolerance that soon exhibits its limits. In the name of educating the boy, one will send him to a specialized school for delinquents despite his young age. Here is what Lacan has called the discourse of the university. Decisions are made for the others in the name of reason, but the rational good is then imposed forcibly to all. To mark a limit to democratic totalitarianism, one needs a new hope, a wish to think a democracy still to come, as Derrida has argued. For this future, a future marked by some pathos, the figure of the child as a quasi-monster full of passion, anarchy, and wild desire is a productive heuristic tool.

The same point was made by Claude Lefort, who contrasted democracy and totalitarianism in view of their antagonistic conceptions of history:

> Democracy proves to be the historical society *par excellence*, a society which, in its very form, welcomes and preserves indeterminacy and which provides a remarkable contrast with totalitarianism which, because it is constructed under the slogan of creating a new man, claims to understand the law of its organization and development, and which, in the modern world, secretly designates itself as *a society without history*.[22]

In order to reconnect a society with its history, it is important to combine the indeterminacy or openness of a democracy to come (to use Derrida's phrase) with a principle as absolute and transcendent as Justice. This is why Simón invokes Justice in the passage preceding the one I quoted:

> I am not trying to save you, he says. [...] Like you I crossed the ocean. Like you I bring no history with me. What history I had I left behind. I am simply a new man in a new land, and that is a good thing. But I haven't let go of the idea of history, the idea of change without beginning or end. Ideas cannot be washed out of us ... [...] The idea of Justice, for instance. We all desire to live under a just dispensation.
>
> (CJ, 114–15)

Even if the workers reach a compromise about a just division of tasks and salaries, the world of Novilla is not perfect as a socialist utopia—for instance, this is not a classless society. There is a police and a powerful bureaucracy; we see idle people living in relative luxury at *La Residencia*, and then discover much worse, with the trophies accumulated by Daga: he has a penthouse in the City Blocks equipped with a television, and besides having a young and sexy girlfriend, he has a spacious apartment with a view. Daga has found short-circuits allowing him to bypass common laws because he embodies the wish to enjoy. He shares with David the fact that he has not renounced his primal narcissism. For instance, when they all meet at Inés's, he wants to have a good time and go out dancing at night (CJ, 191). Earlier, he "tempts" David with the local equivalent of the Disney channel...

However, those material seductions have little force against major issues like the desire to have children, the wish to live in a just world, or the respect for freedom. Inés and Simón agree about these priorities. Throughout the novel, Simón has been yearning for a philosophy "that shakes one. That changes life" (CJ, 238). Acting out the maxim of "You Must Change Your Life," he changes Inés's cosy life of luxury from one day to the next. His main rival is thus the devilish Daga, who is younger, daring, more phallic in his sexuality. He even offered to "give" a child to Inés (CJ, 181) — he is also ready to steal David from both. Simón had accomplished the only possible gift according to Derrida, a free gift of life when he "gave" her a son, David, who then becomes "the light of her life."

In conclusion, I would argue that *The Childhood of Jesus* is not an *Imitatio Christi* but a *Projectio Christi*. At the end of the novel, we do not fall into traditional Christian eschatology. We stay closer to Derrida's concept of "messianicity without a Messiah." If we want to take David as the new Messiah and follow literally the program outlined by the title, it will be only insofar as he announces a "democracy to come." More than the Jesus of the gospels, David appears as a new Adam. Indeed, Adam was called by Romans 5:14 *Adam Forma Futuri:* Adam is the shape of the future, which conveys a generic trope of the "child that gives birth to man." This child has the form of an open-ended future. Because it perpetuates the belief in miracles, the childhood of any child is the childhood of Jesus. Only by paying heed to these strivings and priorities will we keep the door to the future open.

Conclusion

When is a Door Not a Door?

The pathos of distance and the infrathin

Just before opening or closing the eschatological door, let us consider a specific door. Let us stay in front of it, just as Matisse's painting left us in front of a woman who sat forever in front of an aquarium. If we wanted to be inside, we would have to be like Julio Cortázar's axolotl, who ends up changing places with its human observer.[1] To reach this door, I will start from a historical coincidence: Marcel Duchamp and Walter Benjamin both elaborated important theories in Copenhagen. Duchamp spent a fortnight in Denmark in the summer of 1937; it was there that he began taking notes on his new concept of the "infrathin." A year later, Walter Benjamin went to Denmark, for another of his irregular visits to Bertolt Brecht who lived in exile there. Benjamin stayed from June to August 1938. At the end of his stay, needing more quiet and better contacts with the outside world, he went to Copenhagen; it was there that he refined his concept of the aura. It was in the Danish capital that he completed his great study of Baudelaire, a lyric poet in the age of capitalism. I would like to establish a bridge between the two series of thoughts, actions, and interventions.

In July 1937, Duchamp wrote that he was spending two delightful weeks in Denmark. The letterhead bearing the name Hotel Kongen af Danmark carried an enigmatic passage in which he defined the "infra thin" as a minimal difference separating apparently identical objects or people. A second page dated "Copenhagen July 1937" offered more clues: "All identicals, as identical as they may be, and even more the more identical they are, will approach a separative infra-thin difference."[2] These texts remain baffling and endlessly suggestive. Whereas in previous decades Duchamp had worked with the concept of the "ready-made," thinking through the possibility of singling out any mass-produced object, like a bicycle wheel, a porcelain urinal or a metal comb, and then claiming it as work of art by simply signing it, in the late 1930s it seemed that he was going in the opposite direction: he was launching a phenomenology of distance capable of taking into account minute differences between identical objects, quasi-invisible discrepancies commonly forgotten in everyday life, like the distance between the report of a shot from a gun and its impact. This led Duchamp to develop remarks on allegory:

> The possible is an infra thin.
> The possibility for several tubes of color to become a Seurat is the concrete "explication" of the possible as infra thin.
> [sic] allegory on 'forgetting.'[3]

Other notes suggest that according to Duchamp, an allegory is only possible because people forget material differences like the difference between two images (say, a naked woman coming from a well and Truth). They become blended in a single representation: "Allegory (in general) is an application of the infra-thin."[4]

Duchamp and Mary Reynolds may have decided to go to Denmark at the suggestion of Walter Benjamin, who used to stay there with the Brechts, if indeed Duchamp and Benjamin had met earlier in 1937. One critic mentions this possibility. Ecke Bonk refers to the Benjamin archive, quotes Benjamin's memory of meeting Duchamp in the spring of 1937: "Saw Duchamp this morning, some cafe on Blvd. St. Germain ... Showed me his painting: Nu Descendant un escalier in a reduced format, colored by hand en pochoir, breathtakingly beautiful, maybe mention ..."[5] Whether this felicitous encounter of the theoretician of "reproducibility" and its most visible practitioner really took place has been questioned. If it did, Duchamp would have shown Benjamin one of the serial reproductions of his entire *oeuvre* so far, destined to go into the *boîtes en valise*. Whether this was fact or fiction, a year later, Benjamin went to Denmark and stayed for a last time with Brecht in Svendborg, on the island of Iyn. He had come from Paris planning to spend two months with Brecht from June to August 1938. Because of theoretical disagreements, Benjamin left Brecht for a week close to the end of his stay. He went to Copenhagen to finish writing his essay on Baudelaire. Just before, he discussed its theses with Brecht, who had voiced reservations about Benjamin's ideas, as is evident from his journal:

> Benjamin is here. He is working on an essay on Baudelaire. He demonstrates how literature was distorted after '48 by the notion of an immanent, ahistorical epoch. [...] Oddly enough an eccentric idea enabled Benjamin to write it. He assumes something that he calls the "aura" which is connected with dreaming (daydreaming). He says: when you feel someone's gaze alight upon you, even on your back, you respond (!).

The expectation that whatever you look at is looking at you creates the aura. Apparently this has started to disintegrate in recent times, along with rites and rituals. B. discovered this while analyzing films, where the aura is destroyed by the capacity of works of art to be reproduced. All very mystical, despite his antimystical attitudes. This is the way in which the materialistic approach to history is adapted! It is pretty horrifying.[6]

The stay of 1938 was fraught with anxiety over the looming war; there were personal tensions with several friends. It was unlike a happier summer vacation taken by the two writers in Le Lavandou in 1931, during which Benjamin and Brecht had started writing together a detective novel. One idea they had was to stage gangsters communicating messages by making deliberate mistakes when playing chess, an idea that would have delighted Duchamp. What detectives are looking for, above all, are traces. Whereas Brecht reduced history to the traces of capitalistic exploitation and oppression, Benjamin wanted to let traces stand out in their dialectical opposition with the aura, as we have seen with *Blood of a Poet*. Let me quote once more Benjamin's resounding paragraph: "Trace and aura. The trace is the appearance of nearness, however far removed the thing that left it behind may be. The aura is the appearance of a distance, however close the thing that calls it forth. In the trace, we gain possession of the thing; in the aura, it takes possession of us."[7]

This is why the discussion of allegories was so important, as we have seen:

> Allegory recognizes many enigmas, but it knows no mystery. An enigma is a fragment that, together with a matching fragment, makes up a whole. Mystery, on the other hand, was invoked from time immemorial in the image of the veil, which is an old accomplice of distance. Distance appears veiled. Now, the painting of the Baroque [...] has nothing at all to do with this veil. Indeed, it ostentatiously rends the veil and, as its ceiling frescoes in particular demonstrate, brings even the distance of the skies into a nearness, one that seeks to startle and confound.[8]

Not everyone will agree with this definition of the Baroque—it would be contradicted by *La Sapienza* (2014), a film whose main character is obsessed with the Baroque, specifically with the work of the architect Borromini. Eugène Green, the director, has stated in several interviews that he saw the architecture of Borromini as stronger than that of Bernini because it was charged with more "mystical expression." He said: "You are transported toward the summit, the sky, and from outside it's the same thing — a spiraling upward, skyward like a rocket."[9] However, Benjamin's dialectical couple is not limited to this example, and could take into account Cocteau's neoclassical myths and Duchamp's ironical modernism. In these cases, the gaze of the observer will look for the traces of some concept. One will be caught up in proximities, all the while letting oneself be captured by the fascination of irreducible distances. Duchamp's last work exemplifies such a distance; I will even say that it allegorizes a Nietzschean "pathos of distance."

Duchamp's ghostly *Pathosformel*

By general admission, Marcel Duchamp's last work of art, the posthumously unveiled *Given: 1° The Waterfall, 2° The Illuminating Gas*, in the Philadelphia Museum of Art, contains an enigma, even if may not be a mystery. There would be no mystery because the images aim at being as transparent as possible. A while ago, I had believed that I had found the key to the enigma: it would lie in a visual parallel between the first installation ever to be presented as a permanent work of art in a museum and a few tabloid photographs from Los Angeles showing a woman's body cut in two, the ghastly and sensational pictures of the Black Dahlia murder.[10] I had forgotten that the door of "*Etant Donnés*" has no lock. The absence of a lock led me to investigate another consequence of the pathos of distance.

One of the little pleasures afforded by regular visits to the Duchamp rooms of the Philadelphia Museum of Art is to hear visitors commenting on the works, especially when they discuss the last room in which one can see "*Etant Donnés*." I often hear words like: "Let's go, there's nothing to see, it's just an old door." If I tell them: "Go on, take a look, you'll be surprised," which happens once in a while, some thirty seconds later I am thanked for my trouble by a dark look of reproach. Not only have they had to glue their eyes to the two tiny openings in the huge gate, but they have been forced to see in front of their eyes an open vagina, hairlessly gaping, while branches and bricks serve as a realistic background. Behind, a strange lamp turns itself on noiselessly. "Is that all," they often say, implying that this has been too much. It is as if I had become Duchamp's accomplice in his bawdy farce, the installation that he had planned in secret and that he intended to be his posthumous masterpiece. Like Patricia Hampl facing Matisse's portrait of a woman looking at fish in an aquarium, I too was arrested by this work, and meditated about it. I even wrote sections of two books about it in an effort at solving its enigma.[11] I now must admit that I was wrong. The answer is not to be found in the complex allegories inside (the vagina, the woman who looks as if she had been murdered, the allegorical setting) but on the outside—it lies in the very pathos of distance.

I owe to the French art critic Denys Riout to have observed closely the traces left by the sweaty faces of the visitors; for one decade, Riout has taken yearly photographs of the door, which alerted me to a strange phenomenon. Since the opening of the installation in June 1969, the human stain deposited on the wood around the two peepholes has grown. It has created a bigger and darker coloration akin to a gigantic butterfly, quite visible in most reproductions. The ghostly halo keeps a faint trace of the multitude of anonymous viewers who went into the room and gazed inside. One of my friends who worked in the PMA told me that the curators had had to cleanse the door because it started stinking, taking care not to erase the halo altogether. Duchamp, a skilled chess player, foresaw this aspect, calculating in advance the possibility of what might be called a "steatographic inscription", those infinitesimal layers, infra-thin deposits of human skin, sweat and grease, stink and spores.

What result was Duchamp hoping to achieve? The door had to become a literal shroud, a *Sudarium* similar to the famous cloth that Veronica would have used to wipe away the blood and sweat of Jesus. One should not be afraid of performing a blasphemous superposition of the Holy Shroud of Turin, a beautiful myth of the only trace of the Holy Face, with a door barely hiding a naked female sex. Such was Duchamp's Surrealist sense of black humor and mischievous profanation, allied to his very serious assertion that "its viewers make a work of art." Not only had he been the first viewer of his peephole installation, as the detailed instructions for the assemblage prove, but the still life in illusionistic trompe-l'œil was to turn into a "tableau vivant" as well—with the difference that the living person happens to be on the other side of the door.

Unknowingly, viewers glue their faces to the wooden death mask left by the artist. Duchamp's ghost is there, in front of the door, it looks at you when you look inside. Our gazes are attracted by the scandalous object of desire, obviously chosen from a male point of view: the vision of an open woman's vagina. It is visible while being inaccessible. This is not, for all that, where the pathos of distance lies; in a sense, the open sex is all too close for the comfort of the viewer. The point of the work is to materialize art as distance, and this is where we need to mediate on Duchamp's material allegory, as Benjamin had suggested. Thanks to the ghostly signature of the artist, we are united with him, and at the same time an infra-thin distance remains.

When is a door not a door? One answer might be: when it is a Face. The usual response is: when it is ajar. A jar or an aquarium will hold the face looking back at us. The word "ajar" comes from the seventeenth century; it is made up of *a-* as "on" and of *char*, in Old English *cerr*, meaning "turn," or "return." Even if the door is closed and appears first like a stern barn gate, the ghostly auras that inhabit it do return and keep it ajar. "Ajar" would be the motto written on the door, inscribing in its solid wood the unique appearance of a distance, however close it may be, and the endless openness of the future.

Given: :

Duchamp's game with distance and proximity literalizes the most important element of his title: the colon following "Given," which functions as a typographical equivalent of those mischievous peepholes, two spots or dots for our eyes. Typographically, they are vertical, and on the door, horizontal. The word "colon" derives from ancient Greek κῶλον, which means "limb," "member," or "portion of text." One can never get rid of anthropomorphism. Our eyes learn to play with distance, to master its pathos, its proximity when objects are too close, which means that they focus, they play with converging or diverging rays, thus perceiving images reflected or not in an optical system. The need for such a focus should remind us of the need to keep a proper critical rapport, which entails not just optical convergence but also the use of other tools, like Proust's binoculars or the field glasses of the imagination, as Hannah Arendt suggests when talking about understanding and politics:

> Imagination alone enables us to see things in their proper perspective, to be strong enough to put that which is too close at a certain distance so that we can see and understand it without bias and prejudice, to be generous enough to bridge abysses of remoteness until we can see and understand everything that is too far away from us as though it were our own affair. This distancing of some things and bridging the abysses to others is part of the dialogue of understanding, for whose purposes direct experience establishes too close a contact and mere knowledge erects artificial barriers.[12]

Distance marks the critical interval needed to measure the relative objectivity without which there is no understanding; however understanding is not all, and a cynical Nietzschean might reduce it to the Joycean quip: "I overstand you, you understand."[13] Distance should serve as a springboard for creativity, provided it be allowed to remain distance; for distance must remain distance, as a recent poem entitled "Freud's Beautiful Things" by Emily Berry attests:

> It was this childhood scene . . .
> (My mother . . .)

All the while I kept thinking: *her face has such a wild look*
... as though she had never existed
The fact is I have not yet seen her in daylight
Distance must remain distance [...]
Yesterday and today have been bad days
This oceanic feeling, continuous inner monologues
I said: "All the beautiful things I still have to say will have to remain unsaid," and the writing table flooded[14]

Whatever I might add at this point would be superfluous. Just let it flood!

Notes

When no translator is mentioned, I translate from the French and the German.

Introduction

1. Patricia Hampl, *Blue Arabesque: A Search for the Sublime*, New York, Harcourt, 2006. Hereafter in the text abbreviated as BA and page number.
2. Walter Benjamin, "Little History of Photography," in *The Work of Art in the Age of its Technological Reproducibility and Other Writings on Media*, ed. M. W. Jennings, B. Doherty and T. Y. Levin, Cambridge, MA, Harvard University Press, 2008, 285.
3. Walter Benjamin, "The Work of Art: Second Version," in *The Work of Art in the Age of its Technological Reproducibility*, 23.
4. Walter Benjamin, *Das Kunstwerk im Zeitalter seiner technischen Reproduzierbarkeit*, Francfort, Surkamp, 1970, 18.
5. Ibid.
6. Diarmuid Costello, "Aura, Face, Photography: Re-reading Benjamin today," in *Walter Benjamin and Art*, ed. Andrew Benjamin, London, Continuum, 2005, 178. A more critical assessment is provided by Antoine Hennion and Bruno Latour, "How to Make Mistakes on So Many Things at Once—and Become Famous for It," in *Mapping Benjamin: The Work of Art in the Digital Age*, ed. Hans Ulrich Gumbrecht and Michael Marrinan, Stanford, Stanford University Press, 2003, 91–7.
7. See Richard Shiff, "Digitized Analogies," in *Mapping Benjamin*, 63–70.
8. Marcel Proust, "Madame Swann at Home" in *Remembrance of Things Past*, vol. 1, trans. C. K. Scott Moncrieff and Terence Kilmartin, New York, Random House, 1982, 485. *A La Recherche du Temps Perdu*, vol. 1, ed. Jean-Yves Tadié, Paris, Gallimard, Pléiade, 1987, 441.
9. Proust, *Remembrance of Things Past*, vol. 1, 485, *A La Recherche du Temps Perdu*, vol. 1, 442.
10. Walter Benjamin, "The Work of Art: Second Version," in *The Work of Art in the Age of its Technological Reproducibility*, 285.
11. James McFarland, *Constellation: Friedrich Nietzsche and Walter Benjamin in the Now-Time of History*, New York, Fordham, 2013.
12. Friedrich Nietzsche, *Beyond Good and Evil*, trans. Helen Zimmern, New York, New Library, 1906, 197.
13. Friedrich Nietzsche, Notebook 1, autumn 1885–spring 1886, *Writings from the Late Notebooks*, trans. Kate Sturge, Cambridge, Cambridge University Press, 2003, 54.

14 Friedrich Nietzsche, Notebook 9, autumn 1887, *Writings from the Late Notebooks*, 166–7.
15 I want to thank J. Bret Maney for having attracted my attention to this essay.
16 William James, "What Makes a Life Significant," in *The Writings of William James*, ed. John J. McDermott, Chicago, University of Chicago Press, 1977, 648.
17 See Nancy Bentley, *Frantic Panoramas: American Literature and Mass Culture 1870–1920*, Philadelphia, University of Pennsylvania Press, 2009, 269–71.
18 Friedrich Nietzsche, *Ecce Homo* in *On the Genealogy of Morals and Ecce Homo*, trans. Walter Kaufmann, New York, Vintage, 1969, 303.
19 Ibid., 281–2.
20 See Ludwig Binswanger, Aby Warburg, *La guarigione infinita. Storia clinica di Aby Warburg*, eds. Davide Stimilli and Chantal Marazia, Vicenza, Neri Pozza, 2005.
21 Aby Warburg, *Images from the Region of the Pueblo Indians of North America*, trans. Michael Steinberg, Ithaca, Cornell University Press, 1995, 54, and "Bilder aus dem Gebiet der Pueblo-Indianer," *Werke in einem Band*, eds. Martin Treml, Sigrid Weigel, Perdita Ludwig, Suzanne Hetzer, Herbert Kopp-Oberstebrink, and Christina Oberstebrink, Berlin, Suhrkamp, 2010, 561. It is worth looking at Warburg's memories and stray notes, "Reise-Erinnerungen aus dem Gebiet der Pueblo Indianer in Nordamerika," *Werke in einem Band*, 567–600.
22 Gombrich produced an abbreviated edition of Warburg's Atlas in 1937, reduced to 24 panels. He introduced it with a summary of Warburg's philosophy. This Introduction is discussed by Christopher D. Johnson in *Memory, Metaphor, and Aby Warburg's Atlas of Images*, Ithaca, Cornell University Press, 2012, 27.
23 Giorgio Agamben, "Aby Warburg and the Nameless Science," in *Potentialities*, trans. Daniel Heller-Roazen, Stanford, Stanford University Press, 1990, 90.
24 Aby Warburg, "Dürer and Italian Antiquity," in *The Renewal of Pagan Antiquity*, trans. David Britt, Los Angeles, Getty Institute Publications, 1999, 558, and Aby Warburg, "Dürer und die italienische Antike," *Werke in einem Band*, 177.
25 Ibid.
26 Proust, *Remembrance of Things Past*, vol. 1, 603.
27 Ibid.
28 Philippe-Alain Michaud, *Aby Warburg and the Image in Motion*, trans. by Sophie Hawkes, New York, Zone Books, 2007, 251.
29 See Georges Didi-Huberman, *L'Image Survivante, Histoire de l'art au temps des fantômes selon Aby Warburg*, Paris, Minuit, 2002.
30 See Mikhail Bakhtin, "Forms of Time and of the Chronotope in the Novel," in *The Dialogic Imagination: Four Essays*, trans. Caryl Emerson and Michael Holquist, Austin, University of Texas Press, 1981, 84–258.

31 Peter Sloterdijk, *You Must Change Your Life*, trans. Wieland Hoban, Cambridge, Polity, 2013, 36, then 61–5 and 111–17.
32 Sloterdijk, *You Must Change Your Life*, 149–59.
33 Michel Foucault, "Introduction" to Ludwig Binswanger, *Le Rêve et l'existence*, in *Dits et Ecrits, I, 1954–1975*, ed. Daniel Defert and François Ewald, Paris, Gallimard, Quarto, 2001, 134.
34 Ibid., 132.
35 Sloterdijk, *You Must Change Your Life*, 151.
36 I do not agree with Chris Danta, who, in a good presentation of Sloterdijk's "Aesthetics of Verticality," accuses the philosopher of being "insensitive to the emotional implications of the vertical orientation of the humans." See Christ Danta, "Acrobats and Ascetics: Peter Sloterdijk and the Aesthetics of Verticality," *European Journal of English Studies*, vol. 19, number 1, April 2015, 75.

1 "Pathos of Distance"

1 James Huneker, *The Pathos of Distance*, New York, Charles Scribner's Sons, 1913, was republished in 1922, one year after Huneker's death. E-book 2012, Forgotten Books, facsimile reprint of the 1922 edition. Hereafter in the text abbreviated as PD and page number.
2 James Huneker, *Egoists: A Book of Supermen*, New York, Charles Scribner's Sons, 1909. Reprinted in 1918. Hereafter in the text abbreviated as E and page number.
3 Roland Barthes, *Comment Vivre Ensemble, Cours et Séminaires au Collège de France, 1976–1977*, Paris, Seuil, IMEC, 2002; Roland Barthes, *How to Live Together*, trans. Kate Briggs, New York, Columbia University Press, 2013. Hereafter in the text abbreviated as HLT and page number.
4 Camille Henrot, "How to Live Together? An Artist Project Revisiting Roland Barthes's Seminal Lectures on Coexistence," Available online at www.slought.org/resources/how_to_live_together. Last accessed September 22, 2015.
5 Arnold Schwab, *James Gibbons Huneker: Critic of the Seven Arts*, Stanford, Stanford University Press, 1963.
6 James Huneker, *Steeplejack*, New York, Scribner's Sons, 1921, 249.
7 James Huneker "Schoenberg, Musical Anarchist, Who Has Upset Europe," *New York Times*, January 19, 1913, Section 5, 9. Mistakenly quoted by Schwab as from 1912, see Schwab, *James Gibbons Huneker: Critic of the Seven Arts*, 211.
8 Quoted by Schwab, *James Gibbons Huneker: Critic of the Seven Arts*, 210.
9 T. S. Eliot, A review of *Egoists: A Book of Supermen*, *The Harvard Advocate*, LXXXVIII, October 5, 1909, 24.
10 Quoted by Schwab, *James Gibbons Huneker: Critic of the Seven Arts*, 254.
11 Ibid., 79.

12 Ibid.
13 See Friedrich Nietzsche, *On the Genealogy of Morality*, trans. Carol Diethe, Cambridge, Cambridge University Press, 1994, 12.
14 Ibid., 13.
15 See the collection published in 1913, *For & Against: Views on the Infamous 1913 Armory Show*, Tucson, Hol Art Books, 2009.
16 See Schwab, *James Gibbons Huneker: Critic of the Seven Arts*, 224.
17 Huneker, *Egoists*, 6. I presented egoism as Joyce's main philosophy in Jean-Michel Rabaté, *James Joyce and the Politics of Egoism*, Cambridge, Cambridge University Press, 2001.
18 See Schwab, *James Gibbons Huneker: Critic of the Seven Arts*, 197.
19 I discuss this in Jean-Michel Rabaté, "Gender and Modernism: *The Freewoman, The New Freewoman* and *The Egoist*," in *The Oxford Critical and Cultural History of Modernist Magazines, vol. I*, eds. Peter Brooker and Andrew Thacker, Oxford, Oxford University Press, 269–89.
20 Friedrich Nietzsche, *Twilight of the Idols / The Anti-Christ*, trans. by R. J. Hollingdale, London, Penguin, 1990, 102.
21 I discuss this in Jean-Michel Rabaté, *Etant Donné: 1) L'Art, 2) Le Crime*, Dijon, Presses du Réel, 2010, 45–55.
22 See Barthes's note in Barthes, *How to Live Together*, 189.
23 Sigmund Freud, "On Narcissism: An Introduction," in *General Psychological Theory*, ed. Philip Rieff, New York, Collier, 1963, 68–9.
24 Pierre Force, "Beyond Metalanguage: Bathmology," in *Writing the Image after Roland Barthes*, ed. J-M Rabaté, Philadelphia, University of Pennsylvania Press, 1997, 187–95.
25 Gilles Deleuze, *Nietzsche et la philosophie*, Paris, Presses Universitaires de France, 1967, 3. Hereafter in the text abbreviated as N&P and page number.
26 See Gilles Deleuze, *Expressionism in Philosophy: Spinoza*, trans. Martin Joughin, New York, Zone, 1992.
27 Friedrich Nietzsche, *The Will to Power*, trans. Walter Kaufmann and R. J. Hollingdale, New York, Vintage, 1968, 301.
28 Roland Barthes, *The Roland Barthes Reader*, ed. Susan Sontag, New York, Hill and Wang, 1994, 4.
29 Ibid., 15.
30 Nietzsche, *Beyond Good and Evil*, 191.
31 André Gide, *The Immoralist*, trans. David Watson, New York, Penguin, 2001, 7.
32 Roland Barthes, "On Gide and his Journal," in *The Roland Barthes Reader*, 7.
33 Antoine Compagnon, *Les Antimodernes, de Joseph de Maistre à Roland Barthes*, Paris, Gallimard, 2005, 404–40.
34 Roland Barthes, *Writing Degree Zero*, trans. Annette Lavers and Colin Smith, New York, Farrar, Strauss and Giroux, 1968, 50, translation modified.
35 Roland Barthes, "Les Sorties du texte," in *Oeuvres Complètes*, vol. II, ed. Eric Marty, Paris, Seuil, 1994, 1614–22.
36 Roland Barthes, "Outcomes of the Text," in *The Rustle of Language*, trans. Richard Howard, New York: Hill and Wang, 1986, 247.

37 Ibid., 243.
38 Georges Bataille, "The Big Toe," in *Visions of Excess, Selected Writings 1927-1939*, edited by Alan Stoekl, Minneapolis, University of Minnesota Press, 1985, 23.
39 Barthes, "Outcomes of the Text," 239.
40 Ibid., 242.
41 Ibid., 245.
42 Ibid., 246-7.
43 Roland Barthes, "Pouvoirs de la tragédie antique," (1953) in *Oeuvres Complètes*, vol. I, ed. Eric Marty, Paris, Seuil, 1993, 222.
44 Roland Barthes, *Camera Lucida: Reflections on Photography*, trans. Richard Howard, New York, Noonday Press, 1981, 117. Hereafter in the text abbreviated as CL and page number.
45 Donald W. Winnicott, "Fear of Breakdown," publication overseen by Clare Winnicott, *International Review of Psychoanalysis*, 1, 1974, 103-7.
46 Georges Bataille, *The Bataille Reader*, eds. Fred Botting and Scott Wilson, Oxford, Blackwell, 1997, 330 and 340.
47 Roland Barthes, "Preface for an Album of Photographs by Lucien Clergue," in *Oeuvres Complètes*, vol. III, ed. Eric Marty, Paris, Seuil, 1995, 1204.
48 Georges Bataille, *Guilty*, trans. Stuart Kendall, SUNY, 2011, 93.
49 Jacques Derrida, "From Restricted to General Economy," in *Writing and Difference*, trans. Alan Bass, Chicago, Chicago University Press, 1978, 261. Hereafter in the text abbreviated as WD and page number.
50 Benjamin, "Little History," in *The Work of Art in the Age of its Technological Reproducibility*, 276.
51 Ibid., 276-7.

2 "Hard" Modernism

1 I discuss Rimbaud's statement "One has to be absolutely modern" in Jean-Michel Rabaté, *The Ghosts of Modernity*, Gainesville, University Press of Florida, 1996, 194-5.
2 Walter Benjamin, *The Arcades Project*, trans. Howard Eiland and Kevin McLaughlin, Cambridge, MA, Harvard University Press, 1999, 545. Hereafter in the text abbreviated as AP and page number. Walter Benjamin, *Das Passagen-Werk*, edited Rolf Tiedemann, Frankfurt, Suhrkamp, 1983, vol. 2, 677.
3 Charles Baudelaire, *The Painter of Modern Life*, London, Phaidon, 1995, 10.
4 See *The Gender of Modernism: A Critical Anthology*, ed. Bonnie Kime Scott, Bloomington, Indiana University Press, 1990.
5 Virginia Woolf would not belong to international Modernism because she was "an English novelist of manners" according to Hugh Kenner, "The Making of the Modernist Canon," in *Mazes*, San Francisco, North Point Press, 1989, 37.

6   Ezra Pound, "The Hard and Soft in French Poetry" (1918), *Literary Essays*, ed. T. S. Eliot, London, Faber, 1954, 285.
7   Wayne Koestenbaum, *Double Talk: The Erotics of Male Collaboration*, London, Routledge, 1989, 113.
8   T. S. Eliot, *The Waste Land; A Facsimile and Transcript of the Original Drafts Including the Annotations of Ezra Pound*, ed. Valerie Eliot, London, Faber, 1971, 47.
9   Ibid., 97.
10 Ibid., 45.
11 Kimberly Healey, "French Literary Modernism," in *Modernism*, vol. 2, eds. Astradur Eysteinsson and Vivian Liska, Amsterdam, John Benjamins Publishing Company, 2007, 801.
12 Marcel Proust, "Le Pouvoir du Romancier," in *Contre Sainte-Beuve, Pastiches et Mélanges, Essais et Articles*, ed. Pierre Clarac and Yves Sandre, Paris, Gallimard, Pléiade, 1971, 413. The text can be dated from 1895 to 1900.
13 Stéphane Mallarmé, "Crisis of Verse," in *Divagations*, trans. Barbara Johnson, Cambridge, Harvard University Press, 2007, 201.
14 Ibid., 203.
15 See Rabaté, *The Ghosts of Modernity*, 188–93.
16 I have described this moment in Jean-Michel Rabaté, *1913, The Cradle of Modernism*, Oxford, Wiley-Blackwell, 2007, 46–71.
17 Marcel Proust, "Contre l'Obscurité," in *Contre Sainte-Beuve, Pastiches et Mélanges, Essais et Articles*, 390–5.
18 Ibid., 393.
19 Mallarmé, *Divagations*, 236.
20 Ibid., 235.
21 Benjamin B. Bourdon, *L'Expression des Emotions et des Tendances dans le Langage*, Paris, Felix Alcan, 1892.
22 Wilhelm Wundt, *Elements of Folk Psychology* (1900), trans. Edward Leroy Schaub, Project Gutenberg, 2013, 59–64.
23 Alfred Jarry, *Oeuvres Complètes*, vol. III, eds. Henri Bordillon, Patrick Besnier, Bernard Le Doze and Michel Arrivé, Paris, Gallimard, Pléiade, 1988, 531.
24 Léon-Paul Fargue à Alfred Jarry, 5 mai 1893, from Cobourg. Available online at www.alfredjarry.wordpress.com/1893/05/. Last accessed September 22, 2015.
25 See "César-Antechrist" in Alfred Jarry, *Oeuvres Complètes*, vol. I, ed. Michel Arrivé, Paris, Pléiade, 1972, 271–332. Hereafter in the text abbreviated as JOCI and page number. César-Antechrist says: "I am the infinite Intuition ..." (Jarry, *Oeuvres Complètes*, vol. I, 330).
26 *Gestes et Opinions du docteur Faustroll, pataphysicien*, in Jarry, *Oeuvres Complètes*, vol. I, 685–6. See also Marieke Dubbelboer, *The Subversive Poetics of Alfred Jarry: Abusing Culture in the Almanachs du Pere Ubu*, London, Legenda, 2012, 35–7.

27 See their exchange in Jarry, *Oeuvres Complètes*, vol. III, 635-6.
28 Alfred Jarry, *The Supermale*, trans. Ralph Gladstone and Barbara Wright, Cambridge, Exact Change, 1999. Hereafter in the text abbreviated as TS and page number.
29 Juvenal, *The Satires*, Satire VI "Don't Marry," trans. A. S. Kline, 2011. Available online at www.poetryintranslation.com/PITBR/Latin/JuvenalSatires6.htm. Last accessed September 22, 2015.
30 See Alfred Jarry, *Messaline, Roman de l'ancienne Rome*, in *Oeuvres Complètes*, vol. II, eds. Henri Bordillon, Patrick Besnier and Bernard Le Doze, Paris, Gallimard, Pléiade, 1987, 75.
31 Alfred Jarry, *Messalina, A novel of Imperial Rome*, trans. John Harman, London, Atlas Press, 1985, 9. Hereafter in the text abbreviated as MNIR and page number.
32 Sigmund Freud, "Project for a Scientific Psychology" (1895), in *The Invention of Psychoanalysis, Letters to Wilhelm Fliess*, trans. Eric Mosbacher and James Strachey, New York, Basic Books, 1977, 441.
33 Guillaume Apollinaire, "Feu Jarry" (1909), *Oeuvres en prose complètes*, vol. II, eds. Pierre Caizergues and Michel Décaudin, Paris, Gallimard, Pléiade, 1991, 1040.
34 Gilles Deleuze, "An Unrecognized Precursor to Heidegger: Alfred Jarry," in *Essays Critical and Clinical*, trans. D. W. Smith and M. A. Greco, Minneapolis, University of Minnesota Press, 1997, 93.

3 The Birth of Irish Modernism from the Spirit of Nietzscheanism (Yeats, Joyce, and Beckett)

1 See Sam Slote, *Joyce's Nietzschean Ethics*, Houndmills, Palgrave, 2013, and Otto Bohlmann, *Yeats and Nietzsche: An Exploration of Major Nietzschean Echoes in the Writings of William Butler Yeats*, London, Palgrave Macmillan, 1982.
2 See Vincent Sherry's *Modernism and the Reinvention of Decadence*, Cambridge, Cambridge University Press, 2015, 89-91 and 182-189 for astute remarks on Ezra Pound and Nietzsche.
3 Maud Gonne wrote this to Yeats just after her disastrous marriage to MacBride in 1903. Quoted by R. F. Foster, *W. B. Yeats: A Life, I. The Apprentice Mage, 1865-1914*, Oxford, Oxford University Press, 1997, 287.
4 Havelock Ellis, "Friedrich Nietzsche I," *The Savoy* 2, April 1896, 79-94; "Friedrich Nietzsche II," *The Savoy* 3, July 1896, 68-81; "Friedrich Nietzsche III," *The Savoy* 4, August 1896, 57-63.
5 William Butler Yeats, "William Blake and His Illustrations to *The Divine Comedy*," *The Collected Works*, vol. IV, ed. George Bornstein and Richard J. Finneran, New York, Scribner, 2007, 97.
6 Ibid., 377.

7   See Jean Delay, *The Youth of André Gide*, trans. June Guicharnaud, Chicago, The University of Chicago Press, 1963, especially 468.
8   Louis MacNeice, *The Poetry of William Butler Yeats*, London, Oxford University Press, 1941, 40.
9   William Butler Yeats, *Letters of William Butler Yeats*, ed. Allan Wade, London, Rupert Hart-Davis, 1954, 379.
10 Next to Bohlmann's *Yeats and Nietzsche*, see also Richard Ellmann, *The Identity of Yeats*, New York, Oxford University Press, 1964, 91–7; David Thatcher, *Nietzsche in England, 1890–1914*, Toronto, University of Toronto Press, 1970, 139–73; Denis Donoghue, *William Butler Yeats*, New York, Viking Press, 1971, 52–60; and Frances Nesbitt Oppell, *Mask and Tragedy: Yeats and Nietzsche*, Charlottesville, University Press of Virginia, 1987.
11 William Butler Yeats, *The Collected Poems*, London, Macmillan, 1965, 104. Hereafter in the text abbreviated as CP and page number.
12 William Butler Yeats, *The King's Threshold*, in *The Collected Works of W. B. Yeats*, vol. II, The Plays, eds. David R. Clark and Rosalind E. Clark, New York, Scribner, 2001, 148.
13 See Yeats's note in *The Collected Works of W. B. Yeats*, vol. II, The Plays, 686. Yeats was spurred to this revision by the determined hunger strike of Terence MacSwiney, Lord Mayor of Cork, in 1920. MacSwiney was a playwright himself and his courageous death inspired Nehru and Gandhi, among many others.
14 William Butler Yeats, *On Baile's Strand*, in *The Collected Works of W. B. Yeats*, vol. II, The Plays, 160.
15 Zeev Sternhell, with Mario Sznajder and Maia Asheri, *The Birth of Fascist Ideology*, Princeton, Princeton University Press, 1989, and Zeev Sternhell, *Neither Right nor Left: Fascist Ideology in France*, Princeton, Princeton University Press, 1995.
16 *The Gonne-Yeats Letters, 1893–1938*, eds. Anna MacBride White and A. Norman Jeffares, New York, Norton, 1994, 166.
17 Nietzsche, *Writings from the Late Notebooks*, 98.
18 *Yeats's Vision Papers*, vol. 4, eds. George Mills Harper and Mary Jane Harper, New York, Palgrave, 2001, 86. See 31–2 for an earlier version in which Nietzsche figures as "always on the verge of madness" (32).
19 See James Longenbach, *Stone Cottage: Pound, Yeats & Modernism*, Oxford, Oxford University Press, 1988.
20 *A Critical Edition of Yeats's A Vision*, eds. George Mills Harper and Walter Kelly Hood, London, Macmillan, 1978, 211.
21 Ibid., 211–12.
22 James Joyce, *The Day of the Rabblement*, Folcroft Library Reprint, 1974, 17.
23 Ibid., 17.
24 Ibid., 18.
25 Quoted in Foster, *W. B. Yeats: A Life, I. The Apprentice Mage, 1865–1914*, Appendix, Oxford, Oxford University Press, 537.

26 James Joyce, *Ulysses*, ed. H. W. Gabler, New York, Random House, 1986, Chapter 3, line 496. Hereafter in the text abbreviated to U., followed by chapter and line numbers.
27 John Eglington, *Pebbles from a Brook*, Kilkenny, O'Grady, 1901, 115.
28 James Joyce, *Poems and Exiles*, ed. J. C. C. Mays, London, Penguin, 1992, 10 and note 270 and 275.
29 *Dana: An Irish Magazine of Independent Thought*, ed. John Eglington (W. K. Magee), Dublin, Hodges Figgis, 1904–1905, in *The Modernist Journals Project*, an online archive hosted by Brown University and the University of Tulsa.
30 Ibid., 21.
31 Ibid., 182–8.
32 Ibid., 183.
33 Ibid., 184.
34 Ibid.
35 Ibid., 186.
36 Ibid.
37 Ibid., 187.
38 Ibid., 188.
39 James Joyce, *Selected Letters*, ed. Richard Ellmann, London, Faber, 1975, 285.
40 Friedrich Nietzsche, *Jenseits von Gut und Böse*, Munich, Goldmann, n. d., 5.
41 Samuel Beckett, "Dante .... Bruno. Vico .. Joyce" in *Disjecta*, London, John Calder, 1983, 29.
42 Samuel Beckett, *Proust and Three Dialogues*, London, John Calder, 1965, 66.
43 Samuel Beckett, *The Letters, 1929–1940*, vol. 1, ed. Dan Gunn, Martha Fehsenfeld and Lois Overbeck, Cambridge, Cambridge University Press, 2009, 33.
44 Samuel Beckett, *Murphy*, New York, Grove Press, 1957, 178. Hereafter in the text abbreviated as M and page number.
45 See *Arnold Geulincx's Ethics with Samuel Beckett's Notes*, trans. Martin Wilson, eds. Han Van Ruler, Anthony Uhlmann and Martin Wilson, Leiden, Brill, 2006, and David Tucker, *Samuel Beckett and Arnold Geulincx*, London, Bloomsbury, 2012, 42–70.
46 *Arnold Geulincx's Ethics with Samuel Beckett's Notes*, 247 for the text, and 337 for Beckett's typed notes. Beckett quoted the Latin original of *Ethica*.
47 Ibid., 34.
48 Friedrich Nietzsche, *On the Genealogy of Morality*, trans. Keith Ansell-Pearson, Cambridge, Cambridge University Press, 1994, 106.
49 Nietzsche, *On the Genealogy of Morality*, 107–10, and Friedrich Nietzsche, *Zur Genealogie der Moral*, Munich, Goldmann, 1966, 117.
50 I have developed this theme in Jean-Michel Rabaté, "Beckett's Three Critiques: Kant's Bathos and the Irish Chandos," *Modernism/Modernity*, vol. 18, number 4, 2011, 699–719.
51 Martin Heidegger, *Nietzsche*, Pfullingen, Guenther Neske, 1961.

4 *Ethos* vs. *Pathos* of the New in 1910

1. Aristotle, *"Art" of Rhetoric*, trans. J. H. Freese, Loeb, Cambridge, MA, Harvard University Press, 1926, 1856 a, 17–19.
2. Aristotle, *"Art" of Rhetoric*, 1877 b–1882 a, 169–201.
3. Georg Lukács, *Soul and Form*, edited by John T. Sanders and Katie Terezakis, intro. Judith Butler, Columbia University Press, New York, 2010, 197. Hereafter in the text abbreviated to SF and page number.
4. Ezra Pound, *The Spirit of Romance*, New York, New Directions, 2005, 6. Hereafter in the text abbreviated as SR and page number.
5. Adolf Loos, *Ornament and Crime. Selected essays*, trans. Michael Mitchell, Riverside, Ariadne Press, 1997, 3.
6. Jacques Mercanton quotes Joyce in *The Hours of James Joyce*, trans. Lloyd C. Parks in *Portraits of the Artist in Exile: Recollections of James Joyce by Europeans*, ed. Willard Potts, San Diego, Harcourt Brace Jovanovich, 1986, 207.
7. Virginia Woolf, "Mr. Bennett and Mrs Brown," in *A Woman's Essays*, Harmondsworth, Penguin, 1992, 70.
8. I am paraphrasing definitions provided by Howard Kainz in his translation of selections from Hegel's *Phenomenology of Spirit*, Philadelphia, University Press of Pennsylvania, 1994, 107.
9. Woolf, *A Woman's Essays*, 71.
10. Ann Banfield, *The Phantom Table*, Cambridge, Cambridge University Press, 2000.
11. Virginia Woolf, *The Flight of Mind, The Letters of Virginia Woolf*, vol. I : 1888–1912, ed. Nigel Nicolson, London, The Hogarth Press, 1975, 446.
12. Ibid., 440.
13. Ibid.
14. Georg Lukács, "On the Nature and Form of the Essay, A Letter to Leo Popper," in Lukács, *Soul and Form*, 17.
15. See Howard Eiland and Michael W. Jennings, *Walter Benjamin: A Critical Life*, Cambridge, MA, Harvard University Press, 2014, 206–7.
16. Charles-Louis Philippe, *Bubu de Montparnasse*, Paris, Garnier-Flammarion, 1978, 53.
17. Osip Mandelstam, *Prose*, Princeton, Princeton University Press, 1967, 57.
18. Ibid., 59.
19. See Nancy Duvall Hargrove's *T.S. Eliot's Parisian Year*, University Press of Florida, 2009, 35.
20. André Gide, "Charles-Louis Philippe," in *Essais Critiques*, ed. Pierre Masson, Paris, Gallimard, Pleiade, 1999, 475–92.
21. André Gide, *Les Cahiers de la petite dame*, vol. II, 495, quoted by Pierre Masson in *Essais Critiques* 1241.
22. Rainer Maria Rilke, *The Notebooks of Malte Laurids Brigge*, trans. M. D. Herter Norton, New York, Norton, 1964, p 4. Hereafter in the text abbreviated as *Notebooks* and page number.

23 See Martin Heidegger, *The Basic Problems of Phenomenology*, trans. A. Hostadter, Indiana University Press, 1982, 172–3.
24 Ibid., 289.
25 See Rainer Maria Rilke, *Die Aufzeichnungen des Malte Laurids Brigge, Prosa*, Frankfurt, Insel, 1966, 151; and Rilke, *Notebooks*, 48.
26 Franz Kafka, *Diaries 1910–1923*, trans. Josef Kresh, Berlin, Schocken, 1976, 29. Hereafter in the text abbreviated as D and page number.
27 Guillaume Apollinaire, *The Heresiarch & Co.*, trans. Remy Inglis Hall, Boston, Exact Change, 1991.
28 Apollinaire, "Feu Alfred Jarry," in *Oeuvres en prose complètes*, vol. II, 1039.
29 Apollinaire, "Réponse à une enquête," in *Oeuvres en prose complètes*, vol. II, 984.
30 Jules Romains, *The Death of a Nobody*, trans. Desmond McCarthy and Sydney Waterlow, New York, Huebsch, 1914, 122.
31 Apollinaire, *Oeuvres en prose complètes*, vol. II, 960–3.
32 Guillaume Apollinaire, *La Vie Anecdotique*, in *Oeuvres en prose complètes*, vol. III, ed. Caizergues and Michel Decaudin, Paris, Gallimard, Pléiade, 1993, 54.
33 Review of *"Les Copains," Times Literary Supplement*, August 7, 1913, 330.
34 Virginia Woolf, "Les Copains", *Essays*, vol. 2, 1912–1918, New York, Harvest Books, 1990, 17.
35 Ibid., 16.
36 Woolf, *A Woman's Essays*, 74–5.

5 Affect Effects Affects

1 See Ruth Leys, "The Turn to Affect: A Critique," *Critical Inquiry*, vol. 37, number 3, Spring 2011, 434–72.
2 See Melissa Gregg and Gregory J. Siegworth, eds., *The Affect Theory Reader*, Durham, Duke University Press, 2010, 2–4, 11–16, 80–2, 118–21, 242–249, and 292–7. See also Brian Massumi, *Parables for the Virtual*, Durham, Duke University Press, 2002.
3 Colette Soler, *Les Affects Lacaniens*, Paris, Presses Universitaires de France, 2011, 102; the quote, modified by Fink, comes from Lacan's Seminar XX. See Colette Soler, *Lacanian Affects*, trans. Bruce Fink, New York, Routledge, 2016, 101.
4 Gotthold Ephraim Lessing, *Laocoön*, trans. Edward Allen McCormick, Baltimore, Johns Hopkins University Press, 1984, 8.
5 Both were published in 1872, as pointed out by Ulrich Port in *Pathosformeln: Die Tragödie und die Geschichte exaltierter Affekte (1755–1888)*, München, Wilhelm Fink, 2005, 349.
6 Charles Darwin, *The Expression of the Emotions in Man and Animals*, Chicago, University of Chicago Press, 1965, 14.
7 Lessing, *Laocoön*, 15.
8 Lessing, *Laocoön*, 20.

9   To simplify, I will refer to Deleuze as its author, even though Guattari should be considered as a co-author.
10 Gilles Deleuze and Felix Guattari, *What Is Philosophy?* trans. Hugh Tomlinson and Graham Burchell, New York, Columbia University Press, 1994, 163–99. Hereafter in the text abbreviated as WIP and page number.
11 Edith Wharton, *The Hermit and the Wild Woman and Other Stories* (1908). EBook #4533, posted 02/4/2002, Project Gutenberg, produced Charles Aldarondo, HTML version Al Haines.
12 Virginia Woolf, *Mrs Dalloway*, Oxford, Oxford University Press, 2000, 7.
13 Samuel Beckett, *Letters*, vol. I, 1929–1940, ed. Martha D. Fehsenfeld, Lois More Overbeck, George Craig, Dan Gunn, Cambridge, Cambridge University Press, 2009, 540.
14 See Thomas Dommange, "Geulincx ou la mécanique de l'ineffable," in *Notes de Beckett sur Geulincx*, ed. Nicolas Doutey, Besançon, Les Solitaires Intempestifs, 2012, 229–59.
15 In "On the Marionette Theatre" (1810). Available online at www.ada.evergreen.edu/~arunc/texts/literature/ kleist/kleist.pdf. Last accessed September 22, 2015. Heinrich von Kleist argues that marionettes are superior to living dancers because they have no "affectation," no weight, and no mind hindering the grace of their movements.
16 Henry Miller, *Tropic of Cancer*, New York, Grove Press, 1961, 319.
17 Virginia Woolf, *The Diary*, vol. III, 1925–1930, London, Hogarth Press, 1980, 209–10.
18 Ibid., 209.
19 See Sloterdijk, *You Must Change Your Life*, 65–73. See above pp. 12–13.
20 Gilles Deleuze, *Proust and Signs*, trans. Richard Howard, Minneapolis, University of Minnesota Press, 2000, 75.
21 Jean-Paul Sartre, *Esquisse d'une théorie des émotions*, préface d'Arnaud Tomès, Paris, Hermann, 2010.
22 Ibid., 34.
23 Ibid., 35.
24 Beckett, *Murphy*, 107.
25 Gilles Deleuze, *Expressionism in Philosophy: Spinoza*, trans. Martin Joughin, New York, Zone, 1992, 218–21.
26 Benedict de Spinoza, *Ethics*, trans. Edwin Curely, London, Penguin, 1966, 76–7.
27 Darwin, *The Expression of the Emotions in Man and Animals*, 309–46.
28 See Deleuze, *Proust and Signs*, 7–11 and 138–40.
29 See William Shakespeare, *Othello: Texts and Contexts*, ed. Kim F. Hall, New York, Bedford/St. Martins, 2007. Hereafter in the text abbreviated as O and act, scene, and line number.
30 James Joyce, *Exiles*, in *Poems and Exiles*, ed. J. C. C. Mays, New York, Penguin, 1992, 343.
31 Ibid.
32 I have developed this in Jean-Michel Rabaté, *Jacques Lacan: Psychoanalysis and the Subject of Literature*, Houndmills, Palgrave, 2001, 166–9.

33 James Joyce, *A Portrait of the Artist as a Young Man*, ed. S. Deane, New York, Penguin, 1992, 87.
34 Jacques Lacan, *De la psychose paranoïaque dans ses rapports avec la personnalité*, Paris, Seuil, 1975, 1.
35 Ibid., 342–3.
36 Spinoza, *Ethics*, 101.
37 Soler, *Lacanian Affects*.
38 Jacques Lacan, *Anxiety: The Seminar of Jacques Lacan, Book X*, trans. A. R. Price, Cambridge, Polity, 2014. Hereafter in the text abbreviated as S.X and page number.
39 Jakob Bernays, *Grundzüge der verlorenen Abhandlung des Aristoteles über Wirkung der Tragödie (Fundamental Features of Aristotle's Lost Treatise on the Effects of Tragedy)*, 1857, reprinted in 1880, 148.
40 Franz Kafka, *Letters to Friends, Family and Editors*, trans. Richard and Clara Winston, New York, Schocken, 1977, 16.
41 E. Roudinesco, *Jacques Lacan*, trans. Barbara Bray, New York, Columbia University Press, 1997, 226.
42 Jacques Lacan, *Ecrits*, trans. Bruce Fink, New York, Norton, 2006, 197–268.
43 Martin Heidegger, "Logos" (Heraclitus, Fragment B 50)," in *Early Greek Thinking*, trans. David Farrell Krell and Frank A. Capuzzi, San Francisco, Harper and Row, 1984, 77. Hereafter in the text abbreviated as EGT and page number.
44 Lacan, *Ecrits*, 234.
45 Jacques Lacan, *Le Triomphe de la Religion & Discours aux Catholiques*, Paris, Seuil, 2005, 36.
46 Lacan, *Ecrits*, 239.
47 Petronius, *Satyricon*, trans. Michael Heseltine and E. H. Warmington, Loeb Library, Cambridge, Harvard University Press, 1987, 100–1.
48 T. S. Eliot, *The Complete Poems and Plays*, London, Faber, 1969, 65. Hereafter in the text abbreviated as CPP and page number.
49 Ovid's *Metamorphoses* said by Eliot to be "of great anthropological interest". Eliot, *Complete Poems and Plays*, 78.
50 Eliot's notes to *The Waste Land*. Eliot, *Complete Poems and Plays*, 78. Eliot underlines *sees*.
51 Jean-Luc Nancy, *L'"Il y a" du rapport sexuel*, Paris, Galilée, 2001, 14.
52 Nancy, *L'"Il y a" du rapport sexuel*, 17.

6 "Playing Possum"

1 T. S. Eliot, *Inventions of the March Hare: Poems, 1909–1917*, ed. Christopher Ricks, New York, Harcourt Brace, 1996, 56. Hereafter in the text abbreviated as IMH and page number.
2 Bertrand Russell, "A Free Man's Worship," in *Mysticism and Logic, and Other Essays*, London, Allen and Unwin, 1917, 54–5.

3   Ibid., 56–7.
4   Ibid., 53–4.
5   I am alluding to Eliot's definition of a "mythical method" that he saw enacted by Joyce's *Ulysses;* see "*Ulysses*, Order and Myth," *The Dial*, November 1923.
6   Ronald Schuchard describes this moment in *Eliot's Dark Angel*, Oxford, Oxford University Press, 1999, 119–30.
7   T. S. Eliot, "Laforgue and Corbière in our time" (January 1933), in *The Varieties of Metaphysical Poetry*, ed. Ronald Schuchard, New York, Harcourt, 1993, 287. Hereafter in the text abbreviated as VMP and page number.
8   T. S. Eliot, *The Sacred Wood*, London, Methuen, 1976, 52. Hereafter in the text abbreviated as SW and page number.
9   Leo Bersani, *The Death of Stéphane Mallarmé*, Cambridge, Cambridge University Press, 1982.
10 Stéphane Mallarmé, *Correspondance complète, suivi de lettres sur la poésie*, ed. Bertrand Marchal, Paris, Gallimard, 1995, 342. Hereafter in the text abbreviated as C and page number.
11 Jules Laforgue, "Derniers Vers," *Oeuvres Complètes, Tome 2*, Lausanne, L'Âge d'Homme, 306.
12 A different version is given by Peter Dale in Jules Laforgue, *Poems—Poems*, trans. Peter Dale, London, Anvil, 2001, 397.
13 Arthur Symonds, *The Symbolist Movement in Literature* (1899), London, Dutton, 1958, 62.
14 "... mais, heureusement, je suis parfaitement mort."
15 Robert Sencourt, *T. S. Eliot: A Memoir*, New York, Dodd, 1971, 38.
16 Tristan Corbière, *Wry-Blue Loves*, trans. Peter Dale, Anvil, 2005, 45.
17 The story was told by Marcel Schwob to Jules Renard, who jotted it down in his *Journal* for January 1892. See Gérard Gasarian, *De loin tendrement, Etude sur Baudelaire*, Paris, Champion, 1996, footnote 60, 195.
18 Corbière, *Wry-Blue Loves*, 342.
19 Ibid., 343, translation modified.
20 T. S. Eliot, *The Letters of T. S. Eliot, Volume One: 1898–1922*, eds. Valerie Eliot and Hugh Haughton, rev. ed., New Haven, Yale University Press, 2011, 378. Hereafter in the text abbreviated as LI and page number.
21 Translated by Peter Dale in Laforgue, *Poems—Poems*, 19.
22 Jules Laforgue, *Pierrot Fumiste* de Jules Laforgue, Project MUSE, muse.jhu.edu/books/9781400857067/9781400857067-10.pdf.
23 Translated by Peter Dale in Laforgue, *Poems—Poems*, 163.
24 T. S. Eliot, *Letters, Volume II, 1923–1925*, New Haven, Yale University Press, 2011, 627.
25 Paul Valéry, "La Crise de l'esprit," *Oeuvres*, I, Paris, Pléiade, 1965, 988.
26 Ibid., 992 and 996.
27 Mary Hutchinson, "War," *The Egoist*, vol. 4, number 11, December 1917, 169–72.
28 See Vivien Eliot's letter to Mary Hutchinson in Eliot, *Letters of T. S. Eliot, Volume One*, 215.

29 Hutchinson, "War," in *The Egoist*, 171.
30 It was the expression that Bertrand Russell would use when he was tired of a lover. See Carole Seymour-Jones, *Painted Shadow: The Life of Vivienne Eliot, First Wife of T. S. Eliot*, New York, Anchor Books, 2001, 175.
31 Hutchinson, "War," in *The Egoist*, 172.
32 For an account of Kafka's war of attrition against marriage, see Frederick Karl, *Franz Kafka, Representative Man: Prague, Germans, Jews and the Crisis of Modernism*, New York, Fromm International Publishing Corporation, 1993, 308–419.
33 Eliot, *Letters of T. S. Eliot, Volume One*, 54.
34 Eliot, *The Waste Land: A Facsimile*, 73–5.
35 Bertrand Russell's *Autobiography* quoted in Seymour-Jones, *Painted Shadow*, 129.
36 Eliot, *The Waste Land: A Facsimile*, 27.
37 Sigmund Freud, "The Economic Problem of Masochism" (1924), in *General Psychological Theory*, ed. Philip Rieff, New York, Macmillan, 1963, 200.
38 T. S. Eliot, "London Letter: The Novel," *The Dial*, no. 3 (1922), 331.
39 I am summarizing the essay from Hermann Hesse, *Sämtliche Werke, Band 18, Die Welt im Buch, III, Rezensionen und Aufsätze 1917–1925*, Frankfurt, Suhrkamp, 2002, 125–40. The essay was translated by Stephen Hudson (Sydney Schiff) and published, in condensed form, in *The Dial*, no. 6 (1922), 607–18.
40 Hesse, *Sämtliche Werke*, 126.
41 Hesse, *Sämtliche Werke*, 139–40, my translation.
42 Carl Schmitt, *Political Theology*, trans. George Schwab, Chicago, University of Chicago Press, 2005, 5.
43 Schmitt, *Political Theology*, 12.
44 Valéry, "La Crise de l'esprit," in *Oeuvres*, I, 993.
45 T. S. Eliot, *The Annotated Waste Land with Eliot's Contemporary Prose*, ed. Lawrence Rainey, New Haven, Yale University Press, 2005, 199.
46 See Christopher Clark, *The Sleepwalkers: How Europe Went to War in 1914*, London, Penguin, 2013, and Hermann Broch, *The Sleepwalkers*, trans. Willa and Edwin Muir, New York, Random House, 1996.
47 Eliot, *The Waste Land: A Facsimile*, 80.
48 See "Tradition and the Individual Talent," in Eliot, *Sacred Wood*, 50; and John Zilcosky, "Modern Monuments: T. S. Eliot and Nietzsche," *Journal of Modern Literature*, vol. 29, number 1, 2005, 21–33.
49 Samuel Beckett, "Lessness," *The Complete Short Prose*, ed. S. E. Gontarski, New York, Grove Press, 1995, 197–201. The text begins with: "Ruins true refuge…" 197.
50 Jacques Lacan, *The Ethics of Psychoanalysis 1959–1960. The Seminar of Jacques Lacan.* Book VII, trans. Dennis Porter, New York, Norton, 1992.
51 Sigmund Freud, *Jokes and Their Relation to the Unconscious*, trans. James Strachey, New York, Norton, 1989, 65.
52 Eliot, *The Waste Land: A Facsimile*, 113.
53 Ibid.

7 Let the Lips of the Wound Speak

1. See Howard Caygill, "Walter Benjamin's Conception of Allegory," *Cambridge Companion to Allegory*, Cambridge, Cambridge University Press, 2011, 241–53.
2. Jean Cocteau, *Le Sang d'un Poète, Edition anniversaire*, Paris, Editions du Rocher, 2003, 14. Hereafter in the text abbreviated as SP and page number.
3. Jean Cocteau, "La Fin du Potomak", *Oeuvres Romanesques Complètes*, ed. H. Godard and S. Linares, Paris, Gallimard, Pléiade, 2006, 713.
4. Jean Cocteau, *Cocteau on Film: A Conversation with André Fraigneau*, New York, Garland, 1985, 61.
5. See Beckett, "Lessness," *The Complete Short Prose*, 197–201.
6. Jean Cocteau, *Le Livre Blanc*, in *Oeuvres Romanesques Complètes*, 507.
7. See Cocteau, *Le Sang d'un Poète*, 60; plus marginalia in *Oeuvres Romanesques Complètes*, 747, 748. Thus 752, we read this: "Dargelos was a sequence of allegories, and as such, he took the poses of a dead man." Another version of this note gives: "Dargelos was a sequence of allegories, and like people similar to him, he took the poses of a nude model," *Oeuvres Romanesques Complètes*, 1071.
8. Cocteau, *Le Livre Blanc*, in *Oeuvres Romanesques Complètes*, 508.
9. Jean Cocteau, "L'Appartement des énigmes," in *Oeuvres Romanesques Complètes*, 726.
10. Stephen Greenblatt, "The Wound in the Wall," in Catherine Gallagher and Stephen Greenblatt, *Practicing New Historicism*, Chicago, University of Chicago, 2000, 75–109.
11. Jean Cocteau, "Sang d'un Poète," in Jean Touzot, *Jean Cocteau*, Paris, La Manufacture, 1989, 334.
12. One finds a reproduction of panel 28–29 in Charlotte Schoell-Glass, *Aby Warburg und der Antisemitismus: Kulturwissenschaft als Geistespolitik*, Frankfurt, Fischer, 1998, 218 for the panel, and 225–33 for a commentary.
13. Jacques Rancière, *Mute Speech*, trans. James Swenson, New York, Columbia University Press, 2011, 52–61.
14. Cocteau, *Le Sang d'un Poète*, 73, modified; the text has "*corps*" instead of "*travail*" one hears on the soundtrack.
15. Jean Cocteau, *L'Ange Heurtebise*, in *Vocabulaire, Plain-Chant et autres poems*, Paris, Gallimard, 1983, 129–30. My translation is as literal as possible.
16. Jean Cocteau, *Cocteau on the Film*, New York, Dover, 1953, 62–3.
17. Ibid., 103.
18. Ibid., 72–3.
19. Jean Cocteau, "The Secret of Beauty," in Touzot, *Jean Cocteau*, 245. My translation.
20. Nietzsche, *Ecce Homo*, 302.
21. Ibid., 303.
22. See the discussion with Alan Schneider in *No Author Better Served, The Correspondence of Samuel Beckett and Alan Schneider*, ed. M. Harmon, Cambridge, MA, Harvard University Press, 1998.

23 Samuel Beckett, *Watt*, New York, Grove Press, 1953, 254.
24 Jean Cocteau, "Le Sang d'un Poète," *Une Encre de Lumière, Textes Inédits*, ed. F. Amy de la Bretèque and Caizergues, Montpellier, Université Paul Valéry, 1989, 33.
25 Adrian Stokes, *Stones of Rimini* (1935), *Critical Writings*, vol. I, ed. L. Gowing, London, Thames and Hudson, 1978, 184.
26 Benjamin, *The Arcades Project*, 843.
27 See Howard Eiland and Michael W. Jennings, *Walter Benjamin: A Critical Life*, Cambridge, MA, Harvard University Press, 2014, 261 and 448.
28 Translated by William Aggeler, *The Flowers of Evil*, Fresno, Academy Library Guild, 1954.
29 Cocteau, "Le Sang d'un Poète," *Une Encre de Lumière*, 34.
30 See Allan Stoekl's Introduction to Georges Bataille, *Visions of Excess, Selected Writings, 1927–1939*, xiii–xv, about Materialism and Allegory.

8 The Pathos of History

1   Søren Kierkegaard, *Either/Or: A Fragment of Life*, trans. and abridged by Alastair Hannay, London, Penguin, 1992, 56.
2   Siri Hustvedt, "Reliving the Crash." *New York Times*, opinionator.blogs.nytimes.com/2012/02/18/reliving-the-crash. Last accessed January 14, 2015. Italics mine.
3   Cathy Caruth, *Unclaimed Experience: Trauma, Narrative, and History*, Baltimore, Johns Hopkins, 1996.
4   Freud, *Moses and Monotheism*, New York, Random House, 1967, 84, and Caruth, *Unclaimed Experience*, 16–17.
5   Giorgio Agamben, *Remnants of Auschwitz, The Witness and the Archive*, translated by Daniel Heller-Roazen, New York, Zone Books, 1999.
6   Ruth Leys, *Trauma, A Genealogy*, Chicago, The University of Chicago Press, 2000.
7   Ibid., 230.
8   Ibid., 253.
9   I condense a passage from my *Cambridge Introduction to Literature and Psychoanalysis*, Cambridge, Cambridge University Press, 2014, 188–96.
10 Siri Hustvedt, *The Sorrows of an American*, New York, Picador, 2008, 51–2. Hereafter in the text abbreviated as SA and page number.
11 "Under the hermeneutic code, we list the various (formal) terms by which an enigma can be distinguished, suggested, formulated, held in suspense and finally disclosed." Roland Barthes, *S/Z*, trans. Richard Miller, New York, Noonday Press, 1974, 19.
12 Siri Hustvedt, "Old Pictures" in *Living, Thinking, Looking*, New York, Picador, 2012, 263. Hereafter in the text abbreviated as LTL and page number.

13 I am quoting the opening of Lacan's *Television* address: "I always speak the truth. Not the whole truth, because there's no way, to say it all." Jacques Lacan, *Television*, trans. Denis Hollier, Rosalind Krauss and Annette Michelson, New York, Norton, 1990, 3.
14 Arabella Kurtz and J. M. Coetzee, *The Good Story: Exchanges on Truth, Fiction, and Psychotherapy*, London, Harvill Secker, 2015, 9.

9 Pathos of the Future

1 J. M. Coetzee, *The Childhood of Jesus*, London, Harvill Secker, 2013. Hereafter in the text abbreviated as CJ and page number.
2 J. M. Coetzee, *The Master of Petersburg*, London, Vintage, 1995, 225. In the novel, the statement is interpreted as "blasphemy" by Dostoevsky.
3 This Nietzschean theme has been treated eloquently by Robert Pippin, a close friend and colleague of Coetzee at the University of Chicago. Coetzee knew his brilliant analysis. See Robert Pippin, "Nihilism stands at the door: Nietzsche," in *Modernism as a Philosophical Problem* (1991), second edition, Oxford, Blackwell, 1999, 78–113. This chapter offers an excellent discussion of the "Pathos of Distance," 99–109. See also Robert Pippin, "Nietzsche's Alleged Farewell: The Premodern, Modern and Postmodern Nietzsche," in *Idealism as Modernism: Hegelian Variations*, Cambridge, Cambridge University Press, 1997, 346–50.
4 Paul Auster and J. M. Coetzee, *Here and Now, Letters 2008-2011*, New York, Viking, 2013, 65–7. Hereafter in the text abbreviated as HN and page number.
5 Jacques Derrida, *Monolingualism of the Other Or The Prosthesis of Origin*, trans. Patrick Mensah, Stanford, Stanford University Press, 1998, 1.
6 James Joyce, *A Portrait of the Artist as a Young Man*, London, Penguin, 1992, 205.
7 See J. C. Kannemeyer, *J. M. Coetzee, A Life in Writing*, trans. Michiel Heyns, Johannesburg, Jonathan Ball, 2012, 620–1.
8 *The Infancy Gospels of James and Thomas*, trans. Ronald F. Hock, The Scholar's Bible, Santa Rosa, CA, Polebridge Press, 1995, 111. Hereafter in the text abbreviated as IGJT and page number.
9 See J. M. Coetzee, *Life and Times of Michael K.*, New York, Penguin, 1985, 73, 75, 78, 81.
10 J. M. Coetzee, *Doubling the Point, Essays and Interviews*, Cambridge, MA, Harvard University Press, 1992, 98.
11 Miguel de Cervantes, *Don Quixote*, trans. Charles Jarvis, Oxford, Oxford University Press, 1992, 623. Hereafter in the text abbreviated as DQ and page number.
12 Miguel de Cervantes, *El Ingenioso Hidalgo Don Quijote de la Mancha*, ed. Luis Andrés Murillo, Madrid, Castalia, 1978, vol. II, 213.

13 J. M. Coetzee, "Triangular Structures of Desire in Advertising," in Coetzee, *Doubling the Point*, 131.
14 Ibid.
15 Borges, *Collected Fictions*, trans. Andrew Hurley, New York, Penguin, 1998, 94.
16 Ibid.
17 Goethe, "Der Erlkönig," *Wikipedia*, accessed 10/10/2015.
18 Forthcoming in the *Journal of Modern Literature*, 39.2, Winter 2016.
19 Mike Marais, *Secretary of the Invisible: The Idea of Hospitality in the Fiction of J. M. Coetzee*, Rodopi, Amsterdam, 2009.
20 Jacques Derrida and Elisabeth Roudinesco, *De quoi demain . . . Dialogue*, Paris, Fayard/Galilée, 2001, 102.
21 Samir Haddad, *Derrida and the Inheritance of Democracy*, Bloomington, Indiana University Press, 2013, 13. Hereafter in the text abbreviated as DID and page number.
22 Claude Lefort, "The Question of Democracy," in *Democracy and Political Theory*, trans. David Macey, Minneapolis, University of Minnesota Press, 1988, 16. The paper was read in 1982 at Lacoue-Labarthe's and Nancy's Centre for Philosophical Research on the Political, at which Derrida was present. The passage is quoted in Haddad, *Derrida and the Inheritance of Democracy*, 71.

Conclusion

1   Julio Cortázar, "Axolotl," in *Blow-Up and Other Stories*, trans. Paul Blackburn, New York, Collier, 1968, 3–5.
2   Marcel Duchamp, *Notes*, Paris, Flammarion, 32–33.
3   Ibid., 21.
4   Ibid.
5   Ecke Bonk, "Delay Included," in *Joseph Cornell/Marcel Duchamp—in Correspondence*, ed. Anne d'Harnouncourt, Philadelphia, Philadelphia Museum of Art and Menil Foundation, Houston, 1998, 102.
6   Quoted in Momme Brodersen, *Walter Benjamin, A Biography*, trans. Malcolm R. Green and Ingrida Ligers, London, Verso, 1996, 239. Brodersen quotes Brecht's *Arbeitsjournal*, I, 150.
7   Benjamin, *The Arcades Project*, 447.
8   Ibid., 365.
9   Interview of Eugène Green with John Anderson in *The New York Times*, "When the spirit speaks, it whispers," *The New York Times*, March 13, 2015, ARTS 12.
10 This was the thesis of *Given: 1° Art, 2° Crime: Modernity, Murder and Mass Culture*, Brighton, Sussex Academic Press, 2007, and *Etant Donnés: 1. L'Art, 2. Le crime, La modernité comme scène du crime*.

11 "Two" because my Duchamp chapters are different in each version.
12 Hannah Arendt, "Understanding and Politics," in *Essays in Understanding, 1930–1954: Formation, Exile, and Totalitarianism*, New York: Schocken Books, 1994, 323.
13 James Joyce, *Finnegans Wake*, London, Faber, 1939, 444, line 30.
14 Emily Berry, "Freud's Beautiful Things, A cento," in *Poetry*, vol. CCVI, number 3, June 2015, 205.

Index

Adler, Alfred 93
Adorno, Theodor W. 144
Aeschylus 32
Agamben, Giorgio 11, 152–4, 192 n.23
Aiken, Conrad 118–19
Alain-Fournier 118
Allegory 110, 129–30, 143–6, 186–7, 206 n.7, 207 n.30
Allen, Woody 27
Andersen, John 209 n.9
Andre, Carl 13
Antelme, Robert 154
Antigone 73, 77, 114, 127
Anxiety 88–9, 102–4
Aphanisis 98, 122
Apollinaire, Guillaume 18, 42, 48, 82–5
Aragon, Louis 114
Arendt, Hannah 188
Aristotle 31, 60, 62, 69, 87–8, 99
Asheri, Maia 198 n.15
Atget, Eugène 6
Attridge, Derek 178
Auden, Wystan Hugh 141
Aura 3–7, 14, 38, 130, 146–7, 184–5
Auric, Georges 130
Austen, Jane 122–3
Auster, Paul 164, 166

Bakhtin, Mikhail 88, 192 n.30
Balzac, Honoré de 59
Banfield, Ann 73
Barnacle, Nora 165
Baroque 11, 185
Barrès, Maurice 18, 64
Barthes, Roland 14–16, 24–35, 57, 108, 156, 207 n.11
Bataille, Georges 9, 30–4, 46, 50, 55, 146, 207 n.30

Baudelaire, Charles 18–19, 23–4, 37–8, 41, 109–10, 112, 144–5, 184, 204 n.17
Baudrillard, Jean 157
Beardsley, Aubrey 38, 53
Beaufret, Jean 100
Beckett, Samuel 14, 51–2, 63–9, 91–2, 94, 127, 133–4, 143, 167, 177, 205 n.49
Beerbohm, Max 53
Bell, Clive 73–4
Benedict, Saint 26
Benjamin, Walter 3–10, 35–8, 54, 75, 80, 110, 126, 129–30, 144–7, 183–5, 187
Bentley, Nancy 129 n.9
Bergson, Henri 15, 18, 21, 43–4
Berkeley, George 62
Bernays, Jakob 99, 203 n.39
Bernhard, Sarah 5
Bernini, Gian Lorenzo 185
Berry, Emily 188–9
Bersani, Leo 109, 204 n.9
Best, Richard 59
Beuys, Joseph 13
Binswanger, Ludwig 10, 12–13, 93
Bion, Wilfred Ruprecht 64, 164
Bisexuality 39–40, 48–9, 112
Blake, William 18, 53–4, 57, 62
Blanchot, Maurice 33
Bleeding 107, 119, 137
Bohlmann, Otto 197 n.1, 198 n.10
Bonk, Ecke 184, 209 n.5
Borges, Jorge Luis 83, 174
Borgia, Cesare 61
Borromini, Francesco 185
Boulanger, Georges Ernest (General) 56, 64
Bourdon, Benjamin 43–4, 196 n.21
Bourgoint, Jeanne 136

Bradley, Francis Herbert 110
Brahms, Johannes 17
Brecht, Bertolt 183–5, 209 n.6
Breton, André 34
Britt, David 11, 192 n.24
Broch, Hermann 205 n.46
Brodersen, Momme 209 n.6
Browning, Robert 101
Bruno, Giordano 63
Buñuel, Luis 129–30, 141
Bürger, Peter 38
Burnes-Jones, Edward 53
Butler, Judith 200 n.3
Byron, George Gordon, Lord 98

Caillois, Roger 37
Calle, Sophie 157
Camus, Albert 29
Carducci, Giosuè 64
Carlyle, Thomas 73
Carpenter, Edward 53
Carton, Pauline 132
Caruth, Cathy 152–5
Caygill, Howard 206 n.1
Cervantes, Miguel de 172–5, 178, 208 n.11
Cézanne, Paul 22, 74, 89, 91
Chaplin, Charlie 143
Chapman, George 107
Char, René 30
Chekhov, Anton 91
Chopin, Frédéric 17
Clark, Christopher 205 n.46
Clergue, Lucien 34
Cocteau, Jean 14, 126, 129–47, 149, 185
Coetzee, John M. 14, 161, 163–82
Coleridge, Samuel Taylor 62
Common, Thomas 54
Compagnon, Antoine 29
Confucius 70
Conrad, Joseph 150, 170
Corbière, Tristan 108–13
Cortázar, Julio 183
Costello, Diarmuid 5, 191 n.6

Dadaism 13, 83, 114
Dale, Peter 113, 204 n.12
Dalí, Salvador 141
Da Montefeltro, Guido 114
Danta, Chris 193 n.36
Dante (Alighieri) 29, 62–3, 70, 114
Darwin, Charles 43, 60, 62, 87–8, 95
Dauthendey, Karl 35
Decadence 8–9, 18–19, 20, 38, 52–5
De Chirico, Giorgio 129, 144
Degas, Edgar 22
De Gourmont, Remy 18–19
De Jubainville, Arbois 59
Delay, Jean 30, 198 n.7
Delbo, Charlotte 154
Del Castagno, Andrea 136, 143
Deleuze, Gilles 14, 16, 27–32, 49–50, 89–95, 98–9, 105
De L'Isle Adam, Auguste Villiers 53
Della Francesca, Piero 136, 143
Democritus 88
De Noailles, Viscount and Viscountess 130, 134, 136, 139
Derrida, Jacques 34, 109, 164–5, 170, 178–81
Descartes, René 64–6, 95
D'Harnoncourt, Anne 209 n.5
Dickinson, Emily 89
Dickinson, Violet 74
Didi-Huberman, Georges 12, 192 n.29
Disgrace 115–16, 163
Docter, Pete 94
Dommange, Thomas 202 n.14
Donoghue, Denis 198 n.10
Dostoevsky, Fyodor 78, 118, 122–5, 164
Doutey, Nicolas 202 n.14
Doutreleau, Leopold 16
Dowson, Ernest 53
Dubbelboer, Maricke 196 n.26
Duchamp, Marcel 13–14, 23, 25, 50, 79, 132, 183–8, 210 n.11
Dujardin, Edouard 42, 60

Duras, Marguerite 153
Dürer, Albrecht 11

Egoism 15–19, 23–4
Eiland, Howard 200 n.15, 207 n.27
Eliot, George 159
Eliot, Thomas Stearns 14–15, 17–18, 23, 37, 39–40, 71, 73, 76, 78, 101–28, 149–50, 164, 180
Eliot, Vivien 107–13, 115, 117, 119–20
Ellis, Havelock 53
Ellmann, Richard 198 n.10
Ethics 22–7, 31, 72–3, 76–7, 79, 100, 127
Ethos 69, 85, 111

Fargue, Léon-Paul 44, 196 n.24
Faulkner, William 91
Fenollosa, Ernest 70
Ferdinand, Archduke 118
Film 4, 5, 83, 94, 122–47
Fink, Bruce 201 n.3
"Flattening" 8–9, 164
Flaubert, Gustave 15, 18–19, 45, 77, 80
Force, Pierre 26, 194 n.24
Forster, Edward Morgan 158
Foucault, Michel 12–13
Fraigneau, André 133
France, Anatole 18, 42
Franklin, Benjamin 10
Frazer, James 24
Freud, Sigmund 9, 12–13, 25–6, 46, 49–50, 65–7, 87, 95, 99, 101–2, 124, 127, 133, 142, 149–53, 156, 158–60, 167, 177, 188
Frobenius, Leo 70
Fry, Roger 22–3, 74
Futurism 22, 44–6, 49

Gallagher, Catherine 206 n.10
Gardner, Alexander 33
Gasarian, Gérard 204 n.17
Gaudier-Brzeska, Henri 119
Gauguin, Paul 18, 74

Gautier, Théophile 39
George, Stefan 38
Geulincx, Arnold 52, 64–6, 69, 84, 92
Gide, André 23–4, 28–9, 38, 42, 54, 78, 126
Girard, René 174
Goethe, Johann Wolfgang von 25, 59, 61, 101, 159, 176, 209 n.17
Gogarty, Oliver St. John 51
Gombrich, Ernst 10–11, 192 n.22
Gonne, Maude 51, 56, 63–4
Gothic 77, 90, 144
Green, Eugene 185, 209 n.9
Greenberg, Clement 38, 90
Greenblatt, Stephen 137, 206 n.10
Gregg, Frederick James 22–3
Gregg, Melissa 201 n.2
Gregory, Augusta (Lady) 54, 59–60
Guattari, Felix 49, 89–95, 202 n.9

Haddad, Samir 178, 209 n.21
Haigh-Wood, Maurice 120, 123
Hampl, Patricia 1–4, 186
Hannay, Alastair 207 n.1
Hardy, Thomas 91
Hargrove, Nancy 200 n.19
Hauptmann, Gerhart 21, 58
H. D. (Hilda Doolittle) 39
Healey, Kimberley 41, 196 n.11
Hegel, Georg Wilhelm Friedrich 34, 37, 42, 72–3, 75, 85, 114, 116, 117, 200 n.8
Heidegger, Martin 50, 66, 79–80, 93, 99, 100–3, 160, 197 n.34
Hennion, Antoine 191 n.6
Henrot, Camille 15–16, 193 n.4
Heraclitus 42, 100, 111
Hesse, Hermann 124–5, 205 n.39
Hill, David Octavius 5
Hinkley, Eleanor 118, 122–3
Homer 59, 70
Horkheimer, Max 144
Hudson, Stephen 205 n.39
Hugo, Victor 41, 138
Huneker, James 14–24, 29, 32, 62

Hustvedt, Siri 14, 75, 150–1, 154–61, 163
Hutchinson, Mary 116–17
Huysmans, Joris-Karl 18, 24
Hysteria 6, 39–40, 45, 99, 108, 114, 117, 123–4, 153

Ibsen, Henrik 13, 18–19, 58
Infra-thin 25, 183–4

James, William 8–9, 158
Janet, Pierre 93
Jarry, Alfred 31, 38, 41–50, 83–4
Jennings, Michael W. 200 n.15, 207 n.27
Jesus 19, 61, 163–82, 187
Johnson, Christopher D. 192 n.22
Jolas, Eugene 62
Jones, Ernest 98, 122
Joyce, James 14, 22, 24, 37, 40, 42, 48, 51–2, 55, 58–64, 71, 82, 91, 96–8, 114, 116, 165, 167, 188, 204 n.5
Juvenal 45–6, 197 n.29

Kafka, Franz 75, 80–2, 92, 99, 115–17, 205 n.32
Kainz, Howard 200 n.8
Kannemeyer, J. C. 208 n.7
Kant, Immanuel 62, 66, 72, 75
Karl, Frederick 90, 205 n.32
Keats, John 40
Kenner, Hugh 38, 195 n.5
Kierkegaard, Søren 75, 125, 149, 154, 156–7
Klein, Yves 4–5, 7, 13
Kleist, Heinrich von 92, 153, 202 n.15
Koestenbaum, Wayne 39
Kurtz, Arabella 161

Lacan, Jacques 14, 26, 30, 50, 77, 87, 89, 93–4, 99–105, 127, 153, 160, 180, 208 n.13
Lacoue-Labarthe, Philippe 209 n.22

Laforgue, Jules 38, 42, 107–11, 113–14, 118, 125–6
La Mettrie, Julien Onfray de 88
Lanzmann, Claude 153
Larbaud, Valery 42
Larisch, Marie (Countess) 39
Latour, Bruno 191 n.6
Laurencin, Marie 83
Lautréamont (Isidore Ducasse) 41, 43
Lefort, Claude 180, 209 n.22
Leigh, Mike 4
Leopardi, Giacomo 64
Lessing, Gotthold Ephraim 87–8
Levi, Primo 152, 154
Lévi-Strauss, Claude 171
Lewis, Wyndham 24, 58
Leys, Ruth 87, 152–3
Loisy, Alfred (Abbé) 60
Longenbach, James 198 n.19
Loos, Adolf 71
Lukács, Georg 69, 74–8

MacNeice, Louis 54
MacSwiney, Terence 198 n.13
Maeterlinck, Maurice 21
Magee, William 58–61, 63
Mallarmé, Stéphane 24, 38–9, 41, 44, 47, 53, 100, 109–11, 118
Mandelstam, Osip 77–8
Maney, J. Bret 192 n.15
Mann, Thomas 77
Marais, Mike 177–8
Marazia, Chantal 192 n.20
Marchal, Bertrand 204 n.10
Marinetti, Filippo Tommaso 44
Maritain, Jacques 137, 142
Marsden, Dora 23
Marx, Karl 37
Massumi, Brian 89, 201 n.2
Matisse, Henri 1–5, 15, 22–3, 74, 183, 186
Mauthner, Fritz 64
McFarland, James 7
Melville, Herman 91–2

Mendieta, Ana 13
Mercanton, Jacques 200 n.6
Meredith, George 23
Merleau-Ponty, Maurice 100
Messianism 7, 126, 164, 171, 181–2
Michaud, Philippe-Alain 12,
    192 n.28
Miller, Henry 92
Miller, Lee 133, 136, 140, 142
Millevoye, Lucien 54
Modernism 18, 20, 22, 24, 37–43, 45,
    51–67, 73, 85, 103, 116, 143
Monet, Claude 89
Moore, George 18, 51
Morrell, Ottoline (Lady) 123
Morris, William 54
Musil, Robert 85
Mussolini, Benito 56, 138

Nadar (Gaspard-Félix Tournachon) 5
Nancy, Jean-Luc 103–4, 209 n.22
Nietzsche, Friedrich 7–10, 12–13, 16,
    18–21, 23–4, 26–34, 43–4, 50–67,
    72, 78, 88, 95, 124, 142, 164, 179,
    186, 208 n.3
Nordau, Max 18–19
Novalis (von Hardenberg) 59, 62

Oedipus 134–5
Olsen, Regine 75
Oppell, Frances Nesbitt 198 n.10

Pachomius (Saint) 26
Pater, Walter 54–5
Pathos 7–14, 15–16, 20, 26–9, 32–4,
    66, 69, 75–6, 78, 84, 86, 92–5,
    104–8, 115, 123, 129, 138, 150, 164
Pathosformel 10–12, 14, 43, 75, 88,
    129, 138, 201 n.5
Pathos mathos 32, 93, 123
Payne, Lewis 33
Pessoa, Fernando 91
Petronius 101
Phallus 45–9, 102–4, 113
Philippe, Charles-Louis 75–9, 109

Picabia, Francis 22–3
Picasso, Pablo 15, 22–3, 74,
    129, 144
Pierdet, Géry 83
Pippin, Robert 208 n.3
Pisanello, Antonio 136, 143
Pissaro, Camille 89
Pius IX 128
Pius XII 128, 138
Plato 28, 66, 170
Podach, Erich 33
Poe, Edgar Allan 109, 115
Port, Ulrich 201 n.5
Potts, Willard 200 n.6
Pound, Ezra 23–4, 37–40, 52, 57–8.
    69–72, 109, 111, 116, 118–20, 134,
    143
Proudhon, Pierre-Joseph 23
Proust, Marcel 5–6, 11–12, 25, 29, 30,
    41–3, 58, 64, 91, 93, 95–6, 115, 129,
    177, 188

Quinn, John 22, 54

Racine, Jean 42
Radiguet, Raymond 136
Rainey, Lawrence 205 n.45
Rancière, Jacques 88, 138, 169
Redon, Odilon 38
Reich, Wilhelm 26
Renard, Jules 204 n.17
Reynolds, Mary 184
Rilke, Rainer Maria 79–82, 85, 139
Rimbaud, Arthur 24, 37, 41–3, 109,
    195 n.1
Riout, Denys 187
Rock, Joseph 70
Romains, Jules 42, 84–6
Rops, Félicien 48
Rosenzweig, Franz 126
Rossetti, Dante Gabriel 53
Roudinesco, Elisabeth 203 n.41,
    209 n.20
Rousseau, Jean-Jacques 20, 158, 170
Rubens, Peter Paul 89

Russell, Bertrand 105–7, 111, 117, 119–20, 122–3, 205 n.30
Russell, George William (AE) 59
"Russian" pathos 123–5, 163–4
Ryan, Frederick 59

Sade, Donatien A. F. (Marquis de) 84
Sappho 72
Sartre, Jean-Paul 34, 93–4, 100
Schelling, Friedrich Wilhelm Joseph 66
Schiller, Friedrich 62
Schmitt, Carl 125
Schmitz, Ettore (Italo Svevo) 78
Schneider, Alan 206 n.22
Schoell-Glass, Charlotte 206 n.2
Schönberg, Arnold 17
Schopenhauer, Arthur 52, 57, 61, 64, 66, 113
Schuchard, Ronald 204 n.6
Schwab, Arnold 16, 18, 193 n.7
Schwob, Marcel 204 n.17
Seymour-Jones, Carole 205 n.30
Shakespear, Olivia 53
Shakespeare, William 20, 96–7, 107, 125, 149–50, 159
Shaw, Bernard 74
Shelley, Percy Bysshe 53, 62
Sherry, Vincent 197 n.2
Shiff, Richard 5
Siegworth, Gregory J. 201 n.2
Simmel, Georg 8
Simon Magus 173
Slote, Sam 197 n.1
Sloterdijk, Peter 12–13, 92
Smithers, Leonard 53
Soler, Colette 99, 201 n.3
Sontag, Susan 15, 194 n.28
Sophocles 73, 77, 114, 127
Sorel, Georges 56
Spinoza, Benedict de 27, 62, 94–8
Stein, Gertrude 38, 40, 71
Steinberg, Michael 192 n.21
Sternhell, Zeev 56, 198 n.15

Stekel, Wilhelm 93
Stendhal (Henri Beyle) 15, 18, 19, 24, 28
Stieglitz, Alfred 22
Stimilli, Davide 192 n.20
Stirner, Max 18–20, 23–4, 62
Stoekl, Alan 195 n.38, 207 n.30
Stokes, Adrian 143–4
Strauss, Richard 17
Stravinsky, Igor 129, 144
Stuart, Francis 56
Suetonius 44
Surrealism 5–6, 13, 32, 34, 84, 129–31, 187
Symbolism 41–2, 44, 53–4, 108–15
Symonds, Arthur 53, 110
Synge, John Millington 18, 59
Sznajder, Mario 198 n.15

Tacitus 44
Tagore, Rabindranath 70
Tajiri, Yoshiki 177
Thatcher, David 198 n.10
Thayer, Scofield 119
Theocritus 71
Tiresias 39–40, 84, 102–3, 121
Tolstoy, Leo 91
Trauma 14, 123, 141, 149, 151–6, 158–60, 163
Tresize, Thomas 152, 154
Turner, Joseph Mallord William 4

Ucello, Paolo 136–8, 143
Unanimism 39, 84–6
Uncanny 1, 46, 83, 159, 177

Valéry, Paul 101, 116, 125
Van der Kolk, Bessel 152
Van Gogh, Vincent 18, 74
Verdenal, Jean 113, 117–19, 122
Verlaine, Paul 41–2
Verticality 12–14, 30, 32
Vico, Giambattista 63–4, 159

Villon, François 39, 77, 111–12
Virilio, Paul 157
Vittoz, Roger 121
Von Bezold, Friedrich 145
Von Hartmann, Karl Robert Eduard 66, 113

Wagner, Richard 18, 27–8, 32–3, 54
Wallon, Henri 93
Warburg, Aby 9–14, 43, 129, 138, 143, 145
Warhol, Andy 157
Wharton, Edith 89–90
Wilde, Oscar 18, 38, 53
Williams, William Carlos 40
Wilson, Thomas Woodrow (President) 121
Winnicott, Donald 26, 33
Wolfe, Thomas 92
Woolf, Virginia 22, 38, 41, 69, 72–5, 85–6, 91–2
Wright, Orville and Wilbur 10
Wundt, Wilhelm 43

Yeats, Jack 92
Yeats, William Butler 14, 18–19, 38–9, 51, 52–62, 66–7, 70–1

Zilcosky, John 205 n.48
Zola, Emile 76, 126

www.ingramcontent.com/pod-product-compliance
Lightning Source LLC
Chambersburg PA
CBHW052108300426
44116CB00010B/1584